UNHOLY WARF

The Church and the B

And there shall be signs in the sun, and in the moon, and in the stars; and upon the earth distress of nations, with perplexity; the sea and the waves roaring; men's hearts failing them for fear, and for looking after those things which are coming on the earth: for the powers of heaven shall be shaken.

Luke 21:25–6

UNHOLY WARFARE
The Church and the Bomb

Edited by
DAVID MARTIN
and
PETER MULLEN

BASIL BLACKWELL

© in this collection Basil Blackwell Publisher Limited 1983

First published 1983
Basil Blackwell Publisher Limited
108 Cowley Road, Oxford OX4 1JF, England

British Library Cataloguing in Publication Data
Unholy warfare.
1. Atomic weapons and disarmament
2. War and religion
I. Martin, David   II. Mullen, Peter
261.8'73   JX1974.7

ISBN 0–631–13453–0
ISBN 0–631–13454–9 Pbk

Typesetting by System 4 Associates Limited
Gerrards Cross
Printed in Great Britain by
Billing and Sons Ltd, Worcester

Contents

Introduction   viii

The Contributors   xii

Acknowledgements   xix

I The Politicians

Our Capability of Godlike Reason   1
J. ENOCH POWELL

Peace, Politics and Power   9
TONY BENN

Unilateralism, Neutralism and Pacifism   13
LORD CHALFONT

Peace through Arms Control   21
RAY WHITNEY

'No First Use'   28
SIR NEVILL MOTT

II The Strategy of Survival

The 'Normalisation' of Europe   35
E. P. THOMPSON

Reflections on the Debate about the Nuclear Weapons   52
F. H. HINSLEY

Working for Peace: British contributions to
    multilateral nuclear disarmament   62
PAUL ROGERS

Nuclear Weapons in Defence of Western Europe   72
SIR HUGH BEACH

III *A Sociological Perspective*

The Christian Ethic and the Spirit of
    Security and Deterrence   85
DAVID MARTIN

Invisible Religion, Popular Culture and
    Anti-nuclear Sentiment   108
BERNICE MARTIN

IV *Art, Logic and Prophecy*

Why the Bomb is Real but not True   141
PETER REDGROVE

Our Shy Masters   147
ROBERT SIMPSON

False Poles   156
ELIZABETH YOUNG

Armageddon now? Images of the end in
    prophecy and contemporary arts   165
PETER MULLEN

The Church and the Bomb   172
BASIL MITCHELL

V *A Faith for Survival*

The General Synod's Resolutions on
    The Church and the Bomb   181

The Morality of Nuclear Deterrence   183
GRAHAM LEONARD, *Bishop of London*

'...but I say unto You'   197
PAUL OESTREICHER

Conventional Killing or Nuclear Stalemate?   206
RICHARD HARRIES

People and the Bomb   218
JOHN AUSTIN BAKER, *Bishop of Salisbury*

But what about Russia? 223
LORD MACLEOD

The Simplicity of Death and the Complexities of Life 227
DAVID JENKINS

The Heart of the Gospel 236
LORD SOPER

The Epilogue? 238
PETER MULLEN

Index 241

Introduction

We have produced *Unholy Warfare* because the issues set down in the Church of England working party's report, *The Church and the Bomb*, in 1982 and subsequently discussed in the General Synod in the spring of 1983 proved to be of such complexity and importance that a studied and balanced presentation of the whole argument seemed desirable.

Questions of fact and value, of principle and practical politics, are hardly separated in the debate about nuclear weapons, but we have tried to arrange this volume in sections each of which deals with a particular aspect of the whole argument. This procedure should help the reader gain an overview of the issues, so long as it is not imagined that the placing of an article in any one section means it has no relevance to another section.

We have begun with political arguments or, if you will, with the arguments of some politicians. Enoch Powell believes that British unilateralism is not inconsistent with continued membership of NATO and he states his case epigrammatically: 'Britain can use nuclear weapons only in a case of life and death, and in a case of life and death it is too risky to use them.' Tony Benn says secrecy and duplicity about nuclear weapons on the part of the government undermine the very democracy in whose interests those arsenals exist. He adds that the peace movement is growing at such a rate that no government will be able to ignore it for much longer. In 'Unilateralism, Neutralism and Pacifism', Lord Chalfont criticises the proposed alternatives to deterrence, and claims that the two concepts, unilateralism and multi-lateralism, 'are mutually exclusive, and to pretend otherwise is to practise a deliberate deception.' Ray Whitney, a committed multilateralist, claims that negotiated arms reduction is the best policy; and to this end he has helped set up the Council for Arms Control. The Nobel physicist Sir Nevill Mott, who concludes this section, supports a policy of 'no first use'.

The second section contains information and opinion about military and strategic realities and options. E. P. Thompson argues for more cooperation between peace movements in both Eastern and Western Europe. The whole of Europe is under the threat of nuclear war; ideological rivalry must not hamper a common search for peace and arms reduction. Professor Hinsley says that the emerging international system of states is one in which the leading nations will abstain from war. He accepts that this system will always be threatened by 'law-evading bellicose propensities in man', but asserts that it will survive for that very reason. The idea that a unilateral declaration by Britain could help promote the worldwide multilateralist cause is supported by Paul Rogers; but Sir Hugh Beach defends the doctrine of 'flexible response' as one which has proved itself and can continue to prove itself 'for roughly the same amount of money as we spend on drink each year.'

David and Bernice Martin's two articles taken together provide a sociological perspective on the moral arguments in section three. David Martin makes the point that 'If the threat of nuclear weapons makes their use less likely, then the ultimate immorality of nuclear war is by that much less certain. Being motivated to render a grossly immoral act less likely is presumably to be accounted moral rather than immoral.' While Bernice Martin argues that the chants and slogans 'Give peace a chance' and 'You gotta fight to survive' are part of a milieu of symbolic resonances and mythic models which is messy, slippery and ambiguous but which must not be ignored since it provides a way of understanding the emotionally potent dimension of the issue of the bomb.

A poet features in the next section: Peter Redgrove believes that 'the bomb' involves only one way of looking, though a way that is horribly real. He says, 'If we are lucky, and work aright, the deep and shared subjectivity of right feeling can make the bomb's use inconceivable in a world of verified wonders.' Robert Simpson argues that ironically the organisation of multinational companies may help prevent the outbreak of nuclear war purely because it is not in the interests of their profits to have so many of their customers wiped out; but he also argues that the only lasting hope lies in the renunciation of all armaments. Elizabeth Young claims that many of the arguments reveal 'false poles' but she agrees with Robert Simpson that general and comprehensive disarmament needs to be worked for. It does not follow from a state of Britain as 'nuclear free' that it would also be 'nuclear safe'. Peter Mullen writes about the relevance of the Bible's prophetic images to our time and how the theme or the assumption of destruction has been taken up by some contemporary artists. Basil Mitchell makes some illuminating remarks about the Church's report, and concludes that 'The great value of the report is that we can discover in it the true character of our dilemma — one of which there is no resolution possible that is altogether free of risk or moral cost.

The last section assembles the more overtly theological arguments aired in Synod 1983. Graham Leonard, Bishop of London deplores nuclear weapons, but declares that 'their possession and use can be morally acceptable as a way of exercising our moral responsibility in a fallen world.' Canon Paul Oestreicher defends the pacifist case and claims that it is not mere idealism but a practical political option. Richard Harries, Dean of Kings College, London, says that the balance of weapons has proved beneficial for world peace but it is far from being an ideal remedy since injustices abound while it is uncritically upheld. The overwhelming threat of nuclear destruction should not lead us to believe that 'conventional killing' is acceptable.

J. Austin Baker, Bishop of Salisbury, under whose chairmanship the working party produced the report, clears up some misconceptions left uncorrected by the media about what *The Church and the Bomb* actually said. He concludes that 'the question which more than any other those in power in East and West always evade is: why do you cling to the theory that nuclear deterrence demands parity in weapons, when this is demonstrably and patently false?' Lord MacLeod draws attention to the four-day conference of world faiths in Moscow on the issue of peace and claims that the fact this was held in the USSR's capital is evidence of that country's desire for peace. Professor Jenkins accepts that deterrence puts us all under the shadow of the bomb but says that this means we must try to discover better ways of conducting the lives of the nations to the general improvement of everyone's lot. Lord Soper asks us to consider 'the heart of the gospel'.

In a speech on Radio Four during the recent General Election campaign, the Rt Hon. William Whitelaw said that he wished all sides in the debate about the bomb would listen to reason. We hope that the arguments set out in this volume will be judged worthy of an audience in the court of rational discussion.

PETER MULLEN
DAVID MARTIN

The Contributors

The Rt Revd John Austin Baker was Rector of St Margaret's, Westminster and Speaker's Chaplain from 1978 to 1982, and from 1974 to 1977 he was Visiting Professor at King's College, London. He was Chairman of the Defence Theology Working Party of the General Synod which produced the report, *The Church and the Bomb* (1982). Other published works include *The Foolishness of God* (1970) and *Believing in the Church* (1981). He was appointed Bishop of Salisbury in 1982.

General Sir Hugh Beach GBE, KCB, MC was Defence Fellow at Edinburgh University in 1971 and also served as Director of Army Staff Studies in the Ministry of Defence (1971–74). From 1977 to 1981 he was Master of the Ordnance. Sir Hugh is Warden of St George's House, Windsor and is a member of the Security Commission.

Tony Benn was Labour MP for Bristol South-East from 1963 to June 1983. He was Postmaster-General (1964–66), Minister of Technology (1966–70), Secretary of State for Industry and Minister of Posts and Telecommunications (1974–75) and Secretary of State for Energy (1975–79). He has published many books and articles on the theory and practice of politics, including *Arguments for Democracy* (1981) and *Parliament and Power* (1982).

The Rt Hon. Lord Chalfont PC, OBE, MC has made frequent television and sound broadcasts on defence and foreign affairs. He was Minister of State at the Foreign and Commonwealth Office from 1964 to 1970. His publications include *The Sword and the Spirit* (1963), *The Great Commanders* (1973) and *Montgomery of Alamein* (1976).

The Revd Richard Douglas Harries is Dean of King's College, London. His publications include *Prayers of Hope* (1975), *Prayers of Grief and Glory* (1979), *Being a Christian* (1981) and *The Authority of Divine Love* (1983); he has also published in *Theology*, *The Times* and other leading journals. He broadcasts 'Prayer for the Day' every Friday morning on BBC Radio 4's 'Today' programme.

Professor Francis Harry Hinsley OBE, FBA is Vice-Chancellor of Cambridge University, Professor of the History of International Relations, and a contributer to the *New Cambridge Modern History*. Other published works include *Sovereignty* (1966), *Nationalism and the International System* (1973) and *British Intelligence in the Second World War* (2 vols 1979 and 1981).

The Revd Professor David Jenkins was Fellow of the Queen's College, Oxford, from 1954 to 1969, Bampton Lecturer in 1966, and Director of Humanism Studies for the World Council of Churches from 1969 to 1973. From 1976 to 1982 he was joint-editor of *Theology*. He is Professor of Theology at Leeds University and joint-director of the William Temple Foundation. His published works include *Guide to the Debate about God* (1966), *The Glory of Man* (1967) and *The Contradiction of Christianity* (1976).

The Rt Revd and Rt Hon. Graham Douglas Leonard PC is Bishop of London, Dean of the Chapels Royal and Prelate of the OBE. His most recent book is *God Alive: Priorities in Pastoral Theology* (1981).

Lord MacLeod (The Very Revd Dr) George Fielden Mac-Leod MC was Moderator of the Church of Scotland from

1957 to 1958. In 1938 he founded the Iona Community and was its first leader (1938–68). He is a world-famous preacher and lecturer, and the holder of many honorary degrees and fellowships. His published books include *We Shall Rebuild* and *Only One Way Left*.

Bernice Martin is a Lecturer in Sociology at Bedford College in the University of London. She is the author of *A Sociology of Contemporary Cultural Change* (1981) and a contributor to numerous professional journals. Her main research is in the sociology of religion and culture.

Professor David Martin is University Professor of Sociology at the London School of Economics. He was Cadbury Lecturer, Birmingham University (1974), Ferguson Lecturer, Manchester University (1978), Lecturer in Pastoral Theology, Durham (1979), Firth Lecturer, Nottingham University (1980) and Gore Lecturer, Westminster Abbey (1978). In 1975 he became President of the International Conference of the Sociology of Religion. His recent books include *A General Theory of Secularisation* (1978), *Contemporary Dilemmas of Religion* (1979), *Crisis for Cranmer and King James* (ed.) (1979), *The Breaking of the Image* (1980), and *No Alternative: The Prayer Book Controversy* (1981), of which he was co-editor.

Professor Basil Mitchell is a Fellow of Oriel College and Nolloth Professor of the Philosophy of the Christian Religion at Oxford University. He was Gifford Lecturer from 1974 to 1976 and he has been a member of the Church of England's Doctrine Commission since 1978. His publications include *The Philosophy of Religion* (1971), *The Justification of Religious Beliefs* (1973) and *Morality, Religious and Secular* (1980).

Sir Nevill Mott FRS was Cavendish Professor of Physics at Cambridge from 1954 to 1971. He is an honorary Doctor of Science in twenty-two universities. In 1977 he was awarded the Nobel Prize for Physics.

The Revd Peter Mullen has written on theological and general religious issues for *The Times*, the *Guardian* and *The Spectator* and he has published articles and reviews in *Theology*, *Modern Churchman* and *Faith and Freedom*. BBC Radio 4 broadcast his dramatic chorus *St Mark* in 1979. He has also written and presented programmes for Yorkshire TV and Tyne-Tees TV. He is co-editor of *No Alternative: The Prayer Book Controversy* (1981), and his most recent book is *Working with Morality* (1983). He is Vicar of Tockwith, Bilton and Bickerton in the diocese of York.

The Revd Canon Paul Oestreicher was Associate Secretary for International Affairs at the British Council of Churches with special responsibility for East–West relations from 1964 to 1969. From 1968 to 1981 he was Vicar of The Ascension, Blackheath and from 1974 to 1979 British Section Chairman of Amnesty International. Now Assistant General Secretary of the British Council of Churches, he is also a Vice-President of CND. He is editor of several books, including *The Christian –Marxist Dialogue* (1969).

The Rt Hon. John Enoch Powell MBE, MP has held various government posts, including Parliamentary Secretary in Housing and Local Government, Financial Secretary to the Treasury and Minister of Health. A classics scholar and prize winner, he has published many books on the Greek masters, as well as works on parliamentary and social matters, including, *No Easy Answers* (1973), *Wrestling with the Angel* (1977) and *A Nation or No Nation* (1978). He is Ulster Unionist MP for South Down.

Peter William Redgrove is the winner of many literary awards and prizes, including the *Guardian* fiction prize (1973) and *Poetry Book Society* 'Choices' in 1961, 1966, 1979, and 1981. Recent publications (poetry and prose) include *The God of Glass* (1977), *Martyr of the Hives* (1980), *The Apple Broadcast* (1981) and (with Penelope Shuttle) *The Wise Wound* (1978).

Dr Paul Rogers is Senior Lecturer in Peace Studies at the University of Bradford. He was for three years a member of the Catholic Commission for International Justice and Peace. He has published many books and papers on issues of international resource conflict and strategic studies, among them *As Lambs to the Slaughter* (1982) (with Dr Malcolm Dando and Dr Peter van den Dungen).

Dr Robert Simpson joined the BBC Music Division in 1952, where he worked for nearly thirty years. He has written many books including *The Essence of Brückner* and *Carl Nielsen, Symphonist*. One of Britain's foremost composers, Dr Simpson has written eight symphonies and nine string quartets.

Lord Soper (The Revd Dr Donald Oliver Soper) was Superintendent of the West London Mission at Kingsway Hall from 1936 to 1978. He was President of the Methodist Conference in 1953. He is a world-famous preacher and he has written numerous books on the Christian faith, including *Will Christianity Work?* and *Practical Christianity Today*.

E. P. Thompson was the founder and first Director of the Centre for the Study of Social History at Warwick University. His most famous book is *The Making of the English Working Class* (1963), and he has written numerous articles and essays. He is at present a freelance writer, and is loosely involved in the anti-nuclear movement. His recent publications include *Protest and Survive* (1980) and *Zero Option* (1982).

Raymond William Whitney MP served in HM Diplomatic Service as First Secretary in Peking (1966—68), Head of Chancery, Buenos Aires (1969—72), Foreign and Commonwealth Office (1972—73) and Deputy High Commissioner, Dacca (1973—6). He is Conservative MP for Wycombe.

Elizabeth Young is a writer on disarmament and arms control and on maritime policy. Her published works include *Farewell to Arms Control?* (1972) and the Social Democrat Open Forum Pamphlet, *Neither Red nor Dead: The Case for Disarmament* and 'Marxism-Leninism and Arms Control' in *Arms Control*. She is a co-opted member of two SDP policy working groups.

Acknowledgements

The Editors wish to thank the Revd Basil Watson, Vicar of St Lawrence Jewry, for permission to include transcripts of talks given by Lord Chalfont, the Bishop of London and Ray Whitney; the *Cambridge Review* for F. H. Hinsley's article; *Praxis* for that by E. P. Thompson. J. Enoch Powell's article is a transcript of his Brunel Lecture delivered to the British Transport Association in Bristol in October 1982, and first published in the *Daily Telegraph*. Peter Mullen's 'The Epilogue?' appears by permission of the *Guardian*.

Our Capability of Godlike Reason

J. ENOCH POWELL

Great public questions have a way of behaving like an undulant fever; their intensity and imminence rises and falls according to some hidden rhythm. Eventually they either become obsolete, when circumstances are seen to have so changed that they are meaningless; or else they break the surface of decision and are left behind as a thing settled. I have a premonition that the question of Britain's nuclear armament is not only rising towards peak intensity but is this time approaching the point of decision.

For almost a generation the debate has been conducted on the sidelines by and amongst minorities; elsewhere an un-analysed consensus has reigned, which change of party government did not seriously disturb. There are signs now that the nation at large means to take the question up and not set it down again until it has satisfied itself with the outcome. It will do so as usual more by instinct and hunch than by dialectic; but that does not excuse those whose business it is to articulate national questions from proceeding by as rigorous an analysis as they are capable of.

The nuclear weapon was used once in war. It was used in circumstances which bear no comparison with the present. It was used to shorten a war of which the foreseeable outcome could no longer be reversed: it had been won by one side, but the victory had still to be pushed to the point of 'unconditional surrender', to which the victors had committed themselves. There was another attendant circumstance of great importance: those who used the weapon were certain that their enemy could not use it in return, and those against whom the weapon was used had no means of assessing its effects in advance.

Beyond this unique and largely irrelevant actual experience, the whole edifice of thought and argument about nuclear weapons can only subsist on pure theory. Several nations, including Britain, possess and can use the weapon; two nations, the United States and subsequently Russia, have raised the nuclear weapons they possess to a quantity and capability more than sufficient for each to annihilate the other. The only prize henceforward for them to gain by the development of the weapon is to discover a means of preventing the other from using it by either rendering itself physically impenetrable or by attaining the certainty of destroying all the other's weapons first. I doubt if those expert in the relevant sciences and technologies could absolutely exclude such a discovery; but this much can be said about it with reasonable certainty, that neither could ever be convinced of total invulnerability or total pre-emptive efficiency.

There are some who believe that if the United States and Russia had not both possessed these weapons, Russia would have invaded Western Europe at some time in the last thirty years or so. There can in the nature of things be no absolute disproof of this belief; but the structure of assumptions on which it rests is exceedingly rickety. It assumes first that Russia wishes anyhow to conquer Western Europe, and to do so by force of arms. (I remark — only in parenthesis, because it does not affect the general argument — that I do not happen to believe this.) The second assumption is that Russia would assume that the United States would respond to an attack on Western Europe by exerting against Russia the full might of its atomic arsenal, that being the only way to minimize the probability or scale of reprisals.

This last assumption, which is of course the assumption

crucial to the whole case, is of a subtle nature. It cannot be met by retorting that America would not regard even the conquest of Western Europe by Russia as justifying a nuclear exchange, with all its possible or likely consequences for the American homeland. That may well be so; but the assumption is an assumption about an assumption: could Russia be sure enough that the United States would not think that 'Europe is worth a mess'? This is a question which cannot be answered in the abstract. The answer is that everything depends on the scale, nature, circumstances and perceived limits of a Russian attack. If there were uncertainty on the part of Russia, she would, if her intention were to conquer Europe, proceed piecemeal, by creating limited and local *casus belli* as Germany did in 1938–9; so that at each stage the stakes were plainly so low as not conceivably to be regarded by the United States as justifying even semi-suicide.

My conclusion is that the mutually countervailing nuclear armament of Russia and the United States has not been the reason why Russia has not advanced beyond the limits established at the end of the 1940s. If I were asked — what is not germane to my present subject — what then I believe the reason to have been, I would offer two, which are not necessarily alternative to one another: first, Russia does not want to occupy Western Europe; second, Russia's assumption is that to do so or attempt to do so would almost certainly involve her in a long and exacting war, which, even if she could not lose it in the sense that Napoleon, Wilhelm II and Hitler lost, she would, on historical precedent, be in danger of not winning; and Russia does not desire such a war.

All this, however, is only by way of setting the background to the question of *Britain's* nuclear armament; for nothing that Britain does or refrains from doing will affect the behaviour of the United States or Russia. Nevertheless, the argument has made useful progress; for if the nuclear balance between the United States and Russia has not in fact prevented Russia from invading West Germany and, in another theatre, has not prevented the United States from invading

North Vietnam, extreme scepticism must attend the proposition that the possession of nuclear weaponry by Britain
would deter Russian aggression against Western Europe.

Still, there is an extreme case which has not yet been
covered. It is the case that Russia might treat Britain as a
distinct and exclusive objective and either attack it with
nuclear weapons or threaten so to attack it, unless it surren-
dered. The ludicrous improbability of Russia proceeding in
this way and trying to swallow Western Europe tail first,
leaping Europe kangaroo-fashion, must not prevent me from
eliminating this extreme case, because the argument has
wider and more useful applications.

If Russia had any doubt whatever about the American
reaction to an advance by it in Western Europe, no action
that Russia could possibly take would be more calculated to
maximise the risk of the nuclear exchange than for Russia
to plant itself at one fell swoop in the Eastern Atlantic.
That would be the exact opposite to the course of action
which I have already argued Russia would be bound to follow
if it entertained the slightest doubt about American nuclear
reactions. I find myself therefore obliged to conclude that,
quite apart from any argument from the disparity of British
and Russian nuclear armament, the proposition that possession of nuclear weapons deters attack upon, or blackmail of,
the United Kingdom cannot be sustained. The same reasoning,
by the way, though only slightly less conclusively, would
apply to the possession of nuclear weapons by France.

Not all possible grounds, however, for British (or, for that
matter, French) nuclear weapons have yet been examined. I
can discern two.

One is that the weapon might be employed (or threatened)
in a theatre of war so remote as to awaken no apprehension
of reprisal by the victim or by another power possessing
nuclear weapons; in other words, it would be effectively a
Japan 1945 case. Suppose, to illustrate this hypothesis, we
had repossessed the Falkland Islands by using a nuclear
weapon − presumably not on the Falklands but on the

Argentine. In this monstrously inconceivable event, I would not imagine that America, Russia or any other power possessing a nuclear weapon would have punished Britain by bombing London. It was not however this consideration which would, if the thought had ever crossed our minds, have dismissed it instantly. Still leaving aside, as I have succeeded in doing so far, all moral and religious considerations — though the exclusion is itself unrealistic — we should have perceived the means to be inappropriate, indeed contrary, to the end in view, namely, to make good our right to the Falkland Islands by proving that they were tenable by us but not by the trespasser.

It often happens that in this type of inquiry important principles are elucidated by consideration of an extreme improbability, as I have just been doing. One principle which emerges is that the only objective to which the nuclear weapon is even arguably appropriate is one which involves the literally vital interest of the user. Even in the unique historical case of Japan 1945, the justification has to be based upon the avoidance of huge casualties and destruction during what would otherwise have been the remainder of the hostilities against Japan. Therefore the hypothesis of the use of nuclear weapons by Britain in theatres so remote as to be outside the context of Europe and the North Atlantic is automatically self-aborting, since *ex hypothesi* the interests involved are assumed to be of a correspondingly remote or indirect character. Epigrammatically expressed, Britain can use nuclear weapons only in a case of life and death, and in a case of life and death it is too risky to use them.

The last case of the use of nuclear weapons by Britain has not yet been examined. It relates to nuclear weapons so narrowly limited in their scope and effect that they could not, even under conditions of war-fever, be mistaken as evidence of using or being about or prepared to use other nuclear weapons. The mere possibility of such a mistake leads back into the chain of reasoning which we have already followed in exploring what are, and are not, the consequences

of the countervailing possession of nuclear weapons by
Russia and America.

It is not rationally possible to exclude the possibility that
military uses of the nuclear principle so distinctive and
limited as to be virtually an extension of high explosive could
be developed. Provided that the gulf between such weapons
and the nuclear weapons characterised by overhitting and
pollutant side-effects was too wide and deep for any possibility of misapprehension, the reasoning which we have been
tracing would not apply to them; but the very importance of
the proviso would tend to ensure that the increment which
they added to non-nuclear weaponry would be modest.

However, the existence of this possibility is a reminder of
the advantages which might accrue to Britain from remaining
in close touch with the technology of nuclear warheads and
their delivery. It may be that the maintenance of nuclear
armaments on the present scale and their replacement when
obsolete with the new systems are the only means by which
Britain could remain in touch with nuclear military technology. What that price would amount to and whether the
advantages likely to accrue from paying it would be commen-
surate is a judgement requiring expert and far-sighted scientific
and technical advice, which I as a layman cannot command. I
would only say that it could be prohibitive psychologically,
once the deterrent function of a British nuclear armament had
been (if I may be allowed an inappropriate term) 'exploded'.

You will begin to see why I deliberately postponed intro-
ducing the moral or religious dimension. If the use, actual or
threatened, of nuclear weapons by Britain is not logically
sustainable as a rational form of national defence and if, pal-
pably, Britain cannot, if it wanted to, prevent the United
States or Russia, or indeed any other nation, from acquiring
and holding nuclear weapons, the scope left in Britain's case
for moral or religious argument is exiguous indeed. It would
in effect be limited to the question whether Britain should
permit a nuclear power − presumably, in present circumstances, America − to use its territory to locate or maintain

its nuclear weapons. I might also add the question whether Britain should try to bully Ulster out of the United Kingdom so as to secure permission for the island of Ireland to be so used by a nuclear power.

Fortunately, it seems to me that considerations of a similar nature to those used hitherto are sufficient for providing the answers. If, as I have already argued, the defence of Britain cannot be shown to depend upon the existence of America's nuclear weaponry, the only point left to be resolved is whether the assistance of the United States in war would be forfeited by withholding from it the use of our territory for America's nuclear deployment. The point may be expressed another way: would any perceived self-interest of the United States in helping to prevent Britain from being controlled by an enemy in effective possession of the European continent be diminished by the non-availability of Britain to American nuclear weaponry?

I believe the answer to be: 'Yes, it would be diminished, but not critically.' Obviously, if America regards Britain as a good place for nuclear bases from the point of view of America's perception of its own defence, it must attach additional value on that account to Britain not falling under the dominance of a hostile Europe. But there is a mirror-image: on the same hypothesis the UK would be an equally good or still better place for such an enemy to locate *its* nuclear weapons. In 1917 America would not allow Britain and France to lose to Germany; in 1940 America might have allowed Britain to lose to a German Europe; but so long as the present nuclear preoccupation of the United States endures, it would be less likely than ever to allow Britain to lose to an enemy in possession of the European continent, whether or not Britain were available for American nuclear use.

I believe we can thus reach our last conclusion without recourse to morality or religion. That is a great relief; for I do not know how they would have helped us. Christianity lands us either in a dead-end or an argument in a circle — in a dead-end, because the Gospel does not authorise the use of arms or force at all; in an argument in a circle because the appeal to authority to authorise warfare nevertheless is necessarily an appeal to a secular authority, such as the papacy with its 'just war', or the Crown of England with its 'command of the magistrate'. Morality is a less precise concept than Christianity; but I shall venture to make a statement about it which might find acceptance. Whatever may be the limitations and imperatives placed upon human societies by their inner natures and outward circumstances, as a result of which war might be inseparable from the human condition, our 'capability of godlike reason, looking before and after', entails upon us as one of the conditions of humanity that we should apply reason to the best of our capacity even to the consequences which flow from the irrational side of man's nature. The discipline of thinking logically about war is one shape which the performance of this duty can take.

Peace, Politics and Power

TONY BENN

There is no doubt that at the time of writing the government is systematically misleading the people about the military balance. Anyone who thinks that such disingenuousness is never practised by ministers and civil servants should study the lesson of the Falklands campaign. The Ministry of Defence has admitted that deliberate disinformation was used because the military situation demanded it.

Another false impression is being given and it concerns the military balance between the US and the USSR. By selective presentation of the facts — that is, by confusing the strategic with the tactical, and the land base with the submarine base — defence spokesmen are putting it about that the Soviet Union is stronger than the United States. That is not true. Even the Foreign Secretary has been obliged to admit that, if we marshalled British, French and other western weapons, the Russians could reasonably argue that they had a right to further military growth without disturbing the balance of forces. In fact, the United States is by far the most powerful country in the world both technically and militarily; its gross national product is very high, and so is the amount it spends on defence. No wonder its weapons are dominating. But we are being told the opposite.

When people are told that they are under extreme threat from a hostile foreign power, they are quite naturally afraid.

The government is exploiting this fear in order to justify large increases in the arms budget. They also seek to undermine the moral and political authority of their opponents by having minor spokesmen denounce all criticism as treachery and espionage. There is a certain irony about the government's claims that nuclear weapons exist to protect our democracy while all the time that democracy is being destroyed by the possession of these weapons. I mean, the existence of these weapons on our soil guarantees that Parliament is not told the truth. For instance, Dr David Owen has said that Parliament should have the right to debate the nuclear issue, but he has followed that claim with the counter-claim that no vote should be taken. The American Congress was allowed to vote against the MX missile. How impotent is the House of Commons, then, for all the talk about our priceless democratic freedom!

The government constantly undervalues the strong moral base of the peace campaign and the international dimension of the movement. And morality in politics can be more than a righteous gesture, as the British learned when a non-violent campaign drove them from India. It is not necessary to be a supporter of the Left in order to be opposed to nuclear weapons; the movement is growing all over the world from Japan to the US where a million people took to the streets of New York on one day in 1982 to protest about the bomb. The European nuclear disarmament movement has held packed conferences in Brussels and Berlin. Roman Catholic bishops in America have denounced nuclear weapons in a Pastoral letter. Pope John Paul II has condemned these weapons, and he has insisted that the attempt to promote world peace by relying on threats to use them is immoral. This belief is held by many in the Labour Party and in the Liberal Party; and, despite the Synod's refusal to accept frank unilateralism, the desire to be rid of nuclear weapons is widespread in the Church of England. In the debate on the working party's report, *The Church and the Bomb*, Synod resolved against first-use of nuclear weapons, and the distinguished theologian, the Dean of Durham, said that the possession of these weapons is 'morally corrupting'.

Against all the abuse heaped upon the peace movement, I should like to set out very briefly what I think this movement is saying. Its supporters say that nuclear weapons make nuclear war more likely. They do not believe that it is the weapons which have preserved peace in Europe since 1945. And they do not believe that the USSR — a country which lost 20 million people in the Second World War — has shown by anything that it has done that it wants to make an attack on Western Europe. I deplore the attempt to secure a buffer zone around one's territory and I went on a delegation to the Soviet ambassador to say so. I hope that, when Afghanistan is mentioned, critics will remember that in the high days of the British Empire we invaded Afghanistan three times. Nothing in the Russian occupation of that country indicates a plan for the invasion of Western Europe.

The fact is that, while there has been much talk of multi-lateralism and non-proliferation, the number and power of nuclear weapons has increased over the years. Resources which could have been used to feed the world's population have been wasted on nuclear weapons. So many who now die of starvation do so as an indirect consequence of defence spending.

When Catholic bishops and Anglican lay people are united with many in all our political parties and with members of the US Congress in deploring the possession of nuclear weapons, it cannot reasonably be maintained that the peace movement is a communist plot. Have the communists control of the Catholic Church? Is the American Congress a hot-house for the hard Left? Is the Church of England in the hands of the Trotskyists?

The government will not be able to succeed in its attempts to dismiss the peace movement as a bunch of extremists and traitors or as a manifestation of the lunatic fringe. Many people, of all parties and of none, want to see Trident cancelled, and Polaris along with it. They want to see American and British nuclear bases shut down. Above all, they want to see an end to the whole nuclear defence strategy and the so called 'balance of terror'.

No government, Tory or Labour, will be able to ignore such a movement for very much longer.

Unilateralism, Neutralism and Pacifism

LORD CHALFONT

I have chosen the subject of unilateralism, neutralism and pacifism because I believe that the national debate about defence and security — and especially about the role of nuclear weapons — is now entering a decisive phase; and as it does so I believe that those of us whose business it is to analyse and articulate national issues of this kind have a duty to inject some sort of realism into the debate which tends to be disproportionately coloured by idealism. Not that there is anything wrong with idealism; I suggest, however, that in a world of unregenerate nation states, many of whom are prepared to use military force aggressively in the pursuit of their political aims, it has to be tempered, as the Bishop of London suggested in 1982, with a clear appreciation of the realities of power. Our potential enemies do not hesitate to exploit and corrupt our idealism; and it is, I believe, largely as a result of this exploitation that these three elements — unilateralism, neutralism and pacifism — have come to represent a serious threat to the survival of what I insist on calling, in spite of the protests of progressive thinkers everywhere, the Free World.

Let us consider first unilateralism, by which I mean the movement which advocates unilateral nuclear disarmament by the United Kingdom. Here let me take a moment to demolish a myth which is being carefully fostered by some of the leaders of the Campaign for Nuclear Disarmament, namely their suggestion that the distinction between uni-lateral disarmament and multilateral disarmament is a false one — that unilateralism is only a part of multilateralism. This is of course a devious and thoroughly dishonest exercise in semantics, and it should be recognised as such by anyone concerned with clarity of language and thought. Unilateral nuclear disarmament means precisely what it says: the abandonment by one side (in this case Britain) of its nuclear weapons without any simultaneous and corresponding action by anyone else. Multilateral disarmament, on the other hand, means the phased reduction of armaments on *all* sides, subject to verification under international control. The two concepts are mutually exclusive and to pretend otherwise is to practise a deliberate deception. The reason that such deception has become necessary to the CND is that its leadership has had to recognise that there are many people in this country who share an understandable fear of nuclear war but who also know that unilateral disarma-ment carries with it certain risks which are absent from the process of multilateral disarmament.

Now, it has become customary to mitigate criticism of the unilateralist view with careful qualifications about the sincerity and compassion of those who hold it. My own approach is somewhat different. My perception of the unilateralist movement is that it is at best misguided, and at worst extremely dangerous. Furthermore, I find some of its attitudes and assumptions offensive. For example, the concentration of its propaganda on the horrors of nuclear war carries with it the somewhat arrogant assumption that unilateral disarmament is the only way to avoid such a catastrophe. Speaking for myself, I require no instruction from anyone on the effects of nuclear weapons — I would go as far as to say that I know more about the subject at first hand than anyone in the so-called 'peace movement'. There is, however, more than one intelligent, carefully thought-out view as to how nuclear war can best be avoided. There is, indeed (although this will not be explored in detail in this article) a powerful case for saying that unilateral disarmament might make war more, rather than less, likely. I therefore find it cynical and unacceptable that memories of Hiroshima and Nagasaki, images of roasting babies and melting eyeballs, and the dreadful nightmare of death by radiation should be deployed in aid of one side of what is a profoundly serious argument.

The assumption of a monopoly of wisdom is not the only distasteful facet of the unilateralist movement. There seems also to be the implication of a monopoly of moral rectitude and, now that Mr Enoch Powell has entered the debate, the beginnings of a claim to a monopoly of intellectual objectivity as well. It is interesting to note that the position taken both by Mr Powell in his 1982 Brunel address (reproduced in this section) and that arrived at by the Bishop of Salisbury's working party in their report *The Church and the Bomb*, depend on an identical assumption, which if it proves to be false, invalidates most of their elaborately constructed arguments. Let me identify that assumption with quotations.

> First, Russia does not want to occupy Western Europe. Second, Russia's assumption is that to do so or attempt to do so would almost certainly involve her in a long and exacting war which, even if she could not lose it, she would, on historical precedent, be in danger of not winning; and Russia does not desire such a war.

This is one of those definitive statements which leads me irresistibly to wish that I could be as certain of anything as Mr Powell is of everything. That quotation contains five separate propositions. Three of them assume a knowledge of Russia's intentions which Mr Powell, in common with almost everyone in the West, simply does not possess. The other two are, to say the least, based upon insufficient evidence and are certainly not unanimously accepted by those most closely and professionally involved.

In a similar vein, the Bishop of Salisbury's report states 'The Russians do not want war; they recognise that war is not now a viable instrument of Soviet foreign policy.' (p. 24) I beg the Bishop to consider seriously the possibility that he may be wrong, and in doing so I ask him and his colleagues what they think happened to Afghanistan. To predicate our national security upon the assumption that the Soviet Union does not regard military force as an instrument of foreign policy seems to me to ignore reason, logic and most of the history of the last twenty-five years. If the assumption should prove to be invalid, as I firmly believe it to be, the policies which derive from it would be disastrous.

In any case, these assumptions demonstrate that both Mr Powell and the Church's working party have comprehensively misunderstood the nature and function of military power, and by extension the role of nuclear weapons which are an element of that power. The Soviet Union is an imperialist state, and like all imperial powers it would naturally prefer to achieve its ends, if possible, without open conflict. It knows that in order to do this it must be able to confront its potential adversary with an overwhelming manifestation of force with which it can blackmail, terrorise and coerce. Indeed, the real danger of Soviet expansionism is not that it will result in a war, but that it will succeed *without a shot being fired*. And that will certainly happen if the West fails to demonstrate its will and its ability to resist. This, in turn, means rejecting simplistic solutions based entirely on irrational fear or empty logic-chopping. There are important and complex issues to be resolved: we need an informed public debate on such matters as the wisdom of the decision to acquire the Trident missile system; the extent to which the defence of the West can be assured with less dependence on nuclear weapons; the implications of stationing Cruise missiles in Western Europe, and the overriding need to control the nuclear arms race. None of these profoundly important issues will be resolved by the ritual repetition of meaningless slogans like 'Ban the Bomb' — you cannot ban the bomb any more than you can repeal the law of gravity. The ability to manufacture nuclear weapons is now an ineradicable part of human knowledge; and we can never again be certain that some megalomaniac somewhere will not make them and use them in the pursuit of his political design.

I have included neutralism in this analysis for two important reasons. First, it is often an explicit element in the programmes of unilateralists and 'peace' movements; secondly, it is in any case a logical extension of the unilateralist position, however strongly some CND spokesmen may deny this charge. One of the more disturbing features of the current debate is the tendency in some quarters to affect an even-handed objectivity between the Communist world and the Free World. It is, indeed, an especially unpleasant aspect of the book produced by the Bishop of Salisbury and his collaborators, *The Church and the Bomb*. Yet it is not only to Christians that this 'plague-on-both-your-houses' heresy should be repugnant. The people of the Soviet Union and its empire live in the repressive, brutal and degrading twilight inseparable from any attempt to erect the moral squalor of Marxism into a political system. The important difference between our system and theirs is that they believe that the human individual exists to serve the state, and not the state to serve the individual. Furthermore, they are committed to destroying our system and replacing it with theirs. You do not have to take *my* word for that. You only have to read what they say themselves. Sir Winston Churchill once said, in a different context, 'I accept no position of neutrality as between the fireman and the fire'; nor should free men and women accept any position of neutrality as between political democracy and totalitarian communism.

Faced with this argument, many unilateralists protest that it is possible to abandon our nuclear weapons and still remain members of the Western Alliance. They point to Norway or West Germany as examples. It is time, I think, that this irrelevant hypocrisy was firmly challenged. The unilateralist position, as defined in numerous CND documents and, more significantly, in the current position of the Labour Party as adopted at its annual conference, postulates not only the abandonment of the British nuclear deterrent, but also the removal of American missile bases and — and this is the key ingredient — dissociation from any defence policy depending on nuclear weapons. Yet the leading member of the Western Alliance, the United States of America, bases the whole of its defence strategy for the Western world on nuclear deterrence. It seems to me to imply some dubious moral values to suggest that we should wash our hands of nuclear weapons, but still remain in an alliance which depends upon them for the whole of its defensive position. Even for those whose approach to moral imperatives is casual enough to gloss over this difficulty, there must surely be an intellectual dilemma — how do you dissociate yourself from defence policies based on nuclear deterrence while remaining a member of an alliance which relies precisely upon such policies?

If anyone should take up the logic of this challenge and say — 'Very well, let us be neutral — after all, the Swiss and the Swedes are', let me point out that if this happens, the Soviet Union will have achieved one of its principal geopolitical aims — the separation of Western Europe from the United States and the disintegration of NATO. It can be powerfully argued that the vulnerability of the Swiss and the Swedes would be dramatically increased if there were no NATO; and there can be little doubt that if Western Europe were to degenerate into a collection of 'neutral' nation states, they would rely for their continued existence entirely upon the whim of the Soviet Union. This may hold no terrors for those who believe in the pacific and benevolent intentions of the men in the Kremlin — but they must forgive those of us who do not share their comfortable view.

Finally, I turn to the question of pacifism. Once again, as in the debate with unilateralists, it is customary in polite circles to preface any comment on pacifism with deferential qualifications such as 'Of course, I sympathise with the position of the sincere pacifist.' For my part I have no such sympathy. I believe that the pacifist position is selfish and indefensible. The Bishop of Salisbury's working party themselves have conceded that to many Christians the pacifist view is unacceptable on the grounds that the non-violent solution which it proposes might destabilise society to such an extent that even more violence would result. This seems to me to be a decisive argument. As Ray Whitney says (see his article in this section) 'It is useless for the sheep to pass resolutions in favour of vegetarianism while the wolf remains of a different opinion.' The Bishop and his colleagues meet this argument by creating two new categories of pacifist, in an attempt to reconcile Christian ethics with the unilateralist argument. There are the 'prudential pacifists' and 'the pacifists of selective objection', who are, it seems, not pacifists of principle, but who simply believe that violence, especially nuclear violence, is 'essentially counter-productive'. I am bound to say that I find this brand of casuistry totally unconvincing. If the pacifist position, from whatever point of departure it might be arrived at, were to prevail in the West, we should be at the mercy of brute force, and a hostage to any aggressor whose political ambitions included our subjugation. Attempts to obfuscate facts with jesuitical word-play were once the subject of a magisterial rebuke by the Editor of *The Times* when I was the paper's Defence Correspondent. To an earnest young leader-writer who had suggested that, surely, there were two sides to every question, the Editor replied severely: 'No, young man, there are not; some things are evil, cruel and ugly, and no amount of fine writing will make them good, kind or beautiful.'

The pacifist position seems to me to be summed up in the depressing description from an American friend of a young man taking part in a demonstration on an American university campus, who was carrying a banner inscribed 'Nothing is Worth Dying For'. He was a student in a university where freedom of intellectual inquiry is not only permitted, but encouraged; he was enjoying freedom of assembly and freedom to express his dissenting views; he could sleep at night without fear of the midnight knock at the door; he was living in a country with no concentration camps, no slave labour, no psychiatric hospitals designed to reconstruct the dissident. Is it possible that he really believed that none of these things are worth fighting for, and, if necessary, dying for?

Our will to sustain and defend the civilised values of our political system has been eroded by a number of contemporary ills — the decline of moral values; a contempt for authority; the decay of the family; the pervasive cult of mediocrity. I have attempted to analyse briefly three of the principal tendencies of thought and advocacy which I believe are accelerating this process of erosion. The young man on the university campus was not only saying, 'There is nothing worth dying for', he was also, by implication, saying 'There is nothing worth living for'. Speaking for myself, and I believe for many others like me, I reject both these propositions.

Peace through Arms Control

RAY WHITNEY

I had originally intended to say something about the efforts which have been and are being made to reach a more securely based peace through international arms control agreements. This whole process is under attack from those who are impatient with what has been achieved so far and have lost faith in it as a way forward. Yet it is vital that their view does not prevail: for disarmament negotiations offer the only hope for a safer world. And they are not just a matter for governments. We all have a role to play. But in offering a few thoughts on arms control — and doing so from the point of view of someone who tries to be a Christian — I believe it would be wrong if I did not concentrate much of my attention on *The Church and the Bomb*, the report of a working party under the chairmanship of my friend, John Baker, Bishop of Salisbury. This document is keenly debated wherever Christians meet, particularly in the Diocesan Synod and the General Synod, but it has also had a powerful impact in the country at large. Certainly, it is the clear intention of its authors that it should become accepted as the basic Christian response to the problem of securing peace in this nuclear age.

Endorsing as it does the unilateralist position, it will be warmly welcomed by the activists of the Campaign for Nuclear Disarmament, those who would be content to see the collapse of NATO, and by all those on the Left of British politics. As a Conservative politician I must therefore take care to avoid an automatic — should I, in this context, say Pavlovian? — reaction to the report and its findings. I note that the Bishop of Salisbury and his co-authors say they arrived at their joint position from 'widely different starting-points', but I also note that at least three of them started from a firm unilateralist position and that one was, until quite recently, Vice-Chairman of CND.

I believe that the Bishop and the others who started from a non-committed position have been led by their colleagues to the wrong conclusions, and that the report contains worrying errors of fact, of logic and even of theology. I am emboldened to offer views on theological issues only by the many examples we now have of theologians who, quite justifiably, express their own opinions on politics, economics and international relations. This endorsement of the uni-lateralist line is a deeply worrying development because the report, issued in the name of such a respected figure as the Bishop of Salisbury, could do much to build up a political climate which would undermine the whole basis of our position in arms control negotiations. It does not go too far to say that it could lead to the break-up of the Western Alliance. If the Churches helped to carry this country into unilateralism, they would share heavily in the responsibility for endangering world peace and the freedom we have built up so carefully in this country over the years.

Let me start on a point of agreement, a view which I share totally with Bishop Baker and his colleagues, with the Campaign for Nuclear Disarmament and, for example, with Mr Jonathan Schell who, in his widely acclaimed *The Fate of the Earth* wrote 200 pages pointing out that an all-out nuclear war would be a devastating tragedy for the world. Surely no human being — certainly no Christian — could challenge the assertion that the *use* of nuclear weapons would be an evil (and one of the flaws in the logic of *The Church and the Bomb* is that the distinction between the use and the possession of nuclear weapons is frequently blurred). The use of atomic bombs on Hiroshima and Nagasaki was an evil (although there is also the question of whether the prolongation of the war with, perhaps, another million deaths, might not have been the greater evil). The bombing of London, Dresden, Coventry and Hamburg were all crimes against humanity. The use of chemical and bacteriological weapons would also be evil. The use of a piece of wood by an assailant to batter an old lady is an evil act.

As Christians, as sensitive and sensible human beings, we should lament them all. The problem in each case is usually the need to choose between various evils; this is an inescapable part of the human condition. I do not find it nearly as easy as the authors of *The Church and the Bomb* to draw the sharp distinction that they make between nuclear arms and the rest. John Baker, writing in *The Times* (15 October 1982), pointed out that nuclear weapons release radiation in a way which cannot be accurately predicted and cause both somatic and genetic harm which could threaten future generations. It may be that chemical and bacteriological weapons could have equally horrifying effects and yet the report has very little indeed to say about them. I can well understand the case, particularly the Christian case, for the renunciation of the use of weapons of *all* kinds, and it seems to me there is a logic and an intellectual coherence in the pacifist viewpoint and one which I would have expected from one of the authors of the report, Mr Sydney Bailey, who is a Quaker. I respect the Quaker approach of total pacifism, although I neither share it nor do I believe it would be morally right for a democratically elected government to adopt a policy of total pacifism and total disarmament.

Clearly, the authors of the report also recognise this dilemma, but they have chosen something they describe as 'selective objection', 'a variant of prudential pacifism'. They have opted for this 'nuclear pacifism' because they believe that 'outright pacifism…can be dangerously destabilising to such peace as does exist' (p. 23). Sadly, the authors are nowhere able to show that 'nuclear pacifism' would not,

itself, be destabilising. Consideration of how we can maintain
peace inevitably leads to a welter of speculation and theoris-
ing about what might happen in the future; about how other
nations might react should we unilaterally renounce nuclear
weapons; about whether the concept of a limited war is valid
or whether the nuclear combatants really would be ready
totally to destroy each other and the rest. But there is one
unchallengeable fact to which we must cling, namely, that
nuclear deterrence has kept the peace in Europe for thirty-
seven years. We must therefore be very sure of our ground
before we adopt 'nuclear pacifism'. As His Holiness The
Pope pointed out in his statement to the UN Special Session
on Disarmament, 'In current conditions deterrence based on
balance, certainly not as an end in itself, but as a step on the
way towards progressive disarmament, may still be judged
morally acceptable.'

The Bishop's working party does not seem to accept this
proposition. In their view, 'the present balance of terror is
plainly not a secure way of keeping the peace. It becomes
more precarious month by month and will become more
difficult still if horizontal proliferation of nuclear weapons
proceeds.' (p. 159) Now this is the view regularly put forward
by the Campaign for Nuclear Disarmament but it seems to be
one that is very difficult to justify either in logic or by a
study of history. I do not believe the absolute quantity of
nuclear warheads held by either NATO or the Soviet Union
would ever be the significant factor, the difference between
peace and war. Whether the two sides can destroy each other
three times over or one hundred times over is not the point.
The question is whether both recognise that to use nuclear
weapons, or indeed to go to war at all, represents an unacceptable degree of risk for the survival of their own societies.
Wars occur when nations believe they can achieve victory at
a bearable cost rather than because of arms races.

There is one element in the approach of *The Church and
the Bomb* which I have to say I find both wrong and deeply
offensive. This is the determined attempt to treat the Soviet

bloc and the Western nations with total even-handedness.
Honest objectivity in dealing with international issues of such
fundamental importance is surely to be commended as a goal;
to attempt to impose a spurious symmetry where no symmetry exists is, equally certainly, to be rejected. I am not
prepared to equate the democracies of the West with the
totalitarian regimes of the Soviet Union and its satraps. It is
inevitable that any study that approaches the complexities
of international relations from such a position will reach misleading conclusions. As Christians we know that evil exists in
the world and we should be ready to face up to it. The reality
of the Soviet Union is something that the Church working
party does not seem to come to grips with. All the evidence
available, all the facts of history, suggest that the people of
the Soviet Union are burdened with a regime which is far
more unjust, dangerous and poses an infinitely greater threat
to world peace than any in the West. To take any other view
is to devalue Judeo-Christian values and the achievements of
Western societies. These societies have many blemishes and
failings, they are as nothing compared with the failings of
Marxist totalitarianism.

The report yet again dusts down President Eisenhower's
warning of over two decades ago about the 'industrial-
military complex in his own country' (p. 73), and goes on
to say that 'to lie, cheat and deceive, and if need be to kill,
is their business. The Cold War business is big business,
keeping tens and hundreds of thousands in highly-paid, well-
rewarded work. And that dovetails with the even greater
numbers needed to prepare a real war. Britain shares in this
whole process.' What does this imply? Does it betray any
degree of understanding of the political realities today? Are
they suggesting that Britain is a part of 'this whole process'?
It is very sad that the Bishop of Salisbury and his colleagues
should labour under such bizarre illusions.

They are surprisingly confident in their assessment of the
Soviet government and its intentions. They tell us that 'the
Russians do not want war: they recognise that war is not now

a viable instrument of Soviet foreign policy' (p. 24), but the Afghan resistance fighters might well have reached a different conclusion. The most the working party will allow, in its analysis of the Soviet Union, is that 'Afghanistan is a continuing problem' (p. 72). And there is little evidence in *The Church and the Bomb* of the unprecedented growth of Soviet strategic nuclear forces during the 1970s, the decade of détente. Similarly, the Helsinki Agreement is scarcely mentioned, yet Soviet disregard of the accords it signed at Helsinki surely has much to tell us about how we must conduct our search for workable disarmament agreements with Moscow. The authors appear to suffer from a resolute determination to see the world not as it is, but as they wish it to be.

Are we therefore to resign ourselves to the present situation? As the authors point out, 'the Gospel is a gospel of hope' (p. 148); but they then go on to suggest that it is the amassing of nuclear devices which 'threatens the fulfilment of that hope'. If this amassing is to be stopped and the nuclear armoury reduced, it can only be done by careful, determined and persistent efforts to reach arms control agreements. That is where the real hope lies, and where the work has to be done by all of us who are concerned. I find it quite extraordinary that *The Church and the Bomb* devotes just a page or so to international disarmament efforts. It is easy to be critical of arms control negotiations and there are many cynics who will suggest that they have no future, but I should not have expected such indifference or cynicism from Bishop Baker and his colleagues. Over the years nations have reached agreements on the use of outer space, the seabed, Antarctica, a partial test ban treaty, the non-proliferation treaty, and biological and toxin weapons. And there *is* progress to report in the nuclear negotiations. In the decade after 1969 the discussion was about how to put ceilings on the increase in nuclear weapons. Now the Soviet Union is prepared to discuss an actual reduction in numbers and President Reagan has made a proposal for a cut of one-third in the stocks of ballistic missiles.

Of course we can agree that progress has been slow and inadequate. Governments, and particularly their officials, become weary and negative, and there will always be a need for bodies outside government machinery to generate new ideas and new goads to spur on ministers to greater efforts to find genuine, effective and verifiable arms control agreements. It was for this purpose that The Council for Arms Control (CAC), an all-party, non-party organisation dedicated to improving the quality of the peace by a reinvigorated search for ways to multilateral disarmament, was formed in 1981.

At the United Nations Special Session on Disarmament in June 1982, this organisation proposed international self-monitoring arrangements which attracted considerable interest. It also proposed an international convention, based on the Geneva conventions, setting out standards of humane conduct in warfare, which would establish an independent monitoring group for nuclear weapons and their development which would have a status analogous to that of the International Committee of the Red Cross.

Other initiatives and ideas are needed. It is going to be long, complex and difficult work, and it is tempting to slip into the attractive simplicities of unilateralism. But the way forward, the way to the 'multilateral, progressive and verifiable reduction of armaments' called for by the Pope, is the real gospel of hope.

'No First Use'

SIR NEVILL MOTT

It is part of NATO planning that, if a Russian attack with tanks and aircraft could not otherwise be held by its forces, NATO would use nuclear weapons, at whatever level seemed appropriate. The doctrine of 'no first use', on the other hand, proposes that NATO should declare that it would never be the first to use a nuclear weapon. The sole purpose of NATO's nuclear armoury would then be to deter a *nuclear* attack, or the threat of one, by the other side and the defence of Europe would lie in the hands of NATO's conventional forces, built up to whatever level was deemed necessary and politically possible.

The doctrine of 'no first use' has been discussed, at 'Pugwash' meetings and elsewhere, for twenty years or more. More recently arguments for and against it are given in the Green Paper on Defence of the Social Democratic Party, and, most important, in an article published in June 1982 in *Foreign Affairs* advocating the re-examination of the doctrine written by four Americans,[1] former members of the Kennedy administration, who were perhaps more than anyone responsible for present NATO policy. It is therefore perhaps curious that the Bishop of Salisbury's report *The Church and the Bomb* makes no mention of the idea at all. As the proposal seems to have important implications for the morality of nuclear strategy, this article attempts to set them out, and to amplify some of the arguments given by the Bishop of Birmingham in favour of his narrowly adopted motion by the Synod in February 1983.

It is possible that a *limited* nuclear war could be less destructive than a conventional one. A letter in *The Times* (Brian Crozier, 16 November 1982, quoting the French authority, Pierre Gallois) suggested that the Russians could use their SS20 missiles, armed with very low-yield nuclear warheads, to put out of action all NATO bases in Europe with negligible radiation effect or casualties among civilians. On the other hand, there is an absolute difference in kind between the mechanisms of a nuclear and a non-nuclear explosion. Once the nuclear Rubicon is crossed there is no natural barrier against the use of larger and larger warheads and escalation towards the ultimate catastrophe that has been so often described. The illusion that a limited nuclear war can be controlled has been criticised by many authorities, from Lord Mountbatten and Lord Zuckerman onwards, and there is no need to repeat their arguments here.

In discussing the possibility of the adoption by NATO of a policy of 'no first use', I am assuming that the UK remains part of NATO and that those in favour of this policy should urge the British government to initiate discussions within the alliance as to its feasibility. If the UK retains its independent nuclear forces, any such policy would doubtless apply to them too, but this on the whole is a side-issue.

The moral issue on 'no first use' seems to me simple. The side that, in a war, first uses nuclear weapons opens the way to the holocaust. While a modern conventional war, bad enough in all conscience, is something from which a society can recover in a generation, a major nuclear war is not. We do not know if any recovery at all is possible. Any first use of a nuclear weapon, therefore, could be the ultimate crime against humanity, and a defence policy which depends on it as a threat has a very questionable moral basis.

On the other hand, the Russian threat is real, and the Western Alliance needs defence against it. It is not necessary to believe that the present Russian leadership wants war. The official view (*Statement on Defence Estimates*, 1980) is 'We have no reason to believe that the present Soviet leaders are deliberately planning to attack NATO. But they can use Soviet military power to threaten less powerful nations so as to force them to adopt policies which favour the Soviet Union.' I assume this to be correct. The Soviet Union has not hesitated to use military power, in Afghanistan, Czechoslovakia and indirectly in Poland, when it could safely do so. If a nuclear-armed Soviet Union was confronted by a NATO without such weapons one can hardly doubt that in the long run the political results would be profound and such as we would all deplore.

The conclusion is that, if Europe is to be defended, planning must be for a conventional defence, but that NATO should keep a substantial nuclear deterrent, to be used only if the other side crosses the nuclear divide.

There are of course many questions to be asked about this proposal. Would such a policy increase or decrease the risks of war? Is it practicable, and is it possible, to build up conventional forces that could match the Soviet strength in Europe? And finally, what moral basis can it have, since it envisages the retention of weapons which in certain circumstances would be used and lead to the slaughter of millions of innocent people.

A criticism frequently made of 'no first use' is that it would be a declaratory policy only, that it would not necessarily involve an end to the arms race, and that the Russians would have no reason to believe in our sincerity. This could be true; and at first the declaration might be primarily to our own people, appealing for the support of those who are not pacifists but who yet shrink from defence by the threat of world suicide. However, as a no first use policy on the part of NATO would eventually have its effects on the training of the armed forces and procurement of weapons, (there would be more for non-nuclear, anti-tank missiles, less for battlefield nuclear weapons) the policy might come to be believed.

It would be overwhelmingly to the advantage of the Russians to adopt it too. At an informal discussion in Moscow in September 1982 between Soviet and British experts, a principle Soviet thrust was to urge the West to match the Soviet declaration on no first use. But one reason (among many) for the West's hesitation was that the Soviet SS20s are thought to be clearly intended for use against NATO's nuclear delivery system, and therefore make sense only in terms of a first nuclear strike, for which indeed their armed forces are trained (*Bulletin of the Council for Arms Control*, January 1983). On either side, then, 'no first use' will only be believed if training and procurement are consistent with the policy, and it could be a long time before it becomes so credible that it changes to a doctrine of no use at all.

A much more serious criticism of the proposal is that it might increase the risk of war. Present NATO policy is that both sides recognise that a nuclear war would lead to no conceivable gain, and must be avoided at all costs, and so the Russians are deterred from starting any kind of war in Europe. Under 'no first use', the risk to them would be smaller and they might not be deterred. Against this it can be argued that — as between nuclear armed adversaries — the risks of starting any kind of war are enormous, whatever the declaratory policy of the other side. In the real world a 'no first use' declaration would therefore not be an invitation to invade. However, there is the uncomfortable feeling that deterrence works, in so far as no major war has yet occurred. The argument for present policies, given over and over again by government spokesmen and by some speakers at the 1983 General Synod is that deterrence is stable and we should not tamper with it. A particularly cogent exposition of this point of view is given by the historian Professor Hinsley (reproduced in the second section of this volume), who argues that modern technology has reached the point that no nuclear armed power will initiate war against another; that in spite of technical developments the condition is stable, and should not be disturbed. If so, we are much safer than many think.

This is the argument against 'no first use' and it is difficult to refute it.

On the other hand, I believe that 'no first use', as a long-term objective, gives by far the best hope that the nuclear threat will eventually disappear. These weapons have been invented and the knowledge of how to make them will not go away. Therefore, as long as there are armed powers, suspicious of each other, both sides are likely to keep some nuclear capacity whatever level of disarmament is achieved, just in case the other side 'cheated'. This could be so not only for the super-powers and their allies, but for other states which feel threatened and which have — or may soon have — nuclear weapons. If the policy of 'no first use' were adopted by the USSR and the NATO alliance, one could realistically hope that it would be accepted worldwide, and that the threat of their actual use would wither away.

When thirty years ago the United States and her European allies deliberately took the decision to rely on nuclear deterrence for the defence of Western Europe against any kind of Soviet attack, there was one very simple reason: it was cheap. The cost of nuclear weapons and the means of delivery (formidable as they are) were and are less than the cost of recruiting and equipping armed forces to match those of the Soviet Union. With a policy of 'no first use', while some money would doubtless be saved on the nuclear second strike force, more would undoubtedly have to be provided for conventional weapons. How much, neither Bundy and his co-authors nor most other authorities are prepared to say, but it could be substantial, unless an agreement can be reached with the Soviets to limit conventional forces — an exercise that has had no success as yet. Optimists believe that the development of electronically-guided anti-tank weapons is about to revolutionise land warfare, and to make it no longer necessary to match the Warsaw Pact forces, tank for tank, aircraft for aircraft. Defence could thus become cheaper. But even so whether the political will could be found to create and pay for such forces in the NATO countries is the question most in doubt, perhaps particularly in West Germany (the potential battlefield) where for obvious historical reasons a military tradition is suspect.

Any group commending 'no first use' to the British government should not urge that they make a declaration tomorrow — or on the morrow of an election victory. It can only be seen as a fairly long-term objective, consequent on successful discussions with our NATO allies and if necessary some build-up of conventional forces.

Seen from this point of view, the question of an independent British deterrent seems of little importance. One has to ask, what it is for? If it were acknowledged that it is a second strike force, to be used only in the event of a Soviet nuclear strike, then it would seem to me of little importance whether such a force where wholly assigned to NATO and armed with American weapons, or partly in our own hands. The extraordinary contrast with France, with its nuclear forces entirely under its own control and with little opposition to them within the country, is striking. A latent resentment of America does not play a part in that country. 'No first use' is not part of their strategy.

Finally, on the moral issue, *The Church and the Bomb* argues that to destroy millions of people with nuclear weapons is an immoral act; as indeed it is. The theory of deterrence, even under 'no first use', involves a conditional intention to perform an immoral act, and, it is argued, is therefore intrinsically immoral. Even if deterrence works, which is the end in view, can the end justify the means? The 'means' envisages a submarine commander receiving signals from his devastated homeland with orders to press the button, taking action that will lead to the deaths of millions of Russians. That to make plans of this kind is not immoral has of course been argued, not only by governments but by moral theologians. A summary of their arguments was given by Clifford Longley in *The Times* on 7 February 1983. 'If,' to quote from his article,

I intend to do some immoral action only in certain definite circumstances, and suppose I also believe that only by having this intention can I be sure that those circumstances will never occur; and suppose that it is my moral duty to try to prevent those circumstances from occurring; the situation then is that only by intending to do an immoral act can I do my duty of preventing those circumstances from occurring. Is it now clear that that intention is an immoral one?

The snag is that one cannot be certain that the dreaded situation will not arise. But this author believes that with 'no first use' the risk becomes extremely small — smaller than with any other option. Furthermore, whether this is the right way forward or not, the duty of Christians, surely, is to find the way between a surrender to Soviet power and the threat of nuclear war which gives society as much security as possible from the dangers that now threaten us. Above all, their duty is to listen to each other, and to try to see where between the beliefs of a President Reagan and those of an Edward Thompson the next step is to be found.

NOTES

1 McGeorge Bundy, G. F. Kennan, Robert S. McNamara and Gerard Smith, 'Nuclear Weapons and the Atlantic Alliance'.

II THE STRATEGY OF SURVIVAL

The 'Normalisation' of Europe

E. P. THOMPSON

This talk was first given in a private apartment in Budapest on the invitation of the Peace Group for Dialogue, and has been reproduced here without significant alteration.

Friends and colleagues, there is an artificial ideological chasm across our continent, and voices cannot always be heard across it. I will meet this responsibility in the only way proper. I ask your permission to speak with complete frankness. I will not waste your time on platitudes. It is probable that we will have a nuclear war, which will utterly devastate your country and mine, in the next twenty years. This war will bring to an end European civilisation.

Yet expressions of horror or goodwill alone will not prevent this outcome. Goodwill may even be a mask behind which other motives and other interests are at work. We must identify these motives and interests. And we must do so, not as partisans of one 'side' or the other 'side': we must do so together. And then we must find ways of acting together. First of all, we must take off our masks. We must be ready for difficult, uncomfortable arguments. As Gulya Illyes wrote in his 'Ode to Bartok':

> Let there be harmony!
> Order, but true order, lest the world perish
> O, if the world is not to perish
> the people must be free
> to speak, majestically.[1]

I must first explain briefly my personal position. I am not an absolute pacifist. There are circumstances in which I think it to be right to take arms in self-defence. But on nuclear weapons I am an absolutist. A civilisation which rests upon the constant daily threat of mutual extermination is a barbarism. We, in the majority tradition of the Western peace movement, do not just refuse particular weapons — the cruise missile, MX and Trident, the SS20. We refuse them all. And we ask for this refusal on both sides. There are not good democratic Western bombs and evil communist ones, or good proletarian bombs and evil Western imperialist ones. What is the purpose of discussing the 'balance' or 'parity' of two absolute evils?

Nor does talk of 'balance' make for any kind of military sense. For nuclear weapons are not weapons of defence. They are weapons of menace or threat and, in the same moment, of suicide. A nuclear 'deterrent' is like a pistol which, in the very same moment that it is pointed at an antagonist, is also pointed at one's own head. It is to say, 'Don't move, or we will blow us both up!' That is not a credible defence, even though it is what may in the end happen. Meanwhile this fearful threat has rather little effect on the actual behaviour of armed states.

There is a second personal point. I happen to distrust all armed states, for reasons which go beyond the matter of weaponry itself. William Blake wrote, when the French Revolution had passed into its Napoleonic imperial era:

> The strongest poison ever known
> Came from Caesar's laurel crown.

This poison does not come only in the form of plutonium. It is generally true in history that — except in moments of aroused national self-defence — a state of war, or of high military preparedness, is also a degenerative condition in the political and social life of a nation. A military definition of reality is superimposed upon all other human intentions, needs and rights. Certainly — but here I can speak only from Western experience — the long-protracted state of Cold War has encouraged diseases in the body politic — priority given to arms industries over services (education, health, welfare), the strengthening of security services and police, the imposition of ideological conformity and stupidity, 'official secrecy' — which in Britain means keeping secret from the British people facts which are perfectly well-known to the intelligence services of the Warsaw Treaty powers — and all the rest. I used to jest at our own peace meetings that the only growth area of the British economy today is telephone-tapping. Now we have had the Falklands War, and the growth area is building replacements for sunken battleships.

If the present Cold War — or adversary posture of the two blocs — is protracted for a further 20 years, it will not inevitably lead to the final holocaust, although it will probably do so; but it will, very certainly, give rise to two profoundly distorted economies and damaged cultures, to two opposed, warlike societies, ruled by leaders who are intolerant, security-minded persons, and hence to a diminution of every citizen's freedom and right as against the demands of the rival armed states.

That is a dismal outlook. But we must be plain about it. We must not avert our eyes. It gives to this moment of rising peace consciousness, in East and West, a special urgency: this opportunity may be our last before the trap finally closes upon us. Forgive me if I cause offence. I am not talking about the *intentions* of leaders, on your side or on mine. To predict the course of history from the intentions of individual leaders is futile. I am indicating a deep process, quite beyond the intentions of individuals, by which the overfat military establishments of one side continually feed and further fatten the other.

A strange propaganda duel took place in the world's forum in the past year. Caspar Weinberger, the US Secretary of Defense, issued, with an immense sound of tin trumpets, a book prepared in the Pentagon entitled *Soviet Military Power*. This showed a fearsome growth in recent years of Soviet forces — tanks, missiles, aircraft, naval power. The size and technical proficiency of Soviet and Warsaw Pact military resources were shown — with graphs, diagrams, and alarming pictures — to be without precedent.

This goulash was not all made up of lies, although there were some ugly lies within it. What it neglected to do was present any means of comparison: that is, any comparable information on US and NATO military power. This was at once repaired by the Military Publishing House of the USSR Ministry of Defence which issued its own glossy illustrated handbook, *Whence the Threat to Peace?* If anything, the pictures in this one were better — since they are more easy to obtain from Western, than from Soviet, sources — and they were more alarming. They showed a fearsome build-up in recent years of United States and NATO forces.

At the time of the French Revolution, the leading exponent in England of *The Rights of Man* was Thomas Paine, and the leading critic was Edmund Burke, author of *Reflections on the French Revolution.* One philosophical British reformer sent both books to be bound together as one: he said that, when read together, they made up a very good book. In the same way, *Soviet Military Power* and *Whence the Threat to Peace?* should be bound in a common volume. But they do not make a very good book. They make, together, a book so fearsome that the mind and the emotions recoil before it. It is the most barbaric catalogue of the ingenuity of the instruments of murder ever known in the human record. It is an inventory of twin matched evils, a balance-sheet in which every item is loss. The book is a confession of absolute human failure.

But the general shape of the facts is true. I mention this in case there should be anyone here who reads the newspapers upside-down. And the facts of Western military buildup are true not only of the USA. Let me cite the case of my own country. In 1982, a year in which the productive sectors of the British economy have been experiencing great difficulties, in which money for education and services has been cut, in which there are over three millions unemployed, Mrs Thatcher's government has been able to fight an expensive war in the South Atlantic and has also agreed to replace the aging group of Polaris missile submarines with the most expensive of all options possible, the American-designed Trident D5. The British Ministry of Defence reported proudly last week that the quantity of multiple, independently-targeted warheads on the Trident missiles is such that Britain will have 672 warheads to deliver on targets in Eastern Europe and the Soviet Union instead of the 96 in the present Polaris fleet. The new missiles will have a range of 6,000 miles as compared with 2,800 miles for Polaris. And each additional mile will bring 15,000 new square miles into the target area. Britain will therefore be able to target about seven times as many cities and bases as before. And by what analysis have Mrs Thatcher and her military advisors decided that, in fifteen years time, it will be necessary for my country to have forces of extermination seven times more hideous and more menacing? It would seem to be to be a pessimistic deduction. It might even be thought to be unneighbourly. Meanwhile, these Tridents will cost Britain's ailing economy some ten thousand million pounds, and this, with the additions for rebuilding sunken battleships, telephone-tapping and the rest, will, perhaps, destroy my country without any need for Soviet intervention.

I cannot cite with equal accuracy details from the other side of the chasm since matters are not so openly published in the Soviet Union. But we have it on the best authority that, if the growth of weaponry in NATO in the past 20 years has been fearsome, it has been fearsome in the Warsaw Pact also. For President Brezhnev has on several occasions spoken of 'rough parity' in the opposed nuclear weapons systems. If one side is hideous, and the other side is in 'rough parity', then it must follow that the other side is hideous also. There is a reciprocal, mutually-accelerating state of ferocity. The weapons-systems are now the leading sectors of the economy on both sides of the world, and in their interactive stimulation, and in the priority awarded to military needs over all other needs, we may begin, as Zdenek Mlynar has suggested, to discern a 'new mode of development'.

It is against this mode, which is developing a universal death, and which is enforcing — in the increasing sale of arms by both WT and NATO powers to the Third World — its own diseased forms upon the poorer nations of the 'South' that the peace movement has risen — and continues to rise — in the West. It has been epidemic in character, moving swiftly across frontiers like a benign infection: now Holland, now Britain; next Scandinavia, Germany, Italy; and then across the Atlantic. It commenced as a refusal: as Erhard Eppler declared, 'the chain of armaments must be cut through'. But it is more than a refusal. There is, I have been told, some misunderstanding over on this side as to the position of the Western peace movement, or, I should say, that part of the Western peace movement to which I belong. I think I may say that this position is becoming the majority tendency in West Europe and the USA, although there are other minority positions: for example, absolute pacifism, or in some countries pro-Soviet sympathisers. The position which I will explain to you is very widely held in the British Campaign for Nuclear Disarmament which is an association of the mass peace movement in Britain. I have found it widely supported in Ireland, in Iceland, and in Norway. It has been elaborated by the experienced Inter-church Peace Council (IKV) in Holland and by an influential section of the movement in Austria. It is strongly present, for example among the Greens, in the debates now going on in West Germany; and similar arguments are found in Southern Europe, especially in the eurocommunist Italian Communist Party and independent ecological, feminist and left groups.

First, our position on nuclear weapons is absolutist. We refuse them. The human species, the planet itself, cannot afford them. It is essential to the morale of our movement that we should not compromise this refusal by behaving like politicians and arguing about 'numbers'. Now, in many parts of West and South Europe, from Stornoway in the Western Isles of Scotland to Comiso in Sicily, many people are preparing for peaceful direct action: sit-downs, peace camps outside bases, blockades, hunger strikes. I ask you to give your solidarity to these people!

How is this to be done? I do not know your circumstances. I do not wish to intervene in your proper national affairs. But if the destruction of our continent is at stake, then we must consult together and act as Europeans: we must discard narrow national or ideological views. You must know, if you reflect, that this is so, and even for very practical political reasons. The Western peace movement is strong, but it is not yet strong enough to impose its will upon states or military organisations. And it is now reaching the limits of certain ideological/political barriers. What is the question that we are asked most frequently by hostile critics in our countries? 'We agree that disarmament is good', these critics say 'but where is the peace movement on the other side?' And if it is answered that the Soviet Peace Committee, and certain other national peace committees and councils in the East, have organised their own demonstrations and petitions, the critic replies: 'Yes, but these were directed against NATO weapons, not against the weapons and militarism of their own states.' I was present at the great demonstration in Bonn last October which saw the West German movement come to maturity. All afternoon a hostile plane circled overhead drawing behind it a streamer inscribed 'Wer demonstriert in Moskau?' (Who is demonstrating in Moscow?). If the Western peace movement is to break through this barrier, then we must be able to clasp hands with a non-aligned movement, totally independent of the state, on your side also. What has been epidemic must become pandemic.

Yet our own position remains absolutist. Whether an independent movement gains strength on your side or not, we will maintain our absolute refusal. This is unconditional. We are not politicians engaged in clever trading negotiations. Our stand is misinterpreted, not only by hostile critics in the West, but also by some observers in the East. They suppose our stand to be motivated by fear or defeatism — or perhaps by pro-Soviet and anti-American emotions; perhaps the response to Soviet military and diplomatic pressure of a nervous Western intelligentsia and 'petty bourgeoisie'?

No! Of course there may be such minority elements, here and there. But the majority position is grounded not only upon an absolute moral premise. It is also grounded in political logic. Our logic remains one of negotiations: but negotiation *by action*, in which the nations of Europe, East and West, resume an autonomous role. For twenty years the superpowers have imposed their hegemony upon other European nations — have taken all negotiations into their own hands; and all the time the weaponry has gone up and up. Today, once again, negotiations are proceeding behind closed doors at Geneva, on a matter which could scarcely concern all Europeans more — intermediate European 'theatre' weapons, the instruments of a 'limited nuclear war' — and yet there are no European seats at the negotiating table. To refuse these weapons any place on our territory — to refuse any forward launching or air bases from which these weapons might be deployed — is the only option for autonomy left to your people or to mine: the autonomy of survival.

But I spoke of 'negotiating by action'. CND in Britain, like the Dutch peace movement, supports unilateral measures of disarmament. If Holland or Britain refuse any weapons system — and the Dutch and British Labour Parties are pledged to do so — it is not supposed that the matter will end there. It will be the first step in a process of direct

negotiation. We hope to come back then, as better neighbours, to your side — perhaps to the Soviet Union, perhaps to
Hungary or Poland — and say: 'We have stopped that system
and removed these bases of the United States military from
our territory. Now, then, which system will you stop in
exchange, which bases of the Soviet forces will you (politely
of course) remove?'

We are tired of leaving our fate in the hands of the politicians of the superpowers, most of whom are locked into
the inertia of the *status quo*. Nor would our actions endanger
in any way our own nation's legitimate defence. I have already
explained that these are not defensive weapons and that bases
can only invite attack. But there is another point. These
systems are grossly in excess of any military 'needs' in even
the maddest of strategic scenarios. This is not just the view
of some utopian 'pacifist'. It is the clear judgement of senior
military men and arms advisors from both sides, although
they tell us this only when they have retired and are free to
speak. There is a long list of such expert witnesses. A recent
one is Field Marshal Lord Carver, the retired chief of the
British military staff, who published a book called *A Policy
for Peace*. Lord Carver says clearly that 'the number and
variety of weapons systems of the USA and USSR is grossly
in excess of what is needed' for deterrence, and additional
systems are 'superfluous'.

Both sides are as fat with weapons systems as a goose
being prepared for Christmas dinner. Sir Martin Ryle, the
British astronomer royal, has said that there is already
enough nuclear weaponry on our continent to destroy
Europe totally more than 20 times. How can it matter
whether one side can do this 11 times and the other only
9 times? Once is enough. So that even on the premises of
military 'deterrence' there is fat enough to be cut out without any risk.

This is only the first part of our logic. The second part can
only be confirmed, or rejected, by you on this side. Your
generosity in inviting me to speak openly here tonight,

perhaps even in the face of the disapproval of some mis-
informed persons in influential places, moves me very deeply.
We also, in our movement in the West, organise, argue, and
act in the face of official disapproval and misunderstanding;
and despite the many real and important freedoms of press
and opinion in my own country, we often have difficulty
in gaining expression for any full statement of our views in
the most popular television or newspaper media. But your
generosity here tonight makes me have confidence that the
logic of our position may be correct. We believe that if we
continue to act — in this way — even if unilaterally, and that
if we can force one or more Western governments to take
these actions of unilateral refusal, then we will meet, over on
this side, with an equivalent response, equivalent popular
pressure, and action.

I will go further. To suppose that the majority Western
peace movement is motivated by fear or by pro-Soviet
ideological premises is a very great mistake. It could be a
tragic mistake. It could prevent us from gaining the response,
from your side, which is urgent and essential to complete
the logic of the movement for peace and against the armed
states of the world. Soviet leaders must come to understand
that there are now millions in the West whose beliefs and
ideas they would describe as 'anti-Soviet' — that is, who are
severe critics of aspects of Soviet actuality, who are supporters of intellectual and civil rights, who support as a matter
of principle the rights of conscientious objection from military service, or who are, as the majority trade union and
Labour movements of the West are, sympathisers with
Solidarity and the Polish renewal — there are millions of
such people who also support the peace movement, precisely because they believe that a condition of militarism, a
state of preparedness for war, brings out the worst features
of both opposed social and political systems.

Good friends, these people wish to talk with you! How
much they wish to talk, to show goodwill, to defy the
absurd legacies of an old, bad, and dead history, to defy

the antique security and ideological barriers on both sides which hold us apart! But they wish to talk with you directly as I am privileged to talk with you now. They do not wish to talk with you in *any* way and on *any* terms. They wish to talk with you as human neighbours, on an endangered continent, and yet not in such a way as to give advantage or propaganda points to either military bloc. They wish to talk with you honestly and directly, *beneath* the level of the armed states and their ideological caretakers.

This is the reason why many parts of the Western peace movement, including END — the committee for European Nuclear Disarmament of which I am a member — have been shy of direct linkages with national peace councils and committees on your side. To be plain: we do not like the World Peace Council, and we are wary of its affiliated organisations. The WPC has endorsed some good causes in the past, but it has always or very often, acted one-sidedly, as a partisan and sometimes as a captive of Soviet diplomatic interests. It appears to us sometimes as Soviet state interests, wearing the mask of peace and goodwill. We do not suppose the interests of the Soviet state to be inherently aggressive or expansionist, although there have been occasions when — for 'reasons of state' or national 'defence' — aggressions and expansions have taken place. But we cannot accept a situation in which we are contesting, with all our energy and in every moment of our work, the military policies and ideologies of our own states but we are told that the only permissible channel for communication with fellow workers for peace on your side must be committees or councils which in most respects *support* the military policies and ideologies of their own states. That is a bad, unequal, even deceptive relationship between movements and peoples.

Of course, if one side were wholly blameworthy and the other side wholly innocent, there might be some reason in this. But no-one — and certainly no-one of influence in the majority Western peace movement — believes that sort of fairy-tale any more. What are we to make of a 'Peace Committee' which apologised for the harassment of a small independent group of peace workers in Moscow, and did not protest when their leader, Sergei Batovrin, was forcibly sent to a mental hospital and administered depressant drugs? That has become, in the British and American peace movements, an occasion for scandal. The hooligans who acted in this way against this small group are as dangerous to our work for peace as are the manufacturers of nuclear arms.

I am not here criticising the Hungarian Peace Council. This council has been present, as an observer, at several of our conferences in the West; its representatives have made constructive contributions and have attended to criticisms of WTO military policies with courtesy. We are glad to acknowledge their more tolerant and flexible approach. But I wish to explain why it is that, whenever the question of co-operation with organisations on your side comes up, our supporters always ask us at once: 'Is that movement truly independent and non-aligned? Has it criticised the weapons and strategies of its own bloc as well as those of the West?'

At the same time, and all the time, our own supporters do wish to talk with you, so long as the talk is honest, the communication is free and open, and not only what is permitted to be poured through some official funnel into the correct official bottles. I will give you an example. I recently spoke at a meeting of the Campaign for Nuclear Disarmament at Blaenau Ffestiniog, a small town in North Wales. There were some 500 persons at the meeting and many more hundreds of young people at a festival of music and theatre outside. The population of this town is only some 6,000 people, but many had come from the nearby region. The speakers included the MP for the region, the past President of the Welsh National Party, the Archdruid — a leader of Welsh national culture — a Catholic priest, and a member of the Scandinavian Womens Peacemarch who had also visited Mr Batovrin's independent group while in Moscow.

I must explain one further matter. On 23 February 1982,

the whole of Wales was proclaimed a 'nuclear free zone'. This was the culmination of a year-long campaign, in which many thousands took part, and in which, by democratic votes and after much discussion, every major city and every county council in Wales voted to be nuclear free. This means that they refused to have nuclear weapons based on their territory, manufactured within it, and refused also to take part in useless 'cosmetic' gestures at civil defence since reputable authorities agree that there is no defence for populations against these weapons. When the final county in Wales — Clwyd — passed this resolution, there was issued a Clwyd Declaration on behalf of the whole country of Wales:

> ...the whole of Wales, through its democratically elected representatives, has declared itself a nuclear free zone. By this action Wales has given a moral lead to the other countries of Europe and the world.
>
> In passing on to them our message of hope and inspiration, we call upon the other nations of Europe to make known their deep concern for the culture of civilisation. We call upon them to commit themselves to the cause of redeeming Europe from total destruction by taking the initial step of declaring their homelands nuclear free zones.

When I told the meeting that I was coming to Budapest, I was asked to take this message with me. But matters went further. I told them that I had heard that there was a rising spirit of peace-consciousness in your country and new movements taking their own independent positions, willing to act impartially in order to restrain the militarism not only of the West but also of your own side. And it was decided then to place a message in the hall for those present to sign.[2] This message comes to you with the warmest feelings, with the greatest goodwill to all people committed to peace activity in Hungary. I was asked to pass it on to the new Peace Centre which you will form in Budapest.

And this is the most important thing I wish to say about
the new peace movement, West or East. They are movements
which may have commenced in fear, but they are now movements of hope. They are not only contesting particular
missiles — cruise and SS20. They are engaged also in the
recreation of internationalism, by hundreds of different
exchanges between peace activists. They are moving forward
from missiles to contesting the bloc system itself from whose
antagonism the rival militarisms arise. They are setting themselves an astonishing objective: to break down, not in some
distant future which may never arrive, but in the next ten
years, the Cold War itself. The practical objective must now
be the dissolution of both blocs, with intermediate measures
for regional nuclear free zones — the Balkans, the Baltic,
Central Europe — linked to the progressive demilitarisation,
with the withdrawal of contentional forces also, of the whole
continent: that is, the 'normalisation' of Europe.

Friends, our situation today is not only perilous. It is
abnormal and absurd. Here we are, a few hours away from
each other by train or car or plane. We share many elements
of common history and culture. There is no geological chasm
which keeps us apart. The people — and the young people of
both sides especially — share common interests, styles of
dress, tastes in music, concern for the environment and for
the Third World. What keeps us apart is not a line on the
ground but a line inside our heads. Or it is the weight of old
and bad history, which 'weighs like an alp upon the living'.
This unnatural state is the legacy of a particular moment, a
particular balance of forces, at the end of World War II,
which has protracted its moment long after the reasons for
that moment have passed away. A new generation has arisen
on both sides, in Bonn or in Budapest, for whom this artificial segregation — this *apartheid* imposed by senile ideologies
— is an obscenity.

In every moment that we accept the false divisions of the
Cold War in our heads we are guilty of treason to each other.
We allow the armed states — from the inertia of the past — to

arrange us according to military, and not according to human, definitions of reality. We allow the senescent ideologies to say that anyone acting for disarmament by direct unilateral action in the West is somehow 'pro-Soviet', a conscious or unconscious agent of communist power. And we allow them to say that anyone in the East who is critical of your own militarism or who demands certain rights of free communication or expression is a conscious or unconscious agent of Western imperialism. In this way we are held apart from each other, and our strength is bent against each other. The abnormalities of our split civilisation are legitimated and extended into the future in which this state of fission will destroy us all.

But if only we could find some way of bending our strengths together — some force of cultural and political fusion — with difficulties and with risks we could enforce our will upon both armed blocs. How could this be done? This is what the Western peace movement wishes to talk with you about — consult and take your advice. We are clear only on a few matters. First, the Cold War can never be ended by the victory of one side over the other side: there can be no such victory without war. It can be ended only as a result of a 'people's détente' — a détente beneath the level of states — created by popular initiative, above all by the young. Second, no peace movement has any chance of success which serves the interests of only one side: the peace movement must be resolutely non-aligned. Third, it is no part of the peace movement's work to intervene in the complicated questions of the national political life on the other side. The Western peace movement ought not to intervene in your affairs — although, since we are an undisciplined movement of 'individualists', I cannot promise that no one will try to do so. And independent peace movements in the East do not exist to create little moments of drama in the Western press, nor even to give legitimacy to the independent peace movement of the West, but to work steadily for peace according to national conditions and needs, offering their own proposals, and with the single objective of the success of our common work.

I have said, in other places, that the Western peace movement and the forces making for democratisation in the East are natural allies: that the causes of peace and of freedom go together. I believe that this is true, in a profound historical way: here is the force which will combine our strengths. Let us say that the movements should 'recognise' each other. But the Western peace movement is not in the business of being an export agency, seeking to export into the East, along with the ideas of peace, a whole set of other ideas and demands, some of which may be appropriate to your national conditions and some of which may not. And I hope that peace movements on your side will show a similar self-restraint. I will go further. I think the peace movements — our joint peace movements together — should exert their influence as a stabilising force, not as a force making for dramas and emergencies. We may wish to 'de-stabilise' the military structures of both sides, but this does not mean that we wish to throw political life into a turmoil.

I will give you a sensitive example. If the Polish renewal should advance once more and if martial law could be lifted, this would be welcomed by the Western peace movement. We are, after all, most of us trade unionists ourselves. But if the Polish renewal should afford to the Polish nation more space for autonomy then it should be the business of the Western peace movement to use all its strength to hold back those militarist elements in the USA or NATO who might wish to press into these spaces and secure some advantage for NATO from what they might perceive as a 'weakness' in the WTO. This is an example of what I mean by a 'stabilising force'. The proper response of the Western peace movement to the Polish situation ought to be to enforce a relaxation of military tension in Central Europe, to enable there to be space for the Polish people to work out their problems internally and with their neighbours without interference. How can Pershing II missiles, sited on the rim of West Germany, bring freedom or renewal to anyone?

The Western peace movement is not strong enough yet to

give any guarantees that it can restrain NATO adventurers. We are in our childhood still. We must grow stronger. But we have reached a point when we can only gain this strength if we are part of a transcontinental movement, a non-aligned movement stretching across the whole of Europe. And I will not disguise my own advice as to a proper and normal objective. It is time, after 37 years, that World War II was concluded with a normal peace treaty in the Germanies. And this would bring about, as no kind of provocation but as a normal event, the entire withdrawal of foreign military presence and bases, first from Central Europe (including West Germany), and next from our continent: to be specific, of Soviet forces and bases from East Europe and of American forces and bases from the West. We should invite this withdrawal with courtesy: we should thank these forces for their acts of liberation, we should say goodbye with flowers. But 37 years is a long time. It is long enough.

Of course the foreign forces in Europe today are not forces of occupation. But they are still the testimony of an abnormal and unresolved state of affairs and a heavy burden upon the resources of both superpowers. It is in the direct interests of both that this situation should now be ended, and it is our business — the business of a transcontinental peace movement — to provide the conditions in which with the least possible risk or advantage to one side against the other this can be done.

NOTES

1 *New Reasoner*, No. 5, Summer 1958.
2 The message, inscribed in Welsh and English, read: 'At a public meeting of the Campaign for Nuclear Disarmament in Blaenau Ffestiniog in nuclear-free Wales, we, the undersigned, resolved to send this message of friendship and greetings to our fellow workers for peace in Budapest at the new Peace Centre. May all Europe be reunited in peace. By our common efforts we will bring the cold war to an end.' No count was made of the final number of signatories which was several hundreds. The meeting also sent a beautiful slate ornament to the Peace Centre (which may open shortly) and some Welsh daffodil bulbs to the anti-nuclear movement in the Hungarian schools.

Reflections on the Debate about the Nuclear Weapons

F. H. HINSLEY

Three features stand out in the history of relations between the world's leading states since the end of the eighteenth century. Infrequent wars have alternated with long periods of peace. Each of the wars has been more nearly total, more demanding and devastating for all the participants, than that which preceded it. At the end of every war the leading states have made a concerted effort, each one more radical than the last, to reconstruct the international system on lines that would make them more likely to succeed, or so they believed, in avoiding a further war. In these respects international conduct in the past 200 years has differed markedly from international conduct in all earlier times, when states were more or less continuously engaged in wars which remained limited in scale.

The successive attempts to reform the modern inter-national system have come to nothing. The most recent, that which established the United Nations Organisation in 1945, has in itself created no better safeguards against the renewal of war than did its forerunners — the Concert system set up at the end of the Napoleonic Wars in 1815; the arbitration measures that were launched in the 1890s in the aftermath of sixteen years of European wars which had ended in 1871; the League of Nations that followed at the end of the First World War in 1918. But these failures add significance, if they also give poignancy, to the fact that the reforming effort has been so persistently renewed. The leading states embarked on it when they had been brought to recognize that the next war, should there be one, would be still more destructive than the one they were bringing to a close; they resumed it in the knowledge that the latest war had amply confirmed the accuracy of their initial foreboding. It is for the same reason that, even though each period of peace has eventually broken down, the leading states have fought each other only at long intervals: before the outbreak of each war they have shifted and struggled to avert it, and have at least succeeded in deferring it, because they have been reluctant to fight it. Nor is it difficult to understand why in these ways the international conduct of modern states has been marked by an ever-growing pre-occupation with the wish to pursue their interests without engaging in war. Since the end of the eighteenth century they have been caught up in a continuing weapons revolution. The weapons revolution has been but one manifestation of a wider process in which the advance of science has not only intensified the pace of technological, political, social and economic changes but has also quickened awareness of the consequences that must follow.

To the increasingly obvious implications of the weapons revolution, as of wider changes to the structure of society and the capacity of government, which have also steadily raised the scale and reduced the utility of war, industrialised states and societies and the individuals who compose them have necessarily become increasingly alert since 1945; since the end of the Second World War, in thirty-five years, men have made more advances in the application of science and technology than they made between the end of the eighteenth century and 1945, if not in all previous history. The most obvious outcome of this exponential acceleration is the further irreversible stage in the weapons revolution that has resulted from the conquest of atomic and nuclear fission and the development of missile technology. In terms of the consequences for the scale and utility of war, it seems reasonable to conclude – and it is certainly necessary to assume – that the next war between the leading states, should they allow it to occur, will be not only more total than the last, but total *tout court* – so total that all will lose and none will gain.

This necessary assumption is resisted in some quarters. There are strategists who believe that states will not only begin a war with the intention of limiting its scope, but will be able to adhere to that intention when the stakes are down. In the 1930s, in much the same way, the most revered strategists of the day believed that blitzkrieg methods would contain the next war by yielding quick and painless victories. Fifty years later – when for 200 years the industrialised states have become increasingly preoccupied with the wish to avoid another war from the fear, previously always justified in the event, that it would be more total than the last – it seems less unreasonable to conclude that for the governments of those states the need for caution and for precautions has at last become so compelling that they will refrain from fighting each other again, and perhaps could not even if they wished. But to judge from the current debate as to whether the United Kingdom should retain or abandon nuclear weapons, this alternative assumption, far from being resisted in some quarters, is instinctively distrusted or ignored in nearly all.

In this debate there are those who would retain the weapons in the belief that they will deter a nuclear attack but who also believe that the country could not or would not use them against a conventional attack; the country must therefore be ready to oppose a conventional attack with conventional weapons. There are others who share these beliefs, but who question whether the country can afford any, or at any rate the latest, nuclear weapons. They fear that the country, which spends less than 10 per cent of its defence budget on nuclear weapons, must spend even less on them if it is to be effective in a conventional war. Leaving aside the difficulty that the conventional war they envisage is one with a state whose first-line conventional military power exceeds the combined power of all the states which will be at war with it, neither of these arguments allows for the possibility that nuclear weapons have deterred that state from making a conventional attack, and will continue to do so. In preparation for its policy of updating the country's nuclear weapons, the government has gone some way to repairing this omission by letting it be known that it will use them to halt a conventional attack; but it still shrinks from acting on the belief that they ensure that a conventional attack will not take place. Perhaps only political obstacles prevent it from doing so. It could not further reduce its conventional forces without a wrangle with its allies. It could not easily proclaim that it no longer believes, as it once did, that the chief justification for retaining nuclear weapons is that their retention will somehow increase the prospects of securing agreement to their universal abolition; such a confession would gravely disturb the other participants in the debate, those who not merely ignore the possibility that nuclear weapons have eliminated the danger of war, but positively insist that nuclear weapons constitute the sole, or the greatest, danger to peace.

For this last position, which is too easily confused with the reasonable assumption that a nuclear war would be even more terrible than a conventional war, there is no evidence. If anything, the leading states were more incautious between wars before 1914 and before 1939 than they have been since 1945, and the peace between them was more fragile before 1914 and before 1939 than it is today. But this is not to say that their greater caution can confidently be attributed to the nuclear weapons and thus constitutes evidence for the belief that, thanks to these weapons, they will continue to keep the peace. The knowledge that, in contemporary conditions, even a conventional war would be terrible has been enough to account for their keeping the peace so far; and we must look elsewhere for support for the view that the nuclear weapons will persuade them to abstain from war for so long as we need to look ahead.

Before the Second World War states possessed the undisputed right to go to war for any reason whatever — indeed, for no reason at all — as a consequence of their sovereignty. In 1946, in addition to establishing the United Nations Organisation, the states resolved that the renunciation of this right should be a condition of membership of the Organisation. You may be sceptical of the significance of this step. Many states had offered to take it once before, when signing the Kellog Pact in 1928, and even now the renunciation is qualified; it is subject to the right of self-defence and is waived when states are carrying out the instructions of the United Nations. You may be still more sceptical if you recall how easily states have exploited these loop-holes. No state now has a War Office, but all states retain the department and call it the Ministry of Defence. No state of any importance now declares war when it uses force in contravention of its pledge; if it cannot plead self-defence or United Nations' instructions it either resorts to force without admitting that it is doing so or finds some other justification by claiming that it is helping a legitimate government against rebellion, or helping rebels to advance an indubitably moral cause. But I believe these subterfuges confirm rather than weaken the argument that in 1946 the states achieved a great advance. They are subterfuges to which states descend in order to remain within the letter of a new rule of conduct; and you do not make efforts to appear to obey a rule which you do not accept. We must not forget, moreover, the difference between rules and the laws of thermodynamics. You do not make a rule to the effect that water must not flow uphill; but man-made law would not be law — indeed, it would not be made — unless it could be broken or bent. It lays down rules but does not ensure that they will be observed. What came about with the abolition of the right of the state to go to war was a shift of norms; and involving, as it did, the recognition that war had ceased to be a legalised or sanctified form of force, it constituted a greater displacement of assumptions about relations between states than any that has taken place in history.

When a shift is so fundamental we may be sure of two things: it will have been a long time in preparation; and once it has been made, and if it is consolidated, it will have multiple and far-reaching repercussions. In the case of this shift, as I have already argued, it was being prepared for throughout the history of the modern international system: indeed, its completion was nothing less than the logical outcome of those developments, and of those responses to developments, which explain the history of that system and account for its distinctive features. But is it possible to claim that the shift has as yet produced any noticeable repercussions? I believe it is. There has been much evidence to suggest that other displacements of belief or ideology, subsidiary to and consequential upon the first, have been taking place in recent years. And most prominently — and this should cause no surprise since Marxism—Leninism is the most rigorous and self-conscious of all modern ideologies — the evidence is to be found in the steps that have been taken to adjust the doctrines of Marxism—Leninism.

The central doctrine of Marxism—Leninism relating to the issue of peace and war used to be the doctrine that war is inevitable between socialist and capitalist societies. Whether this doctrine issued from the conviction that capitalism would not be satisfied until socialism had been destroyed, or from the conviction that socialism must not be content until capitalism has been abolished, is a question of no consequence; the doctrine was beyond dispute. But in 1956, at the XXth Congress of the Communist Party of the Soviet Union, it was formally cancelled. No less important, another doctrine was made central in its place — the doctrine of peaceful coexistence, which insists that the rivalry that is inevitable between societies with different structures and ideologies, but is supposedly inevitable *only* between such societies, must for ever be kept short of war by the states.

It was perhaps only to be expected that at the time, and for years after, the capitalist societies should regard this change as constituting no more than a dangerous tactical twist in the Bolshevik offensive, one that was designed to lull them into a false sense of security while Stalin's successors rescued Russia from Stalin's excesses and prepared to return to the true Bolshevik path. Even now, this suspicion is not wholly stilled. But this residue of distrust is of little significance compared with the fact that, since the 1960s, capitalist states have embraced the Marxist–Leninist, new-model doctrine of peaceful coexistence and made it their own overriding doctrine in the field of relations between states. At least in this field, East and West, communism and capitalism, now subscribe to a common view for the first time since the Bolshevik revolution of 1917. Nor does China any longer remain outside the consensus. It is sometimes claimed that the Chinese Marxist–Leninists, the fundamentalists of the movement, still proclaim that war is inevitable between socialism and capitalism. On closer inspection it will be found that they now insist only that war will be inevitable unless an expansionist Russia is contained by the combined efforts of other states.

That this adjustment has not been made easily in Russia and China we may be sure from what we know about the rigidity, almost theological, of the Marxist–Leninist laboratory of thought. And we know that the West was hardly less reluctant to make it, for here we may examine in some detail how and why it was brought about when impasse had been reached after a decade of labour in the field of strategic studies. Strategic studies became a major academic industry in the West in the early 1950s. Nor is this surprising; it was then that the nuclear weapons were superseding the atomic bomb; that the missile was superseding the bomber; that the submarine was emerging as the perfect moving missile platform; and that the West's monopoly of these advantages was shattered by developments in Soviet Russia. It is in no way surprising, either, that from the outset until the middle of the 1960s the object of the studies was, as all the literature proclaimed, to reintegrate strategy with policy – to restore to policy the flexibility and the range of options that the latest weapons were taking away from it. Nor is it surprising – the less so in that these years were years of Cold War – that the real, as opposed to the ostensible, objective of the literature was to discover whether nuclear states could evolve strategies and weapons by which they could preserve their options of threatening war with each other and of going to war with each other despite the fact that they had become nuclear states. Techniques of crisis management; theories for the control of escalation; strategies of flexible retaliation; the development of tactical or little nuclear weapons; these suggestions were all advanced in the hope that, by enabling nuclear states to evade the logical outcome of nuclear dead-lock, the strategy of 'the great deterrent', they would preserve for them the possibility of more limited war.

If we read these elaborations today we bring away from them one unmistakable impression. They possess all the cogency, all the intellectual rigour and all the irrelevance of the scholastic writings of the middle ages. And whence their irrelevance? The answer lies partly in the fact that they did not pause to ask whether disciplines accepted by one nuclear state would be accepted by another, or whether disciplines accepted by all nuclear states before the outbreak of hostilities would be observed by all after hostilities had broken out. But it lies mainly in the fact that since the mid-1960s, no doubt as a result of deeper reflection, the response of strategic thinkers has undergone a fundamental change.

Their message since then has been that, should provocation lead to war between the world's most developed states (or should accident or miscalculation do so), there is no reasonable hope of avoiding massive nuclear exchanges and no possibility of providing civil defence against them; that if it is thus imperative to avoid war, then, far from trying to avoid dependence on the great deterrent of massive retaliation, it is imperative to ensure against provocation and miscalculation by seeing to it that all nuclear states shall be able to rely on deterring each other; and that they will be deterred by the risk of massive retaliation if all possess a retaliatory nuclear armoury that is invulnerable to a nuclear first attack. They have concluded – to put this message in other words – that, whereas the chief purpose of military establishments has hitherto been to fight wars, from now on their chief purpose is to avert war, and that the advance of technology has at last made it possible for them to fulfil it.

You may grant the interest and the significance of this development, as of those others I have singled out, and yet remain apprehensive lest they prove to be reversible. The initiative which produced the establishment of the League of Nations was significant; but the League was ineffective and short-lived. It was already a feature of the modern international system before 1945 that its leading states contrived to enjoy long periods of peace; and the fear that the present period of peace between the leading states will break down in its turn is understandable at a time when the world economy is again in serious disarray, détente is again under strain and some voices, however few, are again suggesting that nuclear war would not in the event be so total and so devastating as it could be. There is much force in these points; it would indeed be unwise to assume that the advances to which I have drawn attention could not be reversed. But I derive some comfort from the belief that the conjunction of circumstances which proved fatal to the international system in 1914 and again in 1939 is unlikely to be repeated.

The modern international system collapsed on those occasions because states continued to hold the view that they had the legal right to go to war. It also collapsed because states holding this view were confronted with massive shifts in their relative power which persuaded them in the last resort that war was a reasonable means of defending or advancing their interests. States hold this view no longer, and in the wake of the great acceleration of scientific and technological development that has taken place in the last forty years, and that still continues, they are unlikely ever again to make this judgement. Indeed, they are unlikely, such of them as have been caught up in this acceleration, to be confronted ever again with shifts in their relative power that will disturb the equilibrium between them. That shifts of power will continue to take place — this goes without saying, as does the fact that interests will continue to conflict. But these states have passed so far beyond a threshold of absolute power that changes in relative power can no longer erode their ability to uphold the equilibrium which resides in the ability of each to destroy all.

Such are the grounds for suggesting that we are now witnessing the formation of an international system which will be even more different from the modern system than that system was from all its precursors, and which will be so because its leading states will abstain from war with each other. But since it will also be a system in which conflict and confrontation continue, between those states as between the others, let me conclude by reminding you that Immanuel Kant, he who first foresaw that precisely such a system would one day materialise, allowed that it would remain subject to constant danger from 'the law-evading bellicose propensities in man' but judged that, once constructed, it would survive for that very reason.

Working for Peace:
British contributions to
multilateral nuclear disarmament

PAUL ROGERS

I believe we can take it as read that most people support
the idea of multilateral nuclear disarmament. At present,
however, it is frequently claimed that there is a complete
dichotomy between supporters of unilateral and multilateral
nuclear disarmament. According to this argument, unilateralists are concerned entirely with Britain's possession of
nuclear weapons, and do not appear to be interested in the
wider issues. There is little evidence to support this argument,
yet it remains true that many people believe it to be the
case.

In the context of this debate, this article sets out to
examine the current trends in the nuclear arms race and
the recent experience of attempts to achieve multilateral
nuclear disarmament; it explores Britain's involvement in
the nuclear arms race, and the nature of Britain's commit-
ment to nuclear disarmament; and it concludes by examining
the idea that Britain could promote multilateral nuclear disarmament by means of unilateral initiatives.

It might, first, be useful to summarise the major trends in
the nuclear arms race, giving a context for British initiatives.
There are four principal components to note. First, the

nuclear arsenals currently held by the United States and the Soviet Union are far greater than could conceivably be required by deterrence. Strategic nuclear arsenals run to about 10,000 warheads for the United States and 8000 for the Soviet Union. To this must be added a further arsenal of tactical and theatre weapons running to around 40,000 for the two countries combined. At the strategic level, each country is currently engaged in a massive expansion, likely to result in a 50 per cent increase by the late 1980s.

Secondly, over the next two decades many new countries are likely, on present trends, to acquire nuclear weapons. These include Argentina, Brazil, Iraq, Egypt, Libya, Pakistan, South Korea, Taiwan and Nigeria. (This assumes that Israel and South Africa are already nuclear powers.) Under such circumstances, other countries which have so far refrained from developing nuclear weapons such as Australia and Japan, would no longer exercise restraint, and the degeneration of the world community into a 'nuclearised' state would therefore seem inevitable.

Thirdly, possibly as significant as this horizontal proliferation, is the 'vertical' proliferation, or integration, of nuclear weapons among the armed forces of the nuclear powers. By this is meant the widespread deployment of tactical weapons of diverse types. These include, for example, many different kinds of free-fall nuclear bombs together with nuclear depth bombs, mines, torpedoes, stand-off missiles, artillery shells, ground-to-air missiles and even air-to-air missiles. The effect of this integration is such as to make it almost inconceivable that any major conventional conflict will not escalate into a nuclear war.

Finally, and most significant of all, is the development of new, accurate, long-range missiles suited to the development of a disarming first-strike posture. As counter-silo missiles and anti-submarine warfare capabilities increase the vulnerability of land- and sea-based missiles respectively, so the stability of deterrence through the maintenance of a second-strike ability deteriorates. Far from stabilising a crisis by nuclear deterrence, the new circumstances will destabilise it. The timetable for such a transformation is necessarily unclear. Counter-silo missiles such as the modified Minuteman III ICBM are already deployed in small numbers, but we are, in general, talking about a period of under a decade in which the process of destabilisation of deterrence is likely to be largely complete by the introduction of M-X, Trident D5, and their Soviet equivalents.

This combination of size of nuclear stockpiles, proliferation and weapons which degrade deterrence gives a context in which British unilateral action can be considered. It implies that such action must be geared to stimulating major initiatives in multilateral nuclear disarmament within the present decade.

During the past twenty years there have been many series of negotiations on nuclear disarmament and arms control. Apart from the SALT negotiations, the most significant have been the following: *The Partial Test-Ban Treaty*, which controlled atmospheric testing of nuclear weapons among the then major nuclear weapons powers; *The Non-Proliferation Treaty* (1968–70), which had some limited success in controlling proliferation of nuclear weapons; *The Treaty of Tlatelolco* (signed in 1967), which attempted to maintain a nuclear-free zone covering most of Latin America; and treaties prohibiting nuclear weapons in Antarctica (1959), outer space (1967) and the sea-bed (1971). All in all, though, these treaties are hardly spectacular in relation to the increase in the world's nuclear arsenals witnessed in the same period.

This is true of the much more significant SALT talks. SALT I involved a limit on ballistic missile defences together with a temporary freezing (1972–7) of numbers of strategic missile launchers. SALT II involved ceilings imposed, once again, on launchers (including this time long-range bombers) but not on numbers of warheads. A general framework was agreed in 1977 and the treaty signed in 1979, although it has not, at the time of writing (1983), been ratified in the United States.

The problem has been that the SALT negotiations have typically run several years behind the very weapons developments they might have been intended to control. Thus the SALT talks might involve control of launchers when attention is actually being focused on producing multiple warheads on each launcher. During the seven years of negotiations, the United States increased its numbers of strategic warheads from 5900 to 9200; and the Soviet Union from 2200 to 5400.

In this context, and bearing in mind the erosion of deterrence, we can outline some of the requirements for effective global nuclear disarmament. One initial requirement must be for a comprehensive test-ban treaty. By prohibiting all nuclear weapons testing there would be some limited handicap placed on new weapons developments. A further measure would be an agreement on non-first use of nuclear weapons. Yet another would be the extension of the idea of nuclear-free zones.

Far more important would be a new round of strategic disarmament negotiations involving principally the United States and the Soviet Union, but also Britain, China and France. A number of possible outlines for such negotiations have been discussed elsewhere, and the following serve as examples of how the current problems can be approached: (a) A halt to new weapons developments, including ICBMs, SLBMs, and bombers in relation not just to the United States but also to Britain, France and China. (b) A reduction of strategic arms by approximately one-third, constructed in such a way that the United States and the Soviet Union would each perceive themselves able to maintain their security. (c) A further reduction to about one-quarter of the force levels current at the time of the SALT II signing. (d) Disarmament of all strategic nuclear weapons and delivery systems. Ideally one would wish to see this whole process completed within a decade. The first step is crucial, and must be undertaken in the near future. The second and third steps are also urgent and might be termed SALT III and SALT IV.

In addition to the requirements for strategic nuclear arms

control and disarmament, there is the equally crucial problem of the disarmament of short-range nuclear weapons systems and the prevention of proliferation. The latter is linked to the control of nuclear technology in general, but it must be considered unlikely that any kind of effective international control of proliferation will be forthcoming unless it is in a 'climate' of nuclear disarmament among the major powers. Given that as a basis, with the quite fundamental change in the international climate which it would entail, there would be greater prospects for exercising international control of proliferation, possibly extending to some kind of multilateral policing system.

However, as long as potential nuclear powers in the Third World see the continued growth of nuclear arsenals in other countries, as long as they risk confrontation with those countries (and the Falklands conflict is far from being the only potential example), and as long as the nuclear powers pay no attention to alternative non-nuclear defence policies, then prospects for non-proliferation are bleak.

Negotiations in medium-range or theatre nuclear weapons could proceed parallel to further SALT talks and might be linked to the development of nuclear-free zones in the areas of higher concentration, such as Europe. The greatest problem here lies in the asymmetry in East—West forces, with a single nuclear power, the Soviet Union, facing a combined United States, Britain and France and, in an important sense, China. Unilateral initiatives here might be crucial.

Multilateral nuclear disarmament negotiations have so far produced negligible results, although they have occupied nearly twenty years of diplomatic activity. While Britain has been a party to the limited multilateral initiatives conducted under UN auspices, it has not been involved in the far more important SALT negotiations, nor is it involved directly in the Geneva talks on European nuclear weapons. British nuclear weapons have emphatically not guaranteed us a seat at the conference table.

Unilateral initiatives have also been minimal in the past two decades, although unilateral nuclear armament developments have been the norm. This is an important, yet invariably neglected, point. Obviously, any new nuclear weapons development or deployment is conducted in the context of relations with other nuclear weapons powers, but each such process is essentially unilateral. Opponents do not agree in advance to balanced force increases — they indulge in unilateral increases! Osgood and others have argued that it is also valid to visualise multilateral disarmament processes arising out of a number of small unilateral initiatives producing a 'graduated reduction in tension' (GRIT in Osgood's terminology) and one can argue that a British process of unilateral initiatives would be geared specifically to trying to maximise its effects on the existing multilateral system.

British unilateral nuclear disarmament should not be regarded as an operation to be performed in isolation, a brave but ultimately useless gesture. Rather it should be undertaken in a manner designed to have the maximum impact on the international scene and to stimulate genuine multilateral developments to the greatest extent possible, with each aspect of the process related to other existing nuclear powers, potential nuclear powers and public opinion within Britain and in other countries.

On the negative side this has to be done in the context of two major powers that appear 'locked' into a system of nuclear escalation from which they appear unwilling or unable to break out. On the more positive side, though, there is now a high level of public concern in many Western countries, including the recent developments in the United States, together with evidence of concern within the Warsaw Pact.

Futhermore, there is clear concern on the part of the many non-nuclear and largely non-aligned countries that have been promoting their views through the United Nations. Most important of all, Britain is currently an unpleasantly realistic model of the global nuclear arms race in that we are increasing our strategic weapons enormously by opting for the Trident missile system; and at the same time we are expanding our theatre and tactical forces.

Britain can maximise the effects of its unilateral nuclear disarmament initiatives by action in four different areas. These are management of the actual process of nuclear disarmament; national and international education for disarmament; diplomatic initiatives; and the development of alternative defence policies. Regarding the process of nuclear disarmament, this would not necessarily be an immediate and total event, indeed various practical considerations make this unlikely. Instead there would be a number of linked actions taken over a period of time of maybe two to three years and in such a manner as to maximise the impact of the whole process. Such a procedure would be enhanced by the several different kinds of nuclear weapons currently deployed, and might involve the cancellation of the Trident missile system; the withdrawal of the existing Polaris missile system from service; the withdrawal of the longer-range, aircraft-delivered nuclear weapons, carried by the Buccaneer/Tornado force; the withdrawal of land-based, tactical nuclear weapons such as the Lance missile, nuclear-capable artillery, and weapons delivered by aircraft such as the Jaguar; the withdrawal of tactical nuclear weapons carried by naval forces; the cancellation of US Cruise missile deployment in Britain; the withdrawal of existing US strategic nuclear weapons from Britain; and the withdrawal of US theatre and tactical nuclear weapons systems from Britain.

Each of these actions could be linked to providing a focus for international action. For example, the cancellation of Trident would be an expression of intent, and the withdrawal of Polaris should be accompanied by efforts to persuade the Soviet Union and the United States to conduct negotiations on decreasing their SLBM capabilities. Phased withdrawal of tactical and theatre weapons could be linked with efforts to extend the proposals for nuclear-free zones. The whole process of nuclear disarmament could be undertaken in such a way as to provide a continuing and by no means modest lead for other nuclear powers.

At the level of diplomatic initiatives, Britain could play a number of roles. In practice there has been an unwillingness to participate in international negotiations, Britain preferring to maintain its nuclear weapons and refrain from subjecting them to negotiations. This attitude should be reversed, with Britain making every effort to involve itself in existing and future disarmament negotiations. Moreover, it should seek links with non-nuclear countries, such as Sweden and Canada, attempting to increase corporate pressure on the major nuclear powers through UN organisations and other multi-lateral groups. Such action would involve many factors other than specific disarmament measures, including pressure for a comprehensive test ban, a non-first use agreement and a halt to specific weapons developments.

One can also argue that there is a potentially important role available to the Commonwealth. There is a parallel here with the endeavours of the Commonwealth to improve North—South relations, particularly in the early 1970s, with the Commonwealth serving as a model for the world community. In relation to nuclear weapons, of course, the Commonwealth is a less accurate model, as it does not include a member of the Soviet bloc. Yet it does have a significant nuclear power, Britain, potentially significant nuclear powers such as India and possibly Nigeria, and countries such as Canada which have refrained from developing their own weapons.

The Commonwealth might be particularly significant in the discouragement of proliferation, especially if emphasis were to be put on alternatives to nuclear defence. A unique opportunity would present itself here, although Britain's pursuit of such policies should also be linked to the experience of nations such as Sweden, Switzerland and Yugoslavia.

Finally there is the matter of education. It has not, in general, been the policy of the governments of nuclear powers to encourage the education of their populations in the problems of nuclear weapons. Britain, in undertaking nuclear disarmament, should encourage such education within its boundaries and in the international arena. This could be linked particularly to the major peace movements of Europe and North America, with the process in Britain serving to encourage their further development.

One major query about using unilateral initiatives to stimulate multilateral disarmament is whether the former are to be made conditional on the latter. I would argue strongly against this. Appropriate responses should be demanded incessantly of the Soviet Union, the United States and other nuclear powers, but Britain should persist in its own actions.

The immediate criticism of this position is that no other country will follow Britain's actions. I am not at all convinced that this is the case, especially if these unilateral actions are accompanied by the strongest possible forms of diplomatic pressure and international co-operation with non-nuclear powers and public movements. It is interesting to note that a British academic visit to Moscow in 1982 involved the participants asking Soviet disarmament and defence policy experts whether they would respond positively and specifically to British unilateral moves. The response was that the Soviet government would be foolish not to do so.

To conclude, then, the common perception of organisations such as CND is that they are essentially isolationist in wanting Britain to abandon nuclear weapons with no reference to international developments. This worries people who see Britain being left defenceless while other countries continue with the nuclear arms race. Yet many of the people who feel this are also greatly concerned about the future and want to believe that Britain could help to make the whole world safer.

It is therefore essential to show that unilateral initiatives actually make great sense in terms of leading the world community towards general nuclear disarmament. While a number of countries have refused to develop nuclear weapons, no nuclear power has yet got rid of them. Britain should do so as one part of a massive campaign of international diplomacy and national and international education. It should literally make a nuisance of itself among the nuclear powers, seeing this as its most significant international role in the next decade.

Nuclear Weapons in Defence of Western Europe

SIR HUGH BEACH

If Western Europe has to be defended against anyone it is presumably against the Warsaw Pact, so the obvious first question is: has the Warsaw Pact any intention whatever of attacking us? Or to put the same question in a rather different way, what view is one to take of Russia? Is one to see it as power-hungry and Messianic; intent upon spreading communism by any means, including force of arms, throughout the world; taking a calculated step-by-step approach of which the annexation of Afghanistan is just one move in a remorseless plan? Or is the Soviet Union but a beleagured confederation, terrified of a war on two fronts, whose vast military preparations and apparent paranoia are much more a reaction to the threat of American missiles and bases and trade embargoes than to any residual urge to expand its already shaky frontiers?

It seems that neither of these is correct, although there are elements of truth in both. The Soviet Union is certainly a huge quasi-imperial system, which has much in common with, for example, the Roman empire post-Augustus, or the British empire post-1850, in which the original founding principle, the civilising mission, is fast dying, but in which the reaction to any disturbance around its far-flung borders

— whether it be a danger, a weakness, or an opportunity — is an instinctive reaction to send a legion, a gunboat, a parachute division — or a task force. It is always the most dangerous phase. This accounts for what is happening in South Asia and Poland; why Cuban troops were sent to fight by proxy in Angola and Ethiopia; the navy of Admiral Gorshkov.

On top of that, there is certainly something especially odd about the relationship of the Soviet Union with Western Europe. Why, for example, do they keep, and have kept for the past twenty-odd years, some 600 missiles in Western Russia, each with a nuclear warhead, whose range is such that they can only fall into NATO Europe? Why do they maintain a myriad, in the literal sense, of up to 10,000, low-grade spies in Western Germany? Whenever one goes out with troops on exercise one can see them watching through binoculars, and on your transistor any night you can hear a lady called Magdeburg Annie giving them their instructions in code. The obvious implication is that the Russians, for the simplest of geopolitical reasons, regard Western Europe as belonging rightfully in their sphere of influence. Whenever they have attempted to advance that interest, historically, they have been rebuffed with suffering and loss, particularly at the hands of the Germans.

Having ended the Second World War with an ideal defensive buffer zone, a source of manpower, skills and raw materials in Eastern Europe, no Soviet leader could have contemplated not imposing compliant governments, nor could they subsequently have acquiesced in their overthrow, without engaging the full powers of the Soviet State. The Soviets therefore have no built-in bias in favour of diminishing East—West tension as such — which would be the common-sense meaning of the word détente. On the contrary their aim has been to consolidate their leadership of Eastern Europe and formalise the division of Germany. This is what they wanted and what they largely got out of Helsinki. They recognise, obviously, that the price of this policy is a military stalemate with the West and there is no evidence that they are seriously considering, or have done so for the last thirty years, deliberately upsetting this by military means. There is no need, because they still believe that history is on their side (having discovered the scientific basis for it in their theory) — that the trick is to wait for the mould to be broken by someone else — that it is then their duty either to become active on the side of history; or at the very least, because their legitimacy hinges upon their having read the laws of history correctly, there is a strong temptation to give these laws a helping hand, on the impeccable principle that dialectical materialism helps those who help themselves. Meanwhile, they need only bide their time, undermine and pose a threat.

Undermining is not directly a military problem. What of the threat? Well, it's hardly a threat of economic domination. They dominate Eastern Europe economically. But they need credit to finance an external trade deficit with 'developed capitalist countries'; they have a growing need of western technology; and they have their agricultural Achilles heel. They don't control the Free World's oil supplies, nor any other vital raw material or transportation agency. So the immediate threat is not of economic domination. Cultural? On the contrary, all the signs are that the Soviets are as terrified as ever of exposing their own people to western cultural influence. Censorship is tight — western newspapers and magazines controlled; only a small number of East Europeans are allowed to take holidays in the West; telephone links are minimised. All this despite Helsinki. So, no real challenge here. Where then? The answer is obvious: in the form of the Soviet military overhang.

What is meant by this? A force level — by land and air in Europe, and by sea and air in the Eastern Atlantic — conspicuously greater than could be needed for internal security and to defend themselves against any potential attack. Granted that they have such a superiority (and to this point I shall return), how could it be used? The true pay-off has nothing to do with military 'scenarios', but is here and now in the form of political purchase. In Admiral Gorshkov's words, 'It is an important weapon of diplomacy in time of peace.'[1]

How then could Western Europe lay itself open to such political purchase? The answer is obvious: by becoming detached from the United States; by losing its own cohesion, self-confidence, self-respect. Hence the problem is primarily political, but with a military precondition that is indispensable — not to allow the Soviets any military option to which the West has literally no effective counter. The closest the Soviets could come to such an option would be a massive rolling advance — by surprise or with reinforcement — by land and air in West Germany and by sea and air in the Atlantic. Regardless of likelihood or plausibility this is the worst case for planning. And since the aim is to make all military options unattractive, what can be done about it? This article concentrates on the land battle, but broadly similar arguments apply *mutatis mutandis* to the air and the sea, which are every bit as important. What, then, are the problems?

The first is simply that the battlefield lacks depth. This favours the Russians because it puts objectives of high value within reach. It is a liability to NATO because it commits us to what is called 'Forward Defence'. The second point concerns the military balance. As the following table of force levels shows, at first sight there is a comforting symmetry between the NATO and Russian forces immediately available in the area in question, but when we bring into the balance the non-Soviet Warsaw Pact forces, this begins to swing strongly against NATO.

The question is, of course, whether these forces should be added or subtracted. That is a matter for political speculation on which no man can know the answer in advance. When the mobilisation forces on either side are added on the disparity remains, so that after mobilisation (say after three weeks) there is still an adverse balance against NATO of around 2:1. Now it is surely obvious that in any foreseeable conflict of this type the Soviets will be on the offensive. Even they cannot seriously believe otherwise. And they will aim to succeed quickly, since all the evidence is that they hate the thought of a long war. They have been bled too often; their objective then is to move fast.

LAND FORCES ON CENTRAL FRONT

NATO		Warsaw Pact		
Divisions immediately available			*Soviet*	*Indigenous*
West German	12			
Dutch	2			
Belgian	2	East German	20	6
UK	4	Czechoslovakian	5	10
US	4	Polish	2	15
(French)	(3)			
Total	27	Total	27	31
Total reinforcements				
Belgian	1	Russian (Western		
Dutch	1	military district)	32	
(French)	(3)			
US	8			
Total	13	Total	32	
Totals of all forces	40	Totals of all forces	59	31

As the attackers they possess two priceless initiatives: theirs is the choice of major thrust line (or lines), limited only by the terrain and the availability of suitable routes; theirs is the choice of M-Day, D-Day, and the relationship between the two, that is, whether to opt for an attack 'in place' or after partial or full mobilisation. The table shows how much difference in the ratio of force levels this could make. The special factors on the NATO side are the obverse of these. The NATO aim is to deny the Soviets a quick success, or *fait accompli*. But in regard to the timing of mobilisation and deployment, while the NATO chain of command may call for the declaration of alert measures, this can only be in response to the actions of the Soviets and nothing can happen without governments so deciding. This, almost by definition, is impossible to predict.

Consequently, in looking for a firm basis for planning, the NATO commanders are on shifting sands. They must have a plan both to counter a surprise attack, and to withstand a fully mobilised assault. The assumptions made about the relative timings of M-Day and D-Day (on the two sides) have an immense impact upon planning force levels, which they have to allow for. Equally, lacking the initiative, NATO has to provide a defence along the whole of the Central Front. As a result, not only does the position lack depth but it also lacks strategic reserve.

Arising from these factors there is the very widespread view that if the Warsaw Pact did carry out a massive rolling attack across the North German plain, and if nuclear weapons were used by neither side, then the Warsaw Pact would very likely win — in the sense that they would overrun Western Germany as far as the Ruhr and the Rhine, if not the Channel ports, within days, or at most a week or so — long before the full potential of the NATO countries, and in particular North America, could be mobilised and brought against it.

So, as everyone knows, the doctrine of flexible response explicitly reserves to NATO commanders the freedom to propose, and explicitly assumes that in certain circumstances NATO governments would collectively accede to, what is ghoulishly known as 'nuclear release'. In other words, if there is no other way of stopping the Russians, the NATO nations plan to initiate war at the tactical level in order to do so. But, would they? The plain truth is that nobody knows. But what everyone agrees is that, once any nuclear weapons have been used by either side, the Rubicon will have been crossed. It may not be very logical. Purely as weapons the nuclear are not totally divorced in kind from the conventional. What matters is the perception. Almost everyone who has thought it out, including the Russians, share the perception that once another nuclear weapon has been used, a boundary of almost unimaginable danger has been crossed; because any such use carries with it the gravest risk of escalation, at least within Europe, one should reckon, as the foreseeable consequence of any such use, a European death toll that would run into tens of millions, the overwhelming majority of whom would be civilian.

What possible meaning can one then attach to a phrase like 'the defence of Western values?' What important difference is there between East or West Germany today that could approach by an order of magnitude the difference between either of these societies and what would subsist post-strike? While there is life there is at least the hope of liberty. In this context it is quite literally nonsense to say that it is better to be dead than red. This is what people mean by saying that such a war could not be limited, and in such a war there could be no winners. In this view the military, the politicians, all in authority East or West, are unanimous. Faced with this dangerous and baffling prospect, opinion has always been drawn towards one of two extremes. At one extreme is the school of thought which embraces escalation for the strength it gives to deterrence; this is often called trip-wire theory. At the other extreme is the school which considers that the near certainty of escalation makes flexible response incredible; they therefore advocate a doctrine of no first use. Trip-wire theory argues in essence that all that is needed is the existence of the oft-quoted 6000 theatre nuclear warheads, said to be 'lying around' in North-Western Europe, plus sufficient US ground and air forces and their families (at present they total half a million) to act as the finger in the mangle to ensure they would be used. The example quoted is that of Berlin — impossible to defend conventionally for half a day — preserved for thirty years by precisely the token presence of the three Western nuclear nations' armies and the implicit threat of escalation. If this is true, then the strength, efficiency and military doctrine of the NATO forces is unimportant — and all can save a lot of money!

This argument has at least the merit of recognising one key fact about deterrence: that is, that it is never absolute. One cannot make a general rule and say that in order to deter attack you need, say, an 80 per cent probability that the defence will succeed. The proof is very simple. Consider two more cases. First, that of Hong Kong: Britain has successfully deterred attack by mainland China since 1949, although there is no chance whatever of the defence succeeding (and no nuclear threat there) because the incentive to attack is very low. The second, Israel: she has signally failed, since 1947, to deter attack by Arabs, despite the fact that her defence always succeeds, because the incentive to attack is irresistible. So for deterrence the likelihood of successful defence that is needed in order to deter stands in direct proportion to the incentive to attack.

In Europe, the Soviet incentive to attack is certainly not high (unless we start to crack up) so that a countervailing capability consisting of unspecified thousands of nuclear warheads, plus a token American presence, might indeed be sufficient to deter. The paradox is that such a solution would fail, either because the United States' readiness to remain involved could not be maintained; or because the political self-confidence of Western Europe would collapse. To quote Dr Schlesinger:

> I think that the American contribution is premised on the European nations collectively doing their share. To the extent that the European nations convey to the United States Congress and to the American public that they are unwilling to do their share, because they can rely on the Americans, they have undermined the very motivation for retaining the United States forces overseas and it is that which is a source of concern.[2]

Or, put another way by Professor Laurence Martin:

> Because conventional forces offer many obvious useful
> options, a conspicuous failure to provide them would
> communicate infirmity of purpose to the Soviet Union
> and breed an insidious self-doubt and lack of mutual
> confidence within NATO.[3]

In other words a policy of bluff is self-defeating, and the
only solution is to be able not only to deter, but to be able
to confront a major attack, by land or sea, in a manner that
carries general conviction. This does not necessarily mean to
repel it, or cause it so many casualties, or to hold it up for
so many days. It means to make a convincing response — no
quick, easy gains, no *fait accompli* — so that all can see it is
an unattractive option to the enemy, with unpredictable consequences for him regardless of anyone's assumption about
going nuclear — a move no chess player would make against a
competent opponent. This done, the military overhang has
been neutralised, leaving the main economic, political, cultural contest to be settled on its merits, which is the most
that the military can hope for.

Or is it? There remains the doctrine of nuclear first use if
deterrence fails and if, in the last resort, no other way of
stopping the Russian onslaught would suffice. How much
credibility can one attach to it? Some would say none. Field
Marshal Lord Carver, for example, believes that to invoke
such a policy in support of 'defence or security makes a
mockery of the terms.' He believes that it could not work in
practice: 'if there were a serious rise in tension which made
war in Europe a possibility, NATO itself and its constituent
members would be torn apart by having to face up to the
possibility of nuclear weapons actually being used.' Worse
than that, he believes that in the realm of public opinion, in
peacetime, 'dislike of reliance on nuclear weapons affects
defence generally, and anti-nuclear feelings can and do
become anti-defence and anti-military feelings', leading to

the further danger that 'popular support for NATO's defence and its members' defence policies will be eroded, and this could undermine America's willingness to continue its support for European Defence.' This is a characteristically clear analysis of dangers which are plain for all to see. He goes on to argue for a declaration by NATO that it would never be the first to use nuclear weapons in any conflict, and for 'practical measures to improve our conventional defences' so that we no longer live under the 'delusion... that possession of nuclear weapons...compensates for an inadequate conventional defence.'[4]

Of course, none of this is new, and the consequences of going along with it are enormously disagreeable. It amounts, in the short term, to saying that the only sensible or credible course open to NATO, in the face of imminent or actual defeat at the non-nuclear level, might be acquiescence or surrender. This blows a gaping hole in NATO's deterrent posture. So in the longer term it would mean finding some practical way of redressing the conventional imbalance, so that one could convert a no first use declaration, into a genuine no first use strategy. There are only two ways in which this could be done. One would be to build up the forces of NATO to the point where Soviet superiority no longer existed. As matters stand there is no sign whatever that the European members of NATO are prepared to raise the necessary extra resources — and even if they did, who is to say that the Russians wouldn't simply raise the ante on their side to match? This is what they say they would do, and well they might! So this is a non-starter.

The only other way is to negotiate the Warsaw Pact overhang downwards. This also bristles with difficulties — not least the fact that for nine years there have been negotiations going on in Vienna (the MBFR talks) with exactly this in view, and the results to date have been almost exactly nil! Nevertheless the stage has now been reached where arms control negotiations can — and simply have to — make headway. For the first time there are talks going on — in

Geneva, Vienna and Madrid — across the whole spectrum of force. Economies everywhere are feeling the strain; not least in the USSR. What has been lacking so far, and is still lacking, is collective will on the part of governments for these talks to produce results. If the energies of the unilateral disarmers could be channelled into political pressure for negotiated progress, then real headway could be made.

Meanwhile, until all this can take effect, for the rest of this decade NATO has to make the best of what it's got. It has to nourish the concept of theatre nuclear forces making what the jargon calls a 'political signal' to convey NATO's resolve not to accept defeat, despite the risks of going on. One simply cannot know with certainty how people — politicians and soldiers, even Russian ones — will really act in the unprecedentedly appalling event that nuclear weapons begin to fly. One does not have to dismiss as wholly irrational the option, for NATO leaders facing disaster at the conventional level, of limited nuclear action as an alternative to simple defeat with all its consequences to test the possibility that the Soviet leaders would be so disconcerted at finding that they had miscalculated NATO's resolve, or so appalled at the imminent threat of precipitating the final holocaust, that they preferred to back off from a war that neither side can win; that both sides know they cannot win. It is a counsel of despair to assume that it will never be the Soviet side that backs away, and contrary to history. There is a sense in which any military planner, in the last resort, has to disregard intentions — which can change overnight — and focus upon capability. These nuclear shells, rockets and aircraft bombs exist. The Soviets have to assume that, in the last resort, they might be used. As Denis Healey pointed out, many years ago 'No rational Soviet Government would stake the survival of the Russian people on the guess that, in the event, the US Government would prefer to see its allies occupied and the American Army destroyed, rather than raise the level of the conflict.'[5]

In this sense flexible response, so far from being the

grossly immoral theory that one's instinct labels it, may be for the intervening years the best one can do, simply because it makes the outbreak of any kind of war in Europe, from whatever cause, less likely than it would be if we abandoned this doctrine. A policy for the minimisation of the risk of any war is not a wholly bad one. And if one can have this policy, as we have in the past, for roughly the same amount of money as we spend on drink each year, then that's not a bad bargain!

NOTES

1 *The Sea Power of the State* (Moscow, 1976), p. 152.
2 BBC Radio 4, 24 October 1974.
3 *Survival*, International Institute for Strategic Studies (November/December 1974), p. 272.
4 Talk at the International Institute for Strategic Studies (13 November 1981).
5 6th International Wehrkunde Meeting, Munich, 1–2 February 1969: *Survival* (IISS, April 1969), p. 110.

The Christian Ethic and the Spirit of Security and Deterrence

DAVID MARTIN

One cannot fully understand the present position of influential groups in the Christian Churches on nuclear warfare without considering the long-term moral and political resources on which they draw. These include both the pacifist tradition within so-called alternative Christianity, and the varied applications of natural law as elaborated by established Churches. The alternative tradition has grave reservations about all warfare, which may in the end imply a withdrawal from all political order, and in particular from the state. The established tradition has generally accepted the state and the necessity of force in human affairs, but here too reservations have been expressed in the form of criteria marking out the constraints which combatants ought to recognise. This established tradition is presently undergoing a *crise de conscience*, because it appears very difficult to conduct nuclear warfare within these constraints. Before I develop the joint impact of the alternative and established traditions on contemporary churchmen, I shall say something about Christianity, the political order, and the realities of political process.

The idea of political order and the realities of political process pose problems for Christian faith, which overlap with the twin problems of war between nation states and the ideological war which characterises the twentieth century. The New Testament provides few guidelines for the conduct of everyday political life. The Christian community was, after all, not part of the Hasmonean ruling group, let alone part of the system of Roman overlordship, and thus had no call to work out a moral logic of political decision. All that the Christian community required was a set of norms for its own self-government, and principles to define the claims of faith *vis-à-vis* secular law and authority. Notable among these norms was the injunction not to settle disputes between Christians by resort to secular law, although in relation to secular law and authority the existence of ruling powers was accepted as of divine ordination. Hence it was right both to fear God and honour the King, and the revolt of AD 70 and the rebellion of Bar Kochba AD 132–35 were, therefore, outside the range of Christian options. Christians then could not support the violence of revolutionary or rebellious guerrillas; equally, nowadays, the New Testament does not provide a good basis for any violent form of liberation theology — that has to be sought in the Old Testament. On the other hand, the state can only command a qualified loyalty, since the obligations to God and to Caesar are distinguished. Christians had an overriding duty to the Gospel, which was not compatible, in particular, with worshipping the Emperor, or with the military oath, the *sacramentum*.

These broad norms and principles, though they would prove to be of the utmost importance for the long-term Christian approach to the secular world, did not amount to a Christian understanding of political life. Christians not only aspired to be good citizens — even though their ultimate citizenship was in heaven — they also wished to be part of the total community, even if they belonged also to a unique fraternity in which there was neither Jew nor Gentile, bond nor free. And they cherished virtues such as probity, moderation, and care for the brethren which were compatible with those of a political class. Nevertheless, good citizenship and the practice of virtue do not of themselves constitute an approach to the moral constraints of political existence. Indeed, Christ's death at the hands of the constituted political authorities could be taken to imply that the world of political decision lay on a collision course with the Kingdom of God, His righteousness and His love. Christ was condemned in words which belong to the inner core of political maxims: 'It is expedient that one die for the people.'

Political life is not rooted in a divine love embodied in a carpenter helplessly and scandalously exposed on a gibbet. The New Testament speaks of this 'scandal' as a 'placard', offensive to the natural presuppositions of Greek, Roman or Jew, through which God commends himself to us and to all men.

The essential Christian transaction takes place in a world-view where time was, and is, dramatically foreshortened. Human beings, as political animals, look towards a long term in which they may achieve both possible gain and acceptable loss. They calculate in terms of a secular future, even though the contingencies of accident, disease, death or misfortune may suddenly destroy the basis of all their calculations. But the perspective of the Gospels places a question mark against any calculation by proclaiming the imminence of the Kingdom with its immediate and uncompromising demands. In this perspective, *there is no time*, as there is in political existence.

Christian transactions reverse the processes of authority and assertion in favour of oblation and service. Yet these supreme realities of the spirit cannot be transferred in a simple manner to the political realm. To say they are apolitical is to go much too far, but to believe that the world of grace, oblation and service can be immediately worked out and realised on the political plane is naive. We have to accept our social nature expressed in the political realm, which means that Christians live between the two kingdoms, subject to a continuous and unresolvable tension, or creative dynamism, creatively at odds with the political world.

Of course, this disjunction need not be creative all the time. Interim settlements between grace and nature enable disjunctions to exist by devising temporary viable arrangements, some partial division of spheres, but such arrangements are no solution. The Lutheran Reformation, for example, by penetrating into the Christian mystery of love, handed over the political realm to its own logic and distinctive authorities. The alternative world of sectarian hope, in setting up fraternities under the shadow of imminent judgement, likewise withdraws from the world of political necessity. In the Christian perspective, the problem of the political cannot be finally settled. The problem can be restated by summarising the necessities governing the political kingdom.

Political life is based not on pure gift but on reciprocity — its essence is bargain and exchange. Of course, the whole process may be quite beneficent and simply involve acceptable payment in kind or money for services rendered. But it also involves situations where the partners have unequal resources, and when that is so the stronger will probe the defences of the weaker: the game of exchange is played on the assumption that weakness will be exploited. The rules of the system work inexorably, and are not affected when particular individuals opt out, or decide to abrogate their operation by an act of unrecompensed generosity. Indeed, if the rules were *not* usually followed no reform could ever be calculated.

Political life is just such a system. Whether or not you wish to participate, it will continue. Somebody will be operating according to its necessary constraints. This 'somebody' may constitute a class playing the game for its own advantage rather than for the whole society. Indeed, this is most likely since secular society is hierarchical. Different political systems, no matter whether they involve representative democracy or democratic centralism, result in a political class which becomes inducted into the rules of the system, in particular, the rule which requires they attend to the average tendencies of conduct, which govern internal and foreign affairs alike.

What is meant by this? The rule may be stated as follows. A member of a political class cannot make political decisions on an 'if only' basis. He cannot contradict average tendencies on the assumption that if he acts with uncalculating generosity then a sufficient number of others will act similarly and so abrogate the nature of the system. If a majority were to do so, then a minority could take advantage of the situation, and the bad would triumph at the expense of the good. So a policy in accord with morality, whether abstract or Christian, is impossible. Moral principles remain relevant for the decision-maker, but he is still constrained to work within the system, and indeed if he tries to pretend that the rules of the system are expendable for personal or for national benefit, he acts immorally.

Such a system cannot be immediately presented to the imagination as are the icons of Christian faith. Every Christian picture is personal: mother and child, father and son. These icons do not describe politic trajectories on chess boards. Sometimes conservatives try to express the personal character of Christian imagery by claiming that religion is for the individual. But Christianity has a social dimension too, inaugurating social experiments, including the monastic communities. It would be better to say that everything is mediated through a personalised, particularised mould, the person of Christ, the one unique and particular heavenly city, New Jerusalem. This means that contemporary Christians often try to construct a version of political reason from the personal and the particular.

A Christian will ask: 'Would Christ press the nuclear button?' This is as fatuously personalised as asking 'What would you do if a German raped your sister?' The only answer to the first question is 'No'. But then, can we imagine Christ as a darts or snooker player, a sociologist or an accountant? This sort of Christian argument is paralleled by the personalised style of television presentation in political issues. Television neglects long-term causation and rarely constructs or analyses a pattern. In a way, this is very important. We should be able to see what happens to other human beings, to experience, even vicariously, how a bereft mother feels, how a released bomb causes havoc in people's lives. Yet if policy were to rely on reactions to images of war, it would become utterly unpredictable and extremely dangerous. Without predictability there can be no safety or peace. Armies may be lured to battle by abstract concepts such as democracy, or peace with honour, but to believe that if only the contending individuals could sit down, face to face, the folly of force would be realised, and the malign and incomprehensible apparatus of policy would disappear is untenable.

A member of a political class will act predictably within the system if he has continuing and responsible proximity to decision-making in a situation where he is *directly* involved. At a suitable distance an observer may pass moral judgements because he will never have to put them into effect. The United Nations is in just this position. It may sometimes be right, politically or morally, but remaining structurally parasitic, it can only make moral gestures. Nevertheless these gestures may act in such a way that participants in the system will take them into account, if only at the margin.

If the rule of average likelihoods must be obeyed by members of political classes one may go on to ask more precisely in what the logic of the system consists. It consists basically in variations of the *lex talionis* — an eye for an eye and a tooth for a tooth — the rule of reciprocity. When nations enter into a treaty of mutual support, they are trying to formalise reciprocity. When a nation says it will meet force with force, outrage with reprisal, it is again formally confirming reciprocity. In all such situations it is very important that participants are known to act consistently. Consistency and predictability are essential to the processes of international diplomacy. Once predictability slides towards uncertainty then the perceived wavering in intention may provoke adventurism. Thus, uncertainty over Britain's support of France in August 1914, which was exacerbated by the way

British attention appeared to be focused on Ulster, may have accelerated the slide into war.

The logic of the political process requires a certain solidarity of the political group, whether a nation or a party, in proclaiming collective self-righteousness. Solidarity requires that nobody sacrifice himself for love of his enemies. For example, Mrs Thatcher and her ministers could not back up the Falkland Islands task force and simultaneously insist on truthful and unrestricted reporting throughout the campaign. When pacifists claim that truth is the first casualty in war, they are perfectly correct. Loyalty to party or to nation means that the ninth commandment can only be honoured in the breach, not in the observance.

If I have associated loyalty to party with the solidarities demanded by war, I have done so deliberately in order to emphasise that the constraints on moral action and on personal moral autonomy operate in foreign and internal affairs alike. Political life is a form of restricted warfare, and the state embodies an irreducible residue of violence. Thus all political processes which have to do with party unity or with the integrity of the state or with international relationships will share in the moral constraints brought about by conflict, and to that extent will present a stark contrast to the Gospel.

THE ALTERNATIVE TRADITION

It is unnecessary here to provide a detailed account of the pacifist strain within the alternative tradition (or traditions) of Christianity. Needless to say, that tradition has constantly cited the Gospels, as containing the most unequivocal condemnation of warfare. Enoch Powell, in a recent letter to *The Times* commenting on the Falklands service, made exactly this point. He argued that a disjunction between the state's view of religion and Christianity was inevitable, given the origins of a faith which had first been accepted by the

Roman empire and then become the established belief of the West. Mr Powell described the early Christians as an absolutist pacifist sect, who believed in a divine restoration of the world order in response to an adherence to the new law of the Kingdom of God.

This tradition has surfaced again and again: Quakers and Mennonites have provided the best-known examples of a continuing pacifist witness. Even a millennarian group like the Southcottians, who on the whole believed in a defensive war against the forces of revolutionary atheism, included members who accepted the pacifist position. Such groups have always been outside the ranks of the political class, either by reason of their social origin, or by self-exclusion. And when Quakers, for example, have joined the political class they have usually muted their pacifism: John Bright, George Cadbury and Lord Noel-Baker for example were in favour of peace and disarmament, but they were not pacifists.

It is, perhaps, important to recognise the existence of a pacific attitude, quite distinct from strict pacifism. The broad tenor of the free churches, as voluntary associations of people largely outside the political elites, has been towards this position, and it has complex affinities with liberal optimism. What indeed seems to have happened is that the liberal politics of historic dissent, especially in the period 1860–1940, have now been adopted by large sectors of the various Christian establishments. This approach (short of strict pacifism) is not found exclusively in the modern period. It was adopted for example, by some Lollards. Sir John Clanvowe, the fourteenth-century diplomat and crusader censured a world which pours scorn on those who wish to live simply, away from the noise and strife, and suffer wrongs with patience. This is not pacifism exactly, but it is a Christian austerity which challenges the values of the military caste. It is very much in the spirit of (say) St Martin of Tours, or of St Magnus, who consented to be stoned rather than bloodily to contend for the earldom of Orkney.

The way in which Churches may adopt pacific political

positions when they are not playing their established role is illustrated by the Churches in Japan, especially the Protestant, which have been active in the peace movements of recent years. After all, they are a tiny minority, usually outside the political elite,[1] and they have always been suspected for their western origins and for their resistance to the divinity of the Emperor, as personifying absolute loyalty to the state. Moreover, they are disproportionately concentrated in the educated classes generally, the section of society which entertains liberal reservations about the military caste, in Japan and elsewhere.

THE ESTABLISHED TRADITION

I have been arguing that Christianity cannot offer an unequivocal translation of the gospel of peace, love and universal fraternity into political terms and actions, because the Christian message of reconciliation can only be clear and unequivocal at the level of personal salvation, and also because the early Christians were not usually members of the political class, or brought up to share in its assumptions and experience its imperatives.

But once Christians started living in immediate proximity to the political class, some broad casuistry had to be developed to cross the chasm between peace, joy and love in the Lord and the collective self-righteousness, ruthless calculation and instrumental attitude to truth arising from political pursuits. St Augustine offers an instructive example here as somebody who lived close to political classes and had himself to be responsible for political decisions and their consequences for the integrity and survival of the Catholic Church.

In his *Augustine of Hippo*, Peter Brown describes how, after the sack of Rome in 410 AD, Augustine refused to join those Christians who disassociated themselves from the disaster, which he ascribed to the general human condition, not to the particular vices of Rome. He looked, not to the average man, but to the elite, to exercise the kind of political responsibility he had exercised and understood in Hippo. Traditional pagans had accused the Christians of withdrawing from state affairs and of being potential or actual pacifists, encouraging anarchy, making defeat more likely. For Augustine, however, Catholicism had now to act as the bulwark of civil society, pursuing policies with respect to external enemies as realistic as those he himself pursued against internal enemies. The problem here does not relate to political process as such, which is accepted as necessary in all its moral ambiguity, but concerns the possibility of devising a casuistry which might express ethical reservations. Though it is accepted that peace, atoning sacrifice and non-resistance to evil are not immediately practicable on the political plane, nevertheless, there must be some first principles limiting the 'play' of the system.

These principles constitute the theory of the 'just' war. In sum they do no more than indicate ethical limits on the declaration and the propagation of war. These limits are not in any way especially Christian, though they are compatible with the command: 'Love your enemies, do good to them that despitefully use you.' They involve such notions as 'proportionality', which means that violence should be restricted to what is required to gain certain limited military objectives. Likewise, the direct killing of innocent non-combatants is to be condemned; and any war in which the bad is likely to outweigh the good is to be regarded as immoral.

Clearly such principles are extremely broad, and only make ethical sense in relation to traditional warfare, that of the professional soldier, before modern wars for democracy, communism or Fascism involved whole populations in a total war effort. Thus in the recent Falklands conflict, which harked back to the older kind of war, the Archbishop of Canterbury argued that Britain was engaged in a just war, and he set out certain ethical considerations which he believed should govern its conduct. It is interesting that his article in

The Times omitted any reference to the sinking of the *General Belgrano* outside the military exclusion zone. So delicate a silence would seem to indicate that, in the view of the Archbishop, this particular act of war exceeded what was required by proportionality.[2]

However, the issue currently facing the Churches is not primarily concerned with limited warfare of this kind, but with the special and unique circumstances of nuclear warfare. I have reviewed the general problem of the political process, the alternative pacifist tradition and the established tradition of the just war in order to bring out what resources contemporary Christian bodies have to draw upon. In the past, these resources have not been too carefully enquired into, since war was accepted as a grim but inevitable part of the order of things. If it could be conducted in as humane a way as possible, so much the better; but there was a feeling that once passions were aroused certain outrages were bound to occur. Bishop Bell might rightly protest at 'obliteration bombing', but many would reflect that the Allies did not begin the blitzkrieg, and moreover politicians calculated that whatever brought the war to a rapid conclusion, however frightful, would save more lives than it destroyed.

Two considerations are crucial at this juncture. One is sociological, and concerns the partial separation of even ecclesiastical elites from immediate membership in the political classes and thus from the assumptions which govern political action. The other is more general, and has already been alluded to: the style of Christian thinking faced with the unique destructiveness of nuclear warfare. One does not have to be a progressive to regard nuclear warfare as violating every principle of the theory of the just war. Indeed, one Roman Catholic correspondent to *The Times* framed his rejection of nuclear arms precisely within the traditional and conservative framework provided by an immutable natural law.

I shall begin by expanding the sociological consideration. As I — and others — have argued elsewhere, the clergy are decreasingly recruited from the upper middle class and are, to that extent, less likely to have attended independent schools. Their attitude then is likely to approximate to that found amongst, say, comprehensive school teachers. Teachers at secondary level and clergy exist at parallel points within what sociologists loosely call 'the knowledge class', and share in the left-liberal approach which frequently characterises members of that class. One may add that the professional formation of clergy is relatively self-contained, especially when it is concentrated in a theological college. Within the local parish the older network of natural contacts with, say, the relatively conservative professions of the law, medicine and the armed forces is somewhat attenuated.

When one characterises such a shift in social position, what occurs is not only a distancing from power, its assumptions and its constraints; what follows in many cases is a vigorous repudiation of that social position which is now slipping away, because to stabilise oneself in the midst of a slow but perceptible slide is too painful. It is more satisfying to leave ambiguity behind and opt for 'prophecy'. After all, prophecy will not accelerate deterioration, and may bring notice and interest, even respect. Of course, the prophetic stance may not be motivated in this way at all, or it may have its roots in a desire to say at least something, to act in some way on the world's stage. In more explicit theological vein, some clergy, including Don Cupitt, see the whole period in which religion was established as a divergence from the original faith, not, as others would suppose, the beginning of a mature apprehension of the complexity of civic responsibility. Those who stress the distortion of Christianity brought about by establishment are also inclined to exaggerate the vigour and proselytising success of pristine Christianity, and even to suppose that once establishment is left behind prophecy and success will return. Thus, the prospect of a free, autonomous Church, proclaiming a welcome and prophetic message is contrasted with the situation where the ecclesiastical body is a biddable department of state. In America, the contrast is phrased somewhat differently, given the different historical context. The Episcopal Church there has enjoyed an implicit establishment at the top of American society, and the attractive power of prophecy is in part provided by guilt about wealth.

I would stress that the specialised agencies at national and international level are not without influence upon the opinions of clergy. If the Church is increasingly self-contained as an institution, then a specific viewpoint tends to be generated. This is a viewpoint not only fed by national specialised agencies, but also by the international contacts of churchmen, more particularly through the World Council of Churches. I would hypothesise that there is a continuum running from the most radical in the specialised agencies of the Council, through the bishops, and the specialised agencies of the Church of England, and the British Council of Churches, to the clergy, and last, to the most conservative group of all, the churchgoers. I would expect quite a strong disjunction between one end of that continuum and the other, which means that leaders and local laity are politically at odds. Leaders do not speak for their constituency.

The broad argument just suggested is one which is supported by the views of the *Church Times*. In its leader of 30 July 1982, headed 'God and Caesar', the leader-writer commented: 'To this day many churchgoers share Mrs Thatcher's basic values and instructive reactions. But these churchgoers do not find many ecclesiastical spokesmen whom they can trust completely. The old alliance, once dominant at the top of British life, is visibly disintegrating.' (Parenthetically, I may say that this alliance has been increasingly in abeyance since the time of Archbishop Temple, and was far from monolithic in the interwar period.) The *Church Times* leader-writer adds 'the basic cause of the tension felt on Monday [i.e., the occasion of the Falklands Service at St Paul's Cathedral] is, we believe, that the British Churches have become more internationally minded, interested in the War against Want far more than in territorial disputes.' The same could be said of the Churches in many countries of Western Europe, and of the liberal ecclesiastical establishment in Canada. In the USA it is represented in the National Council of Churches, and in the Roman Catholic Episcopate, which recently drafted a pastoral letter on nuclear weapons. Most notable, perhaps, is the Christian peace movement in Holland, where it takes the form of a shared peace-front of the Dutch Churches.

So far as the British clergy are concerned, the ORC poll organisation conducted, in October 1982, a poll of clerical opinion for the television programme 'Credo'. The results can be summarised as follows. The overwhelming majority of Anglican clergymen hold to the following views: they do not see that any separation can be made between spiritual concerns and political or social activism; they believe that if leading churchmen disagree with the policies of the government, they should say so openly, even when the issues concern defence or economic policy as distinct from such moral issues as abortion and divorce; they are almost equally divided however as to whether the Church of England *as a body* should take up a public position on policy issues; as for their own detailed opinions, most clergy support welfare, overseas aid and employment as the political priorities of the day, not the control of inflation. On issues of defence, nearly one in five takes a pacifist position, and about two in three hold that nuclear arms are, by their nature, immoral; however, only 40 per cent want Britain to abandon her nuclear deterrent as against half who support retention. The Falklands service, with its stress on reconciliation, received overwhelming support.

Some other characteristics of the poll are also worth comment. Disestablishment was only a minority preference, held by 34 per cent. It also showed that politically the clergy had shifted not to the Labour but to the Alliance Party, which now attracts about 50 per cent of Anglican clergymen. It would seem Marxism has a negligible influence, apart from one or two publicly visisble examples: the Alliance voters outnumbered intending Labour voters by four to one. One could infer from the level of Conservative voting that many clergy vote Conservative, yet have fairly 'liberal' attitudes. As for the breakdowns by age and type of parish, the most usual pattern among responses was as one might expect – the older clergy, and those in rural parishes, were somewhat more conservative, at least in their attitudes, though much less so in their voting. For example, an attitude giving primary emphasis to spiritual concerns and moral issues was twice as strong among those aged 51 and over as among those aged 35–50. What is particularly significant is that the 'Falklands factor', which resulted in a sharp rise in general support for the Conservative Party, was not noticeable among clergy: the tide of national feeling left their voting intentions untouched. Since the peace issue has been for nearly a century and a half the litmus paper of liberal attitudes, one can perhaps rephrase the old adage to read 'The Church of England is the SDP–Liberal Alliance at prayer'.

In this context it may be worth quoting an extract from the important paper by Professor Gerard Dekker *Power and Powerlessness of the 'New Clergy'*. He begins by noting the privatisation of religion and the distinction between an abstract, public over-world, which is strange, impersonal in its operation and alienating, and what he calls 'the personal, self-shaped world'. But 'we now see the rise of committees, councils, bureaux, synodical organisations etc.' guided by clerical functionaries, appointed for their expertise, not their piety or charisma. Ecumenism further enlarges the scope of these functionaries. 'The rise of this new bureaucracy, means that church members often feel themselves powerless against the ecclesiastical organisation and against the clergy', but at the same time 'the power of the clergy *vis-à-vis* members is not really great.' The new clergy are 'in danger of living their own lives amidst an alienated membership' for whom the ecclesiastical apparatus has become one more part of the impersonal world.

In so far as the Church preaches at the personal level 'the

words and actions of the Church have to suit people in their
personal world.' Curiously, a large part of the Dutch population thinks the Church should speak on issues like racism
and nuclear armament, but they do not accept ecclesiastical
regulation of their own conduct. Dekker gives two illustra-
tions, one of the Church making pronouncements at the
political level but not really involving many people, and the
other of the Church not daring to pronounce on the personal
morality of smoking. The clergy, argues Dekker, exercise
influence when they speak about nuclear armaments, enter
into discussion with multinationals, and act as mediators
for foreign labourers. But these clergy do not represent the
voice of the Church, taken as a whole, or have much impact
on the personal behaviour and opinions of its members. Thus,
in 1979 the Dutch Council of Churches declared itself against
an updating of nuclear armaments, but at the same time also
said that persons who are members of Churches affiliated to
the Council, but who are also members of the government
(and who even constituted the majority in it), should collabo-
rate in such updating. A similar situation occurs with regard
to the so-called illegal foreign labourers. The Council of
Churches takes a certain view, but the government, in which
the largest Christian political party has a majority, acts
differently.

CONCLUDING AND ALMOST PERSONAL POSTSCRIPT

Finally I come to debateable reflections on ecclesiastical
thinking about issues of national defence, particularly when
traditional arguments about the criteria of a just war are
adduced in the discussion of deterrence and the balance of
nuclear terror. These reflections strongly reflect my personal
viewpoint.

One of the major problems is the nature of much of the
opposition to the shifts in the stance of the Churches on

matters of politics and defence over the past two decades. It is difficult to discover a serious political theology on the Conservative side. Perhaps that is because hitherto the *de facto* position of the Established Church has rendered otiose a theoretical exposition of a politically conservative theology. I am not speaking about generalised statements as to the iniquity of communism and the relationship between a man's dignity and some kind of personal ownership. Those exist in plenty. What has not been attempted is some stark encounter with the realities of power and political process. Reinhold Niebuhr, in the inter-war period, produced a highly sophisticated political theology, which took a left-wing position as its starting-point, but eventually provided the basis for a kind of Christian realism, whether of Right or Left. The neglect of Niebuhr in the last two decades is symptomatic of a general softening of Christian political thought.

Of course, various things are said which point in a realistic direction. Churchmen of conservative mind emphasise that we live in a very imperfect and very dangerous world and one universally tainted by original sin. But there is little enough from them by way of a convincing linkage between the deposit of faith and some rationale of contemporary political action. Mrs Thatcher has revived, in some degree, a two centuries-old tradition of political economy, which has religious underpinnings, and Professor Michael Novak has written *Towards a Theology of the Corporation*. But in general, and especially with regard to the moral rationale of defence and deterrence, argument tends to rely on notions of protecting a Christian civilisation from a godless enemy, and a presumed relationship between Christian liberty and democratic freedom. However, the notions of Christian liberty and democratic freedom are not really cognate, though they could be shown to be compatible. The Christian conscience, and a rejection of any idolatry of the state, certainly run in tandem with western respect for individuality, but the connection with the New Testament or even classical moral theology is loose.

The left-liberal viewpoint normally refers both to moral theology and to the New Testament deposit of faith. In fact, it makes political inferences which exist at several removes from the original texts just as the inferences made by conservative political theologians do. To say that all humankind shares in a common dignity, to affirm the blessedness of the poor, recognise a duty to assist the weak, the widow and the fatherless, prohibit extortion and adding field to field, is to say a great deal. But you can hardly derive a set of political priorities from this, or decide which of your neighbours are most deserving. You have not even begun to work out which preconditions must be fulfilled before peace can be secured, or a war on want successfully embarked upon. You are still at the level of general images and broad ends and imperatives.

One characteristic of left-liberal Christian thinking which has attracted comment is the selectivity of moral indignation. This selectivity is at least as marked as the selectivity of those moral judgements previously used to suggest the moral superiority of the western world. Moreover, such thinkers in the left-liberal tradition are almost paralysed by guilt from making any adverse comment on the politics or activities pursued by certain groups, who are thus exempt from judgement. Western leaders are treated as individually responsible in a way which lays them open to moral obloquy, while criminals are merely 'maladjusted', and adventurers in the Third World are either justly reacting against western exploitation and colonialism, or pursuing justice by understandably, excusably rough methods. Thus the liberal, on the one hand, scales down the scope of the general confession of sin for ordinary, decent people, but adopts a relentless comminatory style and a vocabulary of guilt and responsibility when commenting on the actions of western elites.

At the same time, there is the assumption that the moral score is at best even between representatives of the western and Soviet worlds. This is not true of all ecclesiastical commentators: the Bishop of Salisbury adopts a unilateralist position whilst fully acknowledging the character of the regimes with which we have to deal. But there are plenty of commentators who assume that the Christian is trapped between the Russian devil and the deep-blue, Conservative sea. Bishop Michael Hare Duke, writing in the *Church Times* thinks in precisely this way. His article of 15 October 1982, 'Blessed are the Peace-makers...', begins by contrasting the acts of hard-liners with the 'ordinary person' concerned for peace, and then describes a visit to Hungary to see 'what peace might mean to the ordinary person — and particularly to Christians — in a socialist country.' He described how his colleagues were agreeably received by the State Peace Council 'which was eager to demonstrate that disarmament and reconciliation were as much its business as they were ours.' The arguments offered by the Council were the same as those recently offered by the Foreign and Commonwealth Office in London, only they pointed in the reverse direction. The Bishop went on to say that 'the vaunted peace movements of the East' are not at all just communist propaganda because 'they spring from the Leninist conviction that socialism should be by its nature a force for peace.' 'East and West have much to learn from each other,' he says, with even-handed judgement, though the precise form of this learning is not specified.

The whole article then shifts down precisely to the level of personal contacts, and has that same lack of political insight into systemic processes as that shown by Dr Frank Buchman who thought he could accomplish something by face-to-face talks with Hitler. The Bishop not only thinks that contacts between ordinary people are a good thing — which they certainly are — but supposes that such contacts will erode the unexamined and ignorant prejudices which divide our world. But the existence of power blocs is not dependent on or rooted in misconceptions, but in the logic of accumulated power, and it is just not true, as the Bishop asserts, that what we have to do is accept difference; each different way of political life, being on a rough moral parity.

This liberal presupposition is in total opposition to the view held by those who wield power in the Eastern bloc, who are armed with an ideology in which both liberalism and Christianity are part of the world that is passing away, and must inevitably give place to their system. For the Bishop, Christian charity is taken, quite wrongly, to imply that the rivals are morally much of a muchness, whereas those in the East, who are the sole wielders of power, and who have no need to take note of ordinary people as do western leaders, hold precisely the opposite view.

This personalised and entirely apolitical way of thinking also leans, as I indicated earlier, on the illusory notion that a gesture can break the political log-jam. Now, imaginative gestures are indeed important, but they must be reasoned, calculated and made from a position of strength. The opposing side does not share quasi-Christian presuppositions about the redemptive power of a moral gesture, nor does it understand the notion of 'strength perfected in weakness'. It professes an ideology of proletarian power, not of exemplary vulnerability, and in any case the Christian faith in vulnerable love is precisely one of those notions which cannot be transferred to the political process. In any case, it is very odd, on the one hand, to view the West as much on a par morally with the East, and then, on the other hand, to think that we possess the moral stature to make impressive and effective gestures. Only a state protected against the real pressures of international relations, first by its own imperial position and then by American power, could bring up people to be so deluded. The theology of crucifixion and reconciliation cannot be so reworked that Britain emerges as the innocent corporate agent of redemption, or even as setting an example to lesser breeds without such grace. It is the old imperial *folie de grandeur* transferred to morality. Such delusions are even less well-founded, when they continue to rely on the protection of American power. Indeed, the Bishop of Salisbury, speaking on television, has been entirely frank in acknowledging that the moral example looks somewhat hollow so long as we remain within the ambit of American protection.

I must also say that in my view, ecclesiastical thinking concentrates very much on what would be morally defensible given that nuclear war were to occur. It presumes a reality which the nuclear deterrent is designed expressly to discourage. I do not know to what extent Christian moral theology has concerned itself in the past with the morality of different kinds of deterrence, but I would imagine that the present problem of deterrence is of a magnitude and kind as unique as the kind of war it aims to prevent. The Roman Catholic Bishops of England and Wales appear to hold that not only is the use of nuclear weapons immoral, but so is the threat involved in their possession. If, however, that threat makes their use less likely, then the ultimate immorality of nuclear war is less likely. Being motivated to render a grossly immoral act less likely is presumably to be accounted moral rather than immoral.

Another characteristic of ecclesiastical thinking relates further to this matter of setting an example. It may well be that underlying this is some expectation that a moral action, even one made in the world of politics, is likely to produce a beneficent spiral of responses. Indeed, there may be a link here with the doctrine of divine providence, such as that invoked by Canon John Collins in the original programme of Christian Action. The Call to Christian Action, made in 1946, said

> We boldly reaffirm our faith in the reality of God's providence in human history. We believe that the Cross of Christ and His Resurrection gave us the assurance that history has sense and direction, and that God's justice and His love surely operate in the world. In all national and international affairs the rule of God's love, and not the self-interest of the strong is the ultimate determinant.

In a way, this is a variation of what was clearly believed by some of those who argued for a straightforward celebration of victory in St Paul's. Because our cause was just, why should we not celebrate victory by praising God for His providential blessing on our arms? No doubt those who framed the original statement of Christian Action had a longer term in view in which the relationship between being in the right and being under God's sovereign protection might fructify. Perhaps they supposed that the fruits of righteousness would never have a political reward, but only rewards in heaven, or in the mysterious economy of the kingdom.

Whatever they intended, the statement is very nearly vacuous. Nothing whatever is guaranteed if we obey God's law. God does not underwrite his Kingdom in political terms. What we are here concerned with is not whether a righteous few might bring forth fruit after the collapse of those democratic polities on which we place so great a value, but with the survival of those polities themselves. We do have political responsibility and we cannot off-load it onto the very long run of the divine providence.

Setting an example is not a defensible way of testing the operation of providence by looking for beneficent and cumulative political goodwill and disarmament to spring from our actions. Consider only the following. If we were to adopt unilateralist policies, who would do likewise and so increase the chances of peace? Certainly not France, whose socialist prime minister François Mitterand declared in 1982 that France would not deprive itself of a single missile whatever others may do. All the renunciation of American missile bases in Britain would achieve would be a marginal, but significant, shift in the balance of power away from America to Russia, and by that margin to increase the likelihood of war. The self-interest of the stronger is precisely what *is* crucial in international affairs. Once relative weakness is established every conventional confrontation in any part of the world would be subject to nuclear fiat or blackmail, and, in the last event, America could no longer rationally involve itself in a nuclear confrontation for the sake of a Europe whose conventional arms could be overridden by that fiat. The retreat of the West, worldwide, would begin, with rising fears and apprehension in America, rising expectations of successful nuclear blackmail in Russia, and the concomitant likelihood of eventual nuclear war. However, none of this bears on whether there are rational and financial grounds for Britain forgoing, say, the Trident missile system and retaining Polaris, as is proposed by the Social Democratic Party. It could be argued that Britain could be stronger as an economy and in conventional armaments without that drain on her resources. But as a moral act, it would be entirely self-regarding and utilitarian and would not much impress or affect the world at large, or add in the slightest to our immunity and safety.

NOTES

1 I say usually since the last Japanese prime minister was a Christian, and encountered an agonising dilemma as to whether he should attend the traditional Japanese rites at the Ise shrine in his representative capacity.
2 For a short statement, cf. Gordon Dunstan, *The Artifice of Ethics* (SCM Press, 1974), pp. 101–13.

Invisible Religion, Popular Culture and Anti-nuclear Sentiment

BERNICE MARTIN

'It's unchristian', cried Mrs Varden shaking her head. 'Unchristian!' said the locksmith...'What on earth do you call it unchristian for? Which would be most unchristian, Martha — to sit quietly down and let our homes be sacked by a foreign army, or to turn out like men and drive 'em off? Shouldn't I be a nice sort of Christian, if I crept into a corner of my own chimney and looked on while a parcel of whiskered savages bore off Dolly — or you?'

Charles Dickens, *Barnaby Rudge*[1]

Underground. They want us to go underground.
You got the right to say what you think
You gotta fight 'cos they're leading us to the brink.

There's gonna be a fireball
Never a time like this before

Go down the line
You got the right to stay alive
You gotta fight to survive.

Wishbone Ash, 'Underground'[2]

Someone's gonna work for the CIA
the KGB and the man in red.
I wonder if we're gonna see another day
Somewhere near the future.

We got everything we want for a peaceful time,
Take what you want but you can't take mine,
Everybody's living on the Siegfried line
Worried 'bout the future.
It's so confused
Easy to believe someone's gonna light the fuse.

Rainbow, 'Can't Happen Here'[3]

Two hundred Christians gathered last Sunday for an ecumenical service in unlikely conditions at the 'Green Gate' of the Greenham Common air base — scene of current anti-nuclear demonstrations by women peace activists...There was a strong feeling of Christian support for the demonstration — and for the 'peaceful blockade' of the base on Monday. Several Anglicans and Methodists from Wales who had never participated in any demonstrations before were representative of the many 'non-political' Christians who have felt drawn to the women's peace camp at Greenham...In her sermon, Valerie Flessati observed that Advent recalled the time when Mary waited silently for birth. But, she added, women today could not wait silently for the destruction of life on earth — 'as women were called out of their traditional roles to be first witness of the resurrection, so women are called today to witness to peace and to the non-violent love that makes for peace.'

News item, *Church Times*, 17 December 1982

The world is in a mess
And finished more or less
It doesn't really matter
And maybe it's too late to change it
It's never too late to change it

Now this old sea-dog's gonna get away across the water
This old sea-dog is a-waving you bye-bye
But I don't think God thought we'd get out of order,
This old sea-dog is a-waving you bye-bye.

Status Quo, 'Never Too Late'[4]

While I wouldn't go so far as to term the film a strict
allegory, *E.T.* has — as no doubt others have divined —
an allegorical resonance. A superior being descends to
Earth from his extra-terrestrial sphere. The toolshed in
which he is found will do at a pinch as a modern subur-
ban counterpart to the manger. The only maternal
presence in the film is named Mary. E.T. performs
miracles....His message is one of love. He attracts
disciples among the children, who in a biology class free
the frogs they are expected to chloroform and dissect.
E.T. is hounded by relentless pursuers, dies, is reborn,
and returns at the end, if not to heaven, at least to
outer space. Before departing, he makes a sign of benedic-
tion. 'I'll always be right here,' he says, his luminous
fingertip glowing over Elliot's heart.'

S. Schoenbaum, 'Botanist in the Manger',
Times Literary Supplement, 7 January 1983.

This may seem an ill-assorted set of texts with which to preface
an essay on contemporary Christianity and opposition to
nuclear arms. There is, however, a rationale to the selection:
certain crucial themes connect these quotations within a continuous tradition in English culture. This article will not be an
analysis of the careful theological, philosophical, moral and
political arguments which Christians and non-Christians deploy
in a deliberate and articulate debate on the problem of nuclear
arms. My concern is rather with the inchoate constellations of
imagery, sentiment and identification which form archeological
strata in our culture, sedimented deposits of unconsidered,
implicit meanings lying beneath the surface of reasoned debate.
My premise is that in order to understand the well-springs of
popular sympathy for the anti-nuclear or unilateralist position,

one needs to examine certain long-established models, assumptions and values which are embedded deep in our culture — sometimes so deep that they escape our notice precisely because we take them so much for granted. They stand unanalysed behind what counts as a good story, a proper response in a crisis, and so on. Popular culture is the medium in which these assumptions appear most unselfconsciously as self-evident structures of meaning. The charge that a soap-opera is trite often means just that: it is playing back to us, unmodified by irony or criticism, what we like to assume about how the world works — or ought to work.

Many of these powerful models have the quality of myth and, further, are a direct, though often secularised, legacy of Christianity and, in the case of Anglo-American culture, very specifically of individualistic Protestantism. Partly because they have broken loose from the anchors of coherent theology and institutional location, they have acquired new ambiguities and inner contradictions. The symbols with which I am concerned seldom lead unequivocally to an absolutist pacifism; rather, they cluster problematically around issues of power, authority and coercion as stumbling-blocks equally to an ethic of love and to the politics of individual independence. Secularised Christianity and western individualism are the twin nodes of the constellation which is the subject of my analysis. Together they constitute a major part of what Thomas Luckmann has called 'invisible religion',[5] and of what, by analogy with that concept, I have elsewhere called 'invisible politics'.[6] They are not the only elements in the bedrock of core values in British culture; indeed they are in permanent tension with certain other central values of which two will be important for the discussion below, that is, heroism and group loyalty, more particularly patriotism. The tension is an ancient one which is always rendered especially acute by war and civil disturbance, but it is given a new colour and resonance by the threat of nuclear warfare in which the technology of wholesale death is extravagantly unselective and the individual more than usually impotent.

My first quotation came from Charles Dickens: he is not perhaps the obvious starting-point for an analysis of these contemporary problems. Yet I am not alone in seeing a connection between that most demotic of novelists and the popular culture of today. In a recent television interview[7] the rock music entrepreneur Malcolm McLaren claimed that a direct line connected the author of *Barnaby Rudge* with the rock group the Sex Pistols since both were supreme exemplars of the English tradition of story-telling and social comment. No doubt McLaren expected to create a *frisson* of incredulity in drawing such a parallel, but a variant of his case is far from absurd, provided one ignores the special pleading on behalf of the Sex Pistols. The novels of Dickens are a rich repository of archetypical imagery of English life and values. They may not be wholly accurate accounts of Victorian society[8] but they reflect, and indeed have had no small hand in moulding some of the most condensed and widely recognised symbols of English identity and ideals — one only needs to reflect on the style of the English Christmas to see how deep Dickensian imagery has penetrated. In several of his works, but more explicitly in *Barnaby Rudge*, a central preoccupation is the very tension on which my analysis turns — an ethic of love, and the politics of independent individualism juxtaposed with each other and with the virtues of heroism and patriotism. For Dickens, patriotism encompasses order, duty and Englishness while recognising the frequent inadequacy and corruption of the authorities. Respect for properly constituted authority (parents, masters, the state, the law) vies with the knowledge that our leaders are as often as not little better than licensed rogues, or at the very least, masters of what in *Little Dorrit* he calls, How Not to Do It. Dickens' dislike of chaos and contempt for 'the mob' stands alongside his championship of 'the people'. Modern popular culture, and not least the world of rock music, resonates with the same tensions, although the symbolic vocabulary is somewhat altered and the balance has probably tilted further against authority. There is indeed a direct line connecting

Gabriel Varden and Maypole Hugh of *Barnaby Rudge* with John Lennon, The Jam, Status Quo, Wishbone Ash, Gillen, Rainbow and other English 'anti-nuclear' rock groups of the late twentieth century.

Gabriel Varden, the 'harmonious locksmith' is in many ways the real hero of *Barnaby Rudge*, Dickens' fictional account of the Gordon riots. He is the embodiment of all the English 'yeoman' virtues brought forward in time into this idealised, early bourgeois figure. Varden is a patriot and a supporter of civic order; the exchange with his wife from which I quoted is provoked by his intention to march with the Volunteers: further, he is proud to have made the great lock on the main door of Newgate Prison. Yet his patriotic feelings are not activated by abstractions but by personal loyalties and a fierce private independence. His wife and her malicious, comic maid are members of Sir George Gordon's fanatical Protestant movement which Varden steadfastly refuses to support. Later in the story he faces the No-Popery mob who are intent on sacking Newgate and refuses to help them open the lock of the jail. His refusal stems not so much from a passion for civic order and respect for property — though that too — but rather from the principle of resisting mob coercion. 'Under compulsion I will do nothing,' he repeats, even in peril of his life. Gabriel Varden stands for domestic virtue, loyalty, tolerance, order and individual liberty. It is he and not his cantingly 'religious' wife whom Dickens treats as the real Christian. He is heroic in his unobtrusive protection of the weak, in his exercise of mercy, and in his blunt temerity in recalling his social betters — scheming aristocrat, corrupt magistracy and vacillating government — to their unpalatable moral and civic duty. He is a peaceable man who likes nothing better than to drain his Toby jug of ale, but *in extremis* he is prepared to fight for the sanctity of private life and the right to self-determination. He stands against vicious mob and venal authority as a lone individual and potential martyr.

Varden's *alter ego*, as it were, is Maypole Hugh, one of the leaders of 'Protestant' rioters. He too is courageous and fiercely independent, but these virtues are twisted into negative shapes and become the basis of anarchy and mayhem, public evil and private wrong. Yet Dickens shows a deep sympathy for this anti-hero. He pictures Hugh as a victim of social conditions and, more precisely, of the wilful dereliction of duty of those whose responsibility it should have been to turn Hugh into a civilised being. State, community and family all fail Hugh: the principle of love never applies and he becomes a half-wild creature more at home with horses than people — his unnatural 'natural' father gives him the derisory nickname of 'the centaur'. Yet Hugh's independence and his courage against the odds remain heroic in their own tragic way.

Both figures, Hugh and Varden, are sympathetic characters to English readers because they are two faces of English individualism. A powerful case has been made by Alan Mac-Farlane[9] that such individualism is not only a core value of English culture but that it was established as such long before the onset of modernity and industrialisation. Dickens was merely celebrating what had long been taken for granted as the prime, heroic virtue of Englishness. That same virtue is found at the heart of popular anti-nuclear protest and is a striking feature of the rock music associated with anti-nuclear sentiments. Several current rock styles include anti-nuclear songs among their repertoire. The best-selling ones of the last couple of years are numbers by the veteran heavy-metal group Status Quo and the recently disbanded new mod group the Jam, but anti-nuclear protest is also a frequent element in punk, particularly among the small independent record companies, and among the all-girl groups of the live London circuit[10] as well as in remnants of the 1960s progressive/protest music — vintage Lennon, Dylan and the rest still sell and crop up with fair regularity on the radio. A theme which unites all this music is hostility to leaders: accredited institutions and their representatives and, above all, the state are depicted as hostile to the needs of the private individual. The burden of all these songs is that a nuclear holocaust is likely to come about through the stupidity, corruption and self-interest of political leaders. They stand in privileged positions — first candidates for the nuclear shelters, who meanwhile play lethal power games with all our lives and with the future of mankind itself. Peter Gabriel's 1980 song 'Jeux sans Frontiers' was built entirely on the conceit of world political leaders playing a species of chess game with ourselves and our nations as the pieces. In these lyrics there is never a sense of the state as an institution which embodies and protects the interests of its people: rather, the state is depicted as a privileged club in which pretentious lunatics stride and posture. The individual has to stand on his own feet to oppose this madness in high places.

Two further themes frequently accompany this. The first is that modernity itself — super-tankers, micro-chips and depersonalisation — has somehow sent the world out of control and made it difficult to recapture the human scale of things. The second is a cynical variant on what Daniel Bell once called 'the end of ideology': the leaders of the world super-powers are indistinguishable from each other; there's nothing to choose between capitalism and communism 'the CIA, the KGB and the man in red' are all enemies of the people. In live concerts Ian Gillen prefaces his anti-nuclear song 'Mutually Assured Destruction' (or MAD) by patter which runs roughly as follows: 'We had a personal letter from President [pause] Thingy in America, and from [pause] the other chap in Russia. They said this song had put off a nuclear holocaust for three whole months. But in another three months it will bring one about.'[11] It is a knowing in-group cynicism which presents the world leaders as faceless, inter-changeable, vicarious action-men. Deprive them of their proper names and their proper deference and they are reduced in size; if they treat us as expendable numbers then we shall treat them as nameless puppets. In *Bleak House* Dickens uses a very similar technique to make the same point about the Victorian ruling class: Government and Opposition are identically faceless teams — Boodle, Coodle, Doodle, etc. down the alphabet versus Buffy, Cuffy, Duffy, etc.

I have argued elsewhere[12] that a major cultural legacy of the radical counter-culture of the late 1960s was a simplified, popular version of secular antinomianism which found a niche in youth culture and rock music. The hostility to political leaders which contemporary anti-nuclear songs express, is a continuation of this element in the individualist tradition. John Lennon's hit song 'Imagine' (now 'old' but with a continuing currency) puts the antinomian case as explicitly as possible.[13] All that stands between us and per-petual peace and harmony is society — country, patriotism, property, the state. All the institutional anchors of meaning, identity and ascribed loyalty simply serve to divide us, to corrupt our capacity to recognise our common humanity. In 'Imagine' Lennon resolved the tension he saw between the individual and the social by opting for the personal 'life world' of chosen companions as the only possible haven. In such a view, the private becomes the sacred sphere where peace and harmony would be unproblematic if only the wider structures of society would leave us alone. It is a vision of a world purged altogether of the dimension of power and coercion; it is an *a*political Utopia, the invisible politics of antinomian privatisation.

This is a very frequent theme in youth culture and under-lies most of the anti-nuclear protest rock. The private individual is the proper unit of concern, just as it was for Dickens, but now the level of cynical mistrust of the authorities runs even deeper than it did for Dickens. In the mid-1970s, Bob Marley said: 'The Devil has always come in between politicians and they start quarrelling. Y'have to imagine what really go on, because power become a pride business instead of we live together and trade together and stop the war.'[14] The theology may have been Rastafarian but the sentiment was common to most of the rock music milieu. David Bowie makes a similar point: 'I've seen life and I think I know who's controlling the world. And after what I've seen of the state of this world, I've never been so damned scared in all my life.'[15] A popular song of late 1982 draws the lesson of such beliefs. In 'Gettaway', by Chris de Burgh, the lyric argues that *people* have no quarrels; we are all tired of being threatened with the final big bang so why not lock up the leaders in one room and let them fight it out? The affairs of state and the *amour propre* of politics have no meaning for ordinary folk who are just pawns and victims.

An articulate and self-consciously antinomian philosophy of the kind which was developed in the counter-culture and the 'progressive' wing of youth culture in the 1960s probably characterises only a limited segment of the spectrum today. There are some indications that the generations whose adolescence or early adulthood occurred during the effervescence of counter-cultural radicalism have carried a muted version of sixties' values through into adult life and are notably more radical in a mildly antinomian style than the generations immediately above and below them, that is, the over forty-fives and the under twenty-fives. In a recent poll of its readers, *New Society* found the sixties' generation, among other things, more involved in unilateralist protest than their elders and juniors and more likely to have been involved in demonstrations.[16] The antinomian tradition continues in some youth cultures: a recent hit single by the Jam, 'Going Underground' is an aggressive, anarchic piece which, for instance, includes the line 'I don't want what society wants'. Contemporary punk is the main home of such ideas and is often a hard-nosed repeat of sixties' values. As a total world view, it probably embeds itself in a fairly narrow segment of the current generation. Without further research, however, I would not rule out the possibility that such values have shifted down the social spectrum from the educated young bohemians of the sixties towards the working class and unemployed young today, who after all, will hardly appear in a poll of *New Society* readers.

A full-blown version of antinomianism does still appear
from time to time, more especially on the radical fringe of
the arts. *Any Minute Now*, a musical performed by Wildcat
Stage Productions at Stratford East in February 1983, is a
case in point. The play takes the form of a trial of a young
woman who has strangled her baby, with the audience cast
as the jury. The woman is depicted as the victim of a social
system which subjected her to slum life, a brutal husband
and the ever-present threat of nuclear war. Her compas-
sionate violence on her child is the consequence of society's
wider violence: the structure of the play is an invitation to
the jury/audience to pronounce a verdict of not guilty. Such
theatrical productions — this one began life at the Edinburgh
Festival — seldom reach beyond a small, self-selected audience
of the already converted. Even a humorous anti-nuclear play
such as Spike Milligan's *The Bedsitting Room* — goonish
surrealism on the theme of post-holocaust mutants — will
hardly reach a mass audience. Yet a 1983 revival and updating of this ten-year-old farce has been judged a commercial
proposition for the West End — not least, perhaps, because
political leaders appear in it mutated into parrots, which is
yet another technique of cutting them down to size. Touches
of such surreal humour as well as more explicit anarchism
also figure in New Wave anti-nuclear songs. Their ideal individual is more reminiscent of Maypole Hugh than of Gabriel
Varden. Like *Any Minute Now* they tend to lay the blame
for violence and mayhem with the authorities, but often, as
in the Jam's 'A Bomb in Wardour Street', they nevertheless
seem to take a grisly relish in depicting post-holocaust
horrors. It reminds one sharply of Jeff Nuttall's analysis in
Bomb Culture[17] of the seductive power of sadism even when
employed by disciples of peace.

Anarchic radicalism may be very much a minority phenomenon but there is more than a hint of secular antinomianism
among a wide spectrum of the population, although it is
implicit and unphilosophical in its form. In the course of
conducting research into the beliefs of young people in the

mid-1970s,[18] I found that throughout the range of age, education and social class the young people in my sample expressed a near-unanimous mistrust of politics and politicians. This was not a fundamental radicalism but more a proclivity to assume, as Tom Kitwood found in a similar piece of research more recently, that 'on the large scale nothing can be radically changed.'[19] It was also part of a tendency to regard the formal institutions of Church and State as at best irrelevant to their lives and frequently as hindrances to their personal well-being: in fact, Church and clergy emerged with a more benevolent image than that of the political class. The perspective which these young people had on the world was strikingly individualistic and their positive values clustered around the private and the personal. Kitwood's findings are entirely of a piece with this picture. Such ground is fertile soil for the growth of something between cynicism and fatalistic apathy about the impersonal institutions within which the economy and the polity are organised.

Popular humour shows that such attitudes are part of the common ground of English cultural assumptions[20] and not a mere passing feature of adolescence. A successful television comedy show like *Yes, Minister!* depends for its humour on our being prepared to collude in a knowing cynicism about politicians and civil servants. Sir Humphrey Appleby and his Ministry of Administrative Affairs are worthy successors to Dickens' parasitical Barnacle family and their Circumlocution Office or to Trollope's machiavellian cathedral city, Barchester. I am not suggesting that British democracy is in peril because we have uniformly lost respect for public institutions, but merely that there is a thread in British culture which takes it for granted that the powerful will always be self-interested and pretentious, sometimes even buffoons, but which sees this as as much comic as sinister. It is accompanied by a deep mistrust of missionary zeal and fanaticism. Anyone who takes himself or his cause too seriously is in danger of alienating potential sympathisers.

Among the young people whose beliefs I studied,[21] there was
a pervasive dislike of enthusiasts – both religious and political
– who tried to 'stuff their ideas down your throat'. Proselytising and extremism from the Moonies to the National Front
are seen as embarrassing, un-English and a violation of the
individual's right to privacy and self-determination.

Popular humour mirrors this view, too, treating extremism
as the natural butt of the common man. In a recent television
show, Jasper Carrott, a comedian from the Midlands club
circuit, hit both these targets in a notably effective joke.[22]
He read from a Civil Defence leaflet containing advice about
what to do after a nuclear attack. The base line of the whole
joke was the absurdity of offering homely advice against such
an unspeakable eventuality, but the two biggest laughs came
even-handedly at the expense of the authorities and the anti-
nuclear crusaders. He quoted from the leaflet: 'A nation is
like a forest and the aim of war planning is to secure the
surivival of the great trees and not the brushwood,' and then
added: 'And who's the brushwood? I'm looking at it.' This
was greeted by loud laughter and applause followed by a
gradual uneasy silence as the cameras panned across the
'brushwood' in the audience. There followed some nonsense
about swatting flies as a measure of post-holocaust hygiene,
and then: 'If they wanted to be really useful they'd lock up
all the CND fanatics. They'd be a right pain in the arse running around with tee shirts saying *I told you so.*' Laughter,
applause and cheering followed. The cynicism was uneasy
but pervasive.

What this joke and the audience reaction to it illustrate is
that there is no enormous break in the cultural assumptions
of the mainstream and those of the anti-nuclear activists.
Both see the ordinary citizen as the pig in the middle in the
game of nuclear *realpolitik*. The break lies not in the assumptions but in the seriousness with which they are held and in
the moral drawn from them. A soft-edged, passively fatalistic
and mildly antinomian individualism is what the common
man takes for granted and is probably at least as pervasive as

the hard-edged Darwinian or Manchester School version of competitive individualism which has been the focus of much recent political journalism. It is a syndrome which merits further scrutiny.

In a recent analysis of contemporary best-selling fiction, John Sutherland[23] argued that the major preoccupation in this literature is anxiety about living in a world which is fundamentally unsafe. Neither nature nor society — including, crucially, the properly appointed authorities — can be trusted not to engulf the private individual in horrendous disaster of some kind. The same might be said of the horror/disaster genre of currently popular films. It could be claimed that such themes are merely a sublimation of the perfectly rational fear of nuclear war, but it seems to me more plausible to consider the dread of nuclear disaster as one item in a wider repertoire of contemporary anxieties. Dr Stuart Blanch, Archibishop of York, made a cognate point in the General Synod debate on *The Church and the Bomb* in February 1983.[24] He suggested that in the current wave of public consternation about nuclear arms there may lie a primal fear of cataclysm such as our medieval forebears harboured — an anticipation of Armageddon in which evil triumphs over good. Certainly symbolic reverberations of End-of-the-World mythology are prominent in popular imagery of the nuclear threat: for example, the Status Quo song quoted at the beginning of this article is constructed round the imagery of the flood, the first 'end of the world'. It is certainly the case that such chiliastic hauntings do tend to seize popular imagination in periods of fast and disruptive social change when the causes of personal insecurity and misfortune are abstract, impersonal forces, less than easily amenable to intentional control. Contemporary social systems based on high technology, a minutely complex and ever-changing division of labour and a world political and economic system which is beyond the immediate comprehension of the average citizen, might well spawn such fears. Moreover, a period of world recession in which dread of unemployment and a fall

in living standards haunts a population which only two
decades ago thought it was on an incline of perpetual progress,
is not an inappropriate time for millenarian nightmares. Our
medieval ancestors designated Jews and witches the peculiar
agents of evil: at least the contemporary antinomian preference
for blaming political leaders makes symbolic scapegoats of
the powerful rather than the powerless.

In Sutherland's analysis of *Bestsellers*[25] he found that
salvation usually comes in the guise of specially gifted or
courageous individuals. Perhaps these are secular Messiah
figures (I shall take up the point below) but such mythic
invocation of the *individual* against Armageddon is clearly
also a residue of the individualist morality explored above.[26]
Anti-nuclear rock songs propose the same recipe against the
ultimate disaster. They exhort the individual to fight his own
battle against all the lunatic Dr Strangeloves with their fingers
on the nuclear trigger. 'You gotta fight 'cos they're leading us
to the brink/ You got the right to stay alive/ You gotta fight
to survive' (Wishbone Ash). Even if 'fight' is not intended
literally (and that is ambiguous) the metaphor is 'masculine'
and warlike. The individual is his own best friend; it is every
man for himself: 'Everybody's looking for a little more air';
'Take what you want but you can't take mine' (Rainbow).
It really is not a very far cry, after all, from Gabriel Varden's
defence of hearth and home.

At this point we encounter a complicated set of cross-
cutting resonances. The picture of the independent, private
individual fighting for his rights and his survival calls up not
only the imagery of individualism but also that of heroism,
and heroism is a mythic structure which faces in many
directions. For the anti-nuclear movement the most awkward
of heroism's faces are those which look towards violence and
patriotism respectively. Of course, there is no reason at all
why opposition to nuclear energy or to nuclear arms should
necessarily entail opposition to all forms of violence or to all
war, and in reality it may entail neither. Likewise, a unilateralist
position is not incompatible with intense patriotic feelings.

Nevertheless, in terms of symbolic affinities rather than strict logic, there is something awkward about a movement whose most powerful symbol is *Peace*, employing aggressive, warlike tactics, metaphors or mythic echoes. Further, if my argument so far is correct, a popular mood which involves an antinomian mistrust of the state and its leaders will find many of the obvious mythic modes of heroic patriotism deeply compromised by the state's prior claims on them. The first of these two problems is obviously at its most acute for strict pacifists for whom the 'macho' imagery of heroic independence does not evoke the most appropriate or appealing symbolic connections. (I shall come to the heartland of their appropriate imagery below.) For the rest, however, a *High Noon* solution works very well: in that classic Western the climax involves Gary Cooper as the pacifist sheriff striding along the main street to shoot it out with the villain after all on behalf of the whole town. In this way the lone macho fighter from Agamemnon to John Wayne, taking in Gabriel Varden on the way, can stand behind the anti-nuclear image of fighting for the right to survive.

Perhaps the minimum necessary quality for heroism is that, when the ultimate test or ordeal arises, the hero keeps his personal integrity: the cause, if any, for which he stands is irrelevant at this most basic level, and there is clearly no difficulty in drawing on this strand in the passionate imagery of any cause at all. On another level, however, our culture is saturated with images which focus upon the values or causes which have inspired heroism rather than simply dwelling on the integrity of the individual *in extremis*. Ideals such as individual freedom itself or the protection of the weak, or the value of unquestioning loyalty to the group, are often the real focus of our mythology of heroism. The prime case of the latter is the patriotic heroism which is so important an ingredient in the rituals and symbolism of national solidarity such as the annual Remembrance Day ceremonies. In these powerful common symbols the legitimacy of the state and of its demands upon the loyal citizen are reinforced by association with patriotic heroism. Clearly this can be very problematic for those whose opposition to nuclear arms incorporates an apolitical or anti-political mistrust of the state.

At the height of counter-cultural protest in the late 1960s such antinomian sentiments in popular culture made common cause with opposition to the American prosecution of the Vietnam War as well as with the anti-nuclear cause. It is of the utmost significance that nothing of that order happened in Britain during the Falklands War in 1982. If anything, the opposite occurred. Patriotism and the heroism it inspired and required proved more potent than the antinomian pull which might have been expected to render the war as an illegitimate adventure of an irresponsible colonialist elite: in fact, Mrs Thatcher had never been so popular as she became after the Argentinian invasion of the Falklands in April 1982 and her dispatch of the Task Force. Of course, one must remember that the conflict was brief and cheap compared with Vietnam, and, most important of all, it ended in a British victory: a long drawn-out and costly war might easily have swayed popular sympathies in an anti-state and anti-war direction. Once the armed conflict began, however, the mass media became saturated with heroic images, all working on behalf of British patriotism and the British state and, moreover, couched in terms of a defence of freedom and of self-determination for the Falkland Islanders.

At the time of the Falklands War, I observed many young people — employed and unemployed, as well as university students — who intellectually and morally opposed the war but who found, often to their surprise and consternation, that the heroism of the British troops moved them. Some of them also felt a reluctant anger at what they saw as Argentinian bullying even though they regarded Britain's part in the war as an indefensible imperialist last stand. The Gabriel Varden principle of opposing coercion was called into play on behalf of a patriotism which they had often not even suspected themselves of harbouring. Cynicism about politicians and the state gave way against these more powerful, positive and dramatic enactments of the symbolism of British identity. There was even a parallel to Gabriel Varden's designation of England's potential enemies as 'a parcel of whiskered savages' (not, perhaps, on the face of it, the most likely description of the French) in the phrases which clustered around the popular press's contemptuous reference to 'the Argies!'

I am not suggesting here that the mythic roots of our cultural attitudes in themselves determine such political outcomes as popular support for the Falklands War or popular opposition to the Vietnam War. At most they contribute something to events by providing an emotionally and historically resonant framework which can be invoked to make sense of particular circumstances as they happen. This symbolic vocabulary operates on a plane different from and probably more powerful than that of rational political debate. Mythic models have ambiguous applications, however: the symbolism of individualism and of heroism can combine in several different ways. But the very same combination has led both to what one might call the 'masculine' version of popular anti-nuclear protest, *and* to popular patriotic support for the Falklands War, perhaps even among some of the same population. The latter paradoxical syndrome of individualism and patriotism may go some way towards explaining one of the odder apparent contradictions in the findings of all the late 1982 and early 1983 opinion polls on the subject of nuclear arms. Large to moderate majorities of the British population oppose the siting of Cruise missiles in Britain while even larger majorities are against unilateral disarmament.[27] Could it be that, on the stage of world politics, we see little Britain as the intrepid Gabriel Varden and the Americans as the untrustworthy authorities against whom we need to defend our independence? Such a view would certainly have points in common with that of the anti-Cruise activists, who see Britain as an 'occupied country'.

The rock music charts contain one small index of the complication which ensued from the fact that the individualistic 'masculine' version of anti-nuclear protest shared a symbol system with the imagery of patriotic heroism during the Falklands War. The anti-nuclear songs to which I have made reference all date from before the Falklands War, and all achieved considerable popular success, notably Status Quo's album on which 'Never Too Late' was the title track. (The record sleeve was in the form of a clock on which the finger was a nuclear rocket which a human hand was pushing back from midnight.) The huge public success of The Jam whose vocal support for CND is well publicised, is another indication of the wide spread of popular anti-nuclear sentiment in the rock music world. Yet, in the autumn and winter of 1982 a single by Robert Wyatt, 'Shipbuilding', was given intensive coverage by progressive disc-jockeys on radio. It was an anti-war, and specifically an anti-Falklands War song: here the ships were built which gave *you* employment; but what were they for? — simply to take young men out to their deaths. At New Year 1983, the song was voted number two in a listeners' poll on the Radio One show of the disc-jockey with the best progressive pedigree of all, John Peel. He lamented its sad failure in the wider charts. 'It didn't get the air time it deserved.' Anti-Falklands rock simply did not have sufficient popular appeal, however hard it was promoted.

This is not the end of the lessons to be derived from the Falklands campaign. Let us take a further look at the ambiguities imprinted in the imagery of heroism. It is a simple thing to recognise and respond to the macho heroism of 'our lads' 'yomping' many miles in appalling weather on the uplands of the Falklands to face an enemy who outnumbered them. All that is the stuff of military heroism and the all-male bond from the Sagas to boys' adventure comics.[28] But once one examines the transmutation which occurs when dealing with individual death in war one is drawn to recognise an entirely different ingredient which resonates with Christian significance. In our culture, suffering, sacrifice and martyrdom can hardly fail to conjure images of Christ as the Ur-symbol standing behind and giving reflected meaning to individual human death. When the news of Colonel H. Jones' death was first reported on television it was immediately clear that this had been a major act of heroism and self-sacrifice in battle. No film was then available, so drawings were presented showing colleagues carrying his body on a stretcher. The sketches had the unmistakable quality of a 'Deposition from the Cross', not only in the modelling of the figures but in the sacred manner in which they were presented. The model of innumerable 'Pietàs' similarly lay behind the accumulating images of grief and mourning. To lay down one's life on behalf of others is always a powerful act; in Christian cultures — however secularised — it partakes of something of the numinous quality of Christ's own death and of the deaths of the saints and martyrs because these are the most sacred of all the cultural meanings which historically cluster around both the act itself and representations of it.

Even the fact that the war dead are themselves dealers in violent death does not wholly cancel out the Christ resonance which focuses on death as suffered. It is the victim-hero who has suffered the violence of others who shifts the register of the imagery of heroism into a more specifically Christian mode than I have yet had cause to examine. It is the Christian modes or models which move us from individualism and it's 'masculine' imagery of fierce independence to the more passive or even 'feminine' imagery of suffering love as the ultimate principle. While much, though probably not all, of the individualism which I have discussed above is a product of Protestantism, sometimes at more than one remove, I have not so far done more than indicate that it gives rise to a set of symbols which oscillate uneasily between independent self-determination and antinomianism. I cannot proceed further with my argument — even to a clearer account of why antinomianism so easily fits within the anti-nuclear cause — without becoming more explicit about the basic symbolic models in Christianity itself. To attempt to define the essence of Christianity would be foolish and impossible: my purpose is less ambitious, that is, to suggest some of the lasting elements which Christianity tends to deposit in the culture of societies in which it has been the dominant system of ultimate meaning.

It is often helpful to clear one's view of an over-familiar object by comparing it with one which is similar yet distinct. The cultural deposit of Christianity is so over-familiar, so embedded in what we take for granted, that it has become virtually invisible. A comparison with its parent religion, Judaism, can do a great deal to remind one of the crucial points at which the identity-markers of the two religious cultures diverge and thus reveal to us Christianity's specific legacy.[29] The two religions, of course, share a common core. The first common element is the conception of a transcendent deity who has made man in his own image and is thus able to make demands on his creation: He has also given free will to man, which therefore gives man the power to fail God. (Even the Status Quo song is based on this belief: 'I don't think God thought we'd get out of order'.) The second crucial common feature is an essentially social vision of salvation, with heaven pictured as purified society. This gives rise first to a prophetic tradition of social criticism as actual society is measured against the righteousness of God, and second, to a recurring aspiration to Utopia.

In his novel *The Portage to San Cristobal of A.H.*, George Steiner[30] draws implications from these features which have scandalised many people but which, partly through the shock value of Steiner's literary tactic, throw into high relief those aspects of Judaism and Christianity which are pertinent to my argument. Steiner gives to the aged Adolph Hitler a virtuoso speech of self-justification. The hub of Hitler's case is the argument that the Jews were responsible for bringing into the world 'the bacillus of perfection' and that therefore:

we had to find, to burn out the virus of Utopia before the whole of our western civilisation sickened. [The God of the Jews] is purer than any other. The very thought of him exceeds the powers of the human mind. We are as blown dust to His immensity. But because we are his creatures, we must better ourselves, love our neighbour, be continent, give of what we have to the beggar. Because His inconceivable, unimaginable presence envelops us, we must obey every jot of the law. We must bottle up our rages and desires, chastise the flesh and walk bent in the rain....The Jew invented conscience and left man a guilty serf.

But that was only the first piece of blackmail. There was worse to come. The white-faced Nazarene....What did that epileptic rabbi ask of man? That he renounce the world, that he leave mother and father behind, that he offer the other cheek when slapped, that he render good for evil, that he love his neighbour as himself, no, far better, for self-love is an evil thing to be overcome. Oh! grand castration!...Ask of man more than he is, hold before his tired eyes an image of altruism, of compassion, of self-denial which only the saint or the madman can touch and you stretch him on the rack. Till his soul bursts.

The third act of the drama according to Steiner's *A. H.* is the Marxist Eden.

Sacrifice yourself for the good of your fellowman. Relinquish your possessions so that there may be equality for all. Hammer yourself hard as steel, strangle emotion, loyalty, mercy, gratitude....The Jew had grown impatient, his dreams had gone rancid. Let the kingdom of justice come here and now, next Monday morning. Let us have a secular Messiah instead. But with a long beard and his bowels full of vengeance.[31]

I am not really concerned here with the question of whether Steiner's novel gives a convincing explanation for anti-Semitism and for Nazism (which, after all, was another in the line of western Utopias) but only with his highly persuasive characterisation of the perfectionist utopian strand in the Judeo—Christian—Marxist legacy. (There is no space here to pursue the third, the Marxist, act of the drama.) I want to focus particularly on the tension between the Christian version of that vision and ordinary human and social exigency. It has often been argued — from Frederick Engels to Enoch Powell, in point of fact — that Christianity began as a Jewish sect and its founding characteristics must therefore be expected periodically to reassert themselves. Prominent among these is a heroic ethic which inverts all the conventional categories of social, political and ritual obligations and, with its scandalous ethic of love, places the meek, the poor and the defeated at the centre of the symbol system. The redemptive quality of suffering is a feature which Christianity shares with Judaism, but its transfer from the righteous remnant to the Messiah both individuates and radically alters the idea. Once Christianity appeared, the Messianic element became gradually muted in the mainstream of Diaspora Judaism,[32] which needed to operate as a quasi-tribal religion of cohesion in order to survive, but did so, perhaps, at the expense of an incipient individualism in its spiritual tradition. The exemplary figure in Juadism has long been not the awaited Messiah nor even the prophet, but the patient teacher and, even more importantly, as Freud understood, the patriarch[33] — flawed and all too human like Saul and David. In Judaism, social as distinct from divine authority *does* (*pace* Steiner) wear the fallible human face of the community leader: in Judaism the Incarnate God as perfect man is an alien model. It is Christianity which has carried that 'bacillus of perfection' into the modern world. Moreover, the symbolic legacy of the Christ—Messiah as supreme exemplar in Christianity makes the outsider, the rejected misfit, into the archetypical charismatic figure. Lurking within Christianity is a potent and subversive mixture: love above power and even justice; the spirit above the letter of the law; the degraded criminal, victim of the violence of the state and of the calculus of *realpolitik* as the supreme saviour.

That is not the whole story, of course. Once Christianity became an imperial religion it had need to elaborate the other half of the paradox in its founding texts — not only 'render unto Caesar', but also the whole *political* implication of the social nature of its vision which involves salvation as the City of God and, even more important, God as fully man. Thus the Church developed its complex and subtle traditions of teaching about the Christian as citizen in and of this world. At the level of popular cultural symbolism this has left us images of Christian civic and political virtue, monarchs (and their executioners) as the servants of the Lord, Christian patriotism, crusades, the church militant, and the just war. This is, needless to say, gross simplification, and much of the work of the Church has been an attempt to reconcile and balance the apparent contradictions in the fundamental paradox. I am not concerned here with the popular symbolic legacy of this 'civic' strand in Christianity, though clearly it would be important if the task in hand were to uncover the popular symbolism which might underpin the just war tradition: it certainly played a part in the imagery of the Falklands campaign. But my subject is the principle of love which is the starting-point of anti- or apolitical stances and the whole antinomian tradition. It is this aspect which differentiates Christianity most sharply from Judaism, and even more decisively from the other major religious traditions. Such a legacy of popular subversive imagery is inconceivable in a religion of power like Islam, for example.

The peace movement has available an enormous repertoire of symbol and resonance laid down by this Christian principle of transcendent love. The users of this symbolism are often quite unconscious of the Christian source of the mythic power on which they draw. The effectiveness of such a tradition does not depend on all those who employ it having

automatic access to its directly Christian pedigree, because
for centuries popular culture of many varieties has become
saturated with its themes. In our own secular age, western
rock music would be bereft of much of its power and appeal
if it could not play on the theme of the rejected outsider as
charismatic disturber of the conventional pieties. The Christ
reference can even there sometimes be direct as in The Who's
enormously successful rock opera *Tommy*. Dickens' narrative
structures and moral judgements also rest crucially on the
power of love and the redemptive qualities of the poor and
meek: Florence Dombey, Little Nell and Little Dorrit may
additionally show feminine dutifulness but in masculine
figures like Smike and Barnaby Rudge who are 'despised and
rejected', broken innocence acts as the instrument of redemption for others through love. The phenomenal success of the
Tolkien fantasies owes much to the same theme. The weak
and insignificant Hobbits become the instrument of common
salvation: through suffering, Frodo attains a Christ-like
stature while in Sam — the Gabriel Varden of the story —
the theme of yeoman independence and an unmistakable
Englishness is organically attached to the myth of the defeat
of power by love.[34] The Tolkien *oeuvre*, incidentally, is an
instructive popular instance in which this theme is comple-
mented rather than contradicted by the counterpoint of Holy
War — a strand which draws not only on the alternative
Christian tradition but on the Sagas and European folklore.
I mention this partly to illustrate the lack of exclusiveness
which symbolic traditions display: no cause, group or tendency can lay exclusive claim to them. (It may, however, be
worth remarking in parentheses that the juxtaposition
worked easily for Tolkien because he took the precaution of
making The Enemy wholly outside the human pale and
irredeemably evil — an expedient which works better in
fantasy than in human politics.)

The film *The Extra-Terrestrial* (*E.T.*) which is currently
breaking box office records is another instance of the same
kind — my list is indicative not exhaustive. Schoenbaum's

somewhat sardonic review of *E.T.* quoted at the beginning of this article, is perhaps meant to puncture portentous claims which have been made for the film as 'profound' or 'art', but I would simply restate what I argued above — that such a film could not conceivably produce the same response in a culture which had never been saturated in Christian imagery. Perhaps it takes a Jew to recognise it as a carrier of the boundary-markers of Christian culture. At all events, Bernard Levin hailed the film as warmly as he had earlier enthused about the Royal Shakespeare Company's production of *Nicholas Nickleby*, and for the same reasons — that they are both celebrations of the power of love, innocence and weakness. In a recent column in *The Times* he wrote:

> Steven Spielberg... [seizes] as did Dickens and his interpreters at the R.S.C., on the crucial principle at the heart of the universe: *the Manichee is wrong.* Though hate, cruelty, pain and fear abound, love is stronger.[35]

In the film children are the agents of this principle and E.T. himself, in his innocence is a 'child emeritus', as it were. The adult world, and more particularly the male world of power, is set to crush this fragile creature in the interests of reason, science and politics. The children's refusal to dissect frogs in school as well as their protection of E.T. are gestures rejecting that world of power and calculation. Levin ended his column by quoting directly: 'Verily I say unto you, Except ye be converted and become as little children, ye shall not enter into the kingdom of heaven.' The case could hardly be clearer.

I should be very surprised if Bernard Levin were in favour of unilateral disarmament. I am not arguing that there is an irresistible translation from such themes and values to anti-nuclear sentiment or strict pacifism. I am only suggesting that they offer a powerful reservoir of symbols with an in-built legitimacy on which the peace movement can draw. The structure of reasoned argument employed by unilateralists can encompass strategic and political as well as moral and theological considerations, but at the level of symbolic rhetoric the gesture of throwing away the ultimate in coercive weapons has a clear affinity with the repertoire of values which places love above power in the final hierarchy of spiritual priorities. The clearest example of this process is found in the Women's peace camp at Greenham Common which opposes the siting of Cruise missiles on European soil. The mass demonstration organised there on 12 and 13 December 1982 by Women For Life On Earth might have taken as its text the same fragment of the Gospel as Bernard Levin quoted, or equally well, the ubiquitous Sunday School wall frieze of my childhood 'Suffer the little children to come unto Me'. The demonstrators 'embraced' the whole nine-mile perimeter fence of the air base — a terminology and a ritual act redolent with imagery of love. The leaflet which advertised the demonstration stated:

> Each gate will have a theme, and on Sunday [sic] morning women will gather at the gates they find express their feelings about life on earth and the nuclear threat. Bring personal things to decorate the fence with — objects that express our lives, our joy, our anger, our fears and feelings about the threat of nuclear war: photos, banners, writing, toys, children's clothes, ribbons, balloons, cardboard tombstones bearing the names of victims of violence and war. At one o'clock we'll begin to form a circle and link around the base, singing the same songs, linked with joined hands, scarves, wool, ribbons. Then return to the gates, and as dusk falls we will light candles and hold closing ceremonies.[36]

Those present, whether as demonstrators or observers, found it a powerfully moving occasion, which is hardly surprising given the closely textured and unmistakably liturgical deployment of the 'feminine' symbolism of love.

Valerie Flessati was not alone in drawing the parallels with Mary particularly since the whole occasion vibrated with transmuted Christmas references. Christmas as the secular festival of family love and child-centred celebration was echoed in the toys, balloons and children. The lighting of the peace candles in the closing ceremonies conjured Christmas trees, carol singers and the whole Christmas card and *Christmas Carol* world through which we traditionally view our own ideal selves at this season. Peace candles have taken on a ritual significance of their own, too, in recent years. The spontaneous lighting of the peace candles was the most powerful moment during what one can only regard as the secular requiem which took place in the main square of Liverpool after John Lennon was shot, again close to Christmas in 1980. (The Christ resonances there were, incidentally, as unmistakable as in the reports of the death of Colonel H. Jones in the Falklands.)

These symbolic features carry a stronger charge than a coldly rational statement of the case against allowing American Cruise missiles on English soil, not least because the symbols seem to transcend the vocabulary of political calculation. The ritual expressions of 'love not war' make a pre-emptive strike in claiming the vocabulary of love and the dimension of the personal as their exclusive property: they make the political calculus look shabby and mean. On 9 February 1983 when the American Vice-President, George Bush, met CND demonstrators in London the peace marchers deployed very similar symbolic props to those used at Greenham Common. In an exchange with Monsignor Bruce Kent, Bush was provoked to protest at the expropriation of such themes — especially that of the vulnerability and innocence of childhood — by CND: 'I've got grandkids, I've got children! Do you think we want peace any less than you?'

The rhetorical imagery of the personal as opposed to and transcending the political dimension is one of the more potent residues of the incipient antinomianism of the doctrine of love when it is pulled out from the rest of the fabric of Christian social theology. It underlies what was taken for granted by the journalist of *The Church Times* when he wrote of the many 'non-political' Christians who had been drawn to the women's peace camp. This 'non-political' valuation of the personal as the fundamental dimension of values has long been a particular characteristic of women's attitudes to politics in this country. It may be worth noting that in Britain women are far more likely than men to oppose Cruise missiles and to support unilateralism.

The high value placed on the personal and the private, on sincerity and the feeling heart, is one point at which the Christian and the individualist traditions intersect, and, indeed, in English culture the two have frequently fused indissolubly. The Protestant tradition of individual conversion is one example of this. It is a model to which the peace movement is clearly indebted in its style of turning individual hearts to the cause of peace. It also surfaces in the Status Quo song quoted above with its refrain 'It's never too late to change'. By one of the many paradoxes in this tangle of symbol systems, the missionary effort to convert individual hearts and minds has a capacity for turning into a crusade. Once a movement takes on the quality of a crusade (or for that matter, the absolute conviction of the sect that it possesses the only truth) one frequently finds that the individual and the personal sink beneath the pressures for group cohesion. The symbols of love and innocence march behind increasingly military-looking banners. When the massed young women of Greenham dance ring-a-roses around a small group of policemen, singing John Lennon's 'Give Peace A Chance', there is a thin line between the invocation of innocent children's games and the coercive circle of playground bullying. Even passive resistance can evolve into active struggle and by February 1983 some of those same women were prepared to punch and kick the newly-appointed Defence Secretary, Michael Heseltine, in their anxiety to convey the urgency of their message: 'You gotta fight to survive.'

The milieu of symbolic resonances and mythic models is messy, slippery, ambiguous. But my case is that it is important because it provides a conventionally 'invisible' but emotionally potent dimension to issues such as the debate on nuclear arms policy. It supplies a hidden vocabulary which may be just as significant to the outcome of such debates as is the more carefully modulated vocabulary of rational argument. Indeed it may say more to the man and woman in the street and in the pew — and even in the pulpit — than he or she is aware of having heard.

It may seem tasteless, implausible and even blasphemous that I have placed the deeply serious cheek by jowl with the ephemera of popular culture, and claimed that they share a set of meanings. The juxtaposition was deliberate. Profound messages can resonate in the apparently trivial, and the popularity and persuasive power of the latter arise precisely from the echoes and reverberations which are set up in and by the former. This is why the 'invisible religion' of our society is as important as either the visible variety or reasoned argument in affecting choices and decisions of great moment. Yet because the structures of symbolism so often operate subliminally, they tend to escape our notice. They combine and regroup in shifting and complex patterns of which we have only glimpsed a few here. It may well be that particular groups and movements at specific times have a natural affinity with distinctive symbolic constellations, but we understand too little of these processes to do more than hazard a guess about what the dominant patterns may currently be. At all events, I do not believe the patterns are random; I do believe that they are available, however partially, for rational reflection if we care to look for them. And it is surely preferable to confront directly the implicit values so richly embodied in the cultural forms of our society rather than to allow them to act on us as hidden persuasions.

NOTES

1 Charles Dickens, *Barnaby Rudge* (Penguin Books: Harmondsworth, 1973), p. 383.

2 Wishbone Ash, 'Underground', copyright.

3 Rainbow, 'Can't Happen Here', copyright.

4 Status Quo, 'Never Too Late', Copyright Rossi/Frost, Dump Music/Eaton Music.

5 Thomas Luckmann, *The Invisible Religion* (Macmillan: New York, 1967).

6 Bernice Martin, 'Not Marx but Lennon', *Encounter*, vol. 56, no. 6., June 1981.

7 *Whatever You Want*, Channel 4, 3 January 1983.

8 A point made effectively by Krishan Kumar, *Prophecy And Progress* (Allen Lane: London, 1978).

9 Alan MacFarlane, *The Origins of English Individualism* (Basil Blackwell: Oxford, 1979). This argument has important implications. For example, it renders very dubious the popular Marxist view that capitalism itself created an ethic of competitive individualism.

   The American and English traditions of individualism do have many points in common but also some important differences. The English tradition is held within a culture of historical depth and continuity in which Durkheimian elements of social solidarity — from a popular constitutional monarchy to a tradition of class solidarity and of the dignity of manual labour — soften its competitive edge. American individualism, whether of the frontier or of Yankee commerce, is more extreme in its implications. Dickens was well aware of the differences as his merciless caricatures of the American variety in *Martin Chuzzlewit* can testify. The issue may be pursued in: Seymour M. Lipset, *The First New Nation: The United States in Historical and Comparative Perspective* (Heinemann: London, 1964); Richard Sennett and Jonathan Cobb, *The Hidden Injuries of Class* (Cambridge University Press: Cambridge, 1977).

   In contemporary popular culture the North American component is of course a considerable ingredient and although I have taken my main instances of anti-nuclear rock music from English bands, many of the other media from which I take examples have a transatlantic provenance. I would point out that the British and American traditions have enough in common to be instantly accessible to each other; and my concentration is on what British users make of the common tradition.

10 I am indebted for this information to Philip Wark, an MPhil student at Bedford College who is studying these all-girl bands.

11 From a report supplied, like many other leads for this article, by my sons Izaak and Magnus, to whom much thanks.

12 Bernice Martin, *A Sociology of Contemporary Cultural Change* (Basil Blackwell: Oxford 1981).

13 Bernice Martin, 'Identity in the Modern World: a sociologist on John Lennon', in *Kairos* no. 5, Easter 1982.

14   Quoted in Jonathon Green (ed.), *The Book of Rock Quotes* (Omnibus Press: London 1977), p. 69. One can find such quotations all the time in rock music press, but I have used this source — a best-selling paperback — simply because of its appeal to mainstream readership. I have concentrated on mainstream anti-nuclear rock music rather than specialist extreme sub-cultures for the same reasons: it is easy to study extreme sub-cultures because they exist in discrete pockets, but very difficult to find an accept-able and effective methodology for studying mainstream culture. Hence my essay takes the form of an artful trawl rather than 'scientific' research.

15   Green (ed.), op. cit., p. 65.

16   Paul Barker, 'Radicals in a Generation Gap: New Society Readers' Survey' *New Society*, vol. 62. no. 1045, 25 November 1982. *New Society* readers were more in favour of unilateralism than the general population. The findings of this survey are supported by the work of Jonathan Chandler, a PhD student at Bedford College who is analysing responses to John Lennon's death.

17   Jeff Nuttall, *Bomb Culture* (McGibbon & Kee, London, 1968).

18   Bernice Martin and Ronald Pluck, *Young People's Beliefs* (General Synod Board of Education: Church House Westminster, 1976).

19   Tom Kitwood, *Disclosures to a Stranger: Adolescent Values In An Advanced Industrial Society* (Routledge & Kegan Paul: London, 1980), p. 3.

20   For an effective analysis of the social significance of humour, see e.g. Christie Davies, 'Ethnic Jokes, Moral Values and Social Boundaries', in *The British Journal of Sociology*, vol. 33, no. 3, September 1981.

21   Martin and Pluck, op. cit.

22   'The Best of Jasper Carrott', BBC2, Christmas week 1982. My sons drew my attention to this joke.

23   John Sutherland, *Bestsellers: Popular Fiction of the 1970s* (Routledge & Kegan Paul: London, 1981).

24   The debate of the General Synod of the Church of England on the report of the working party of the Board of Social Responsibility, *The Church and the Bomb: Nuclear Warfare and the Christian Conscience*, (Hodder & Stoughton: London, 1982). The debate was broadcast live on both television and radio.

25   Sutherland, op. cit.

26   Cartoonists who have caricatured Mrs Thatcher as Superman may be nearer the mark than they suppose. I suspect that one wholly positive aspect of her image (and one which intellectuals tend to see negatively) is her refusal to regard *any* problem, whatever its provenance, as *not* amenable to decisive, individual action.

27   Gerald Kaufman, Labour MP for Manchester Ardwick, pointed this out in *The Times*, February 1983.

28   In Anglo-American culture much of this male bonding takes the form of what, adapting Troeltsch, one might call 'a parallelism of individualism'. It is quite distinct from, say, Mediterranean or oriental styles of all-male cohesion.

29   An abortive attempt to assist a potential research student to delineate 'Jewish identity' which she regarded as threatened with assimilation to the implicit Christianity of English culture, did much to focus this point for me.

30 George Steiner, *The Portage to San Cristobal of A. H.* (Faber & Faber: London and Boston, 1981).

31 Steiner, op. cit., pp. 122—4.

32 Movements of Jewish Messianism did in fact occur, with the usual disastrous outcomes, alongside the other millenarian movements of the middle ages in periods of disruptive social change. My point — over-condensed in the text — is that: Christianity's having expropriated the Messianic principle led mainstream Judaism to de-emphasise the theme as a mark of its own distinctiveness against the dominant Christian culture; and the social system of the Jewish ghetto communities was, *faute de mieux*, relatively undifferentiated. Under pressure Jewish identity and culture were held together by the Durkheimian virtues of everyday ritual and the sanctity of tradition.

33 I am indebted to Basil Bernstein for pointing this out.

34 Tolkein himself protested against the idea that *The Lord of the Rings* (Allen & Unwin: London, 1969, 1 vol.) was a directly Christian allegory, perhaps in order to insist on the difference between his work and that of his friend and rival C. S. Lewis, whose Narnia cycle was designed to be a Christian allegory for children. Readers can often detect implicit structures better than authors, however.

35 Bernard Levin, 'A Night of Magic With the Little Invader' *The Times*, 22 January 1983.

36 Printed by Spider Web (TU) Sussex Way, London N.7.

IV ART, LOGIC AND PROPHECY

Why the Bomb is Real
but not True

PETER REDGROVE

Somehow it would be a relief if Einstein turned out to be wrong, since his physics seems to have created a world in which the atomic bomb not only exists, but in which his ideas and authority appear to make it easier to use that bomb.

What I mean by this I can only sketch, and it would be better for a professional physicist to describe these ideas. I hope the reader will forgive any gross errors I make here. But as I understand the matter, there seems to be not only a connection but also a feedback between a certain monstrous cosmic detachment there is in Relativity, which is held to describe the ground of our universe, and modern behaviour. Relativity has not only given us the bomb, but its mechanistic aspects are no improvement on other cold-blooded systems of thought which bring despair into the world. Without Einstein's work, the bomb would not have seemed possible, and so would not have been looked for; and he himself got caught up in the terrible accident of the weapon's creation, and recommended its first use to Truman.

Should one blame Einstein? It is such a curiously-named theory: 'Relativity'. As Bertrand Russell remarked of it, the theory is 'wholly concerned *to exclude what is relative* and arrive at a statement of physical laws that shall in no way depend on the circumstances of the observer' (my italics). Einstein was not able to obtain a unified field theory which *related* human beings to the universe or each other. In David Bohm's words, the theory 'still retains the essential features of a mechanistic order, for the fundamental entities…are assumed to be connected with each other only through external relationships…relativity theory requires strict causality (or determinism)…'[1] So it appears that Einstein's basic work should be called 'Irrelativity', and like other mechanistic theories it is a recipe for alienation.

To the honest scientist, professing truth at all costs, this shouldn't matter, if the theory can predict experimental results which verify it. But does it? Because the physical universe seems to correspond to certain of its predictions, including the prediction that the atom can be split to release enormous power, that in itself means no more than that the theory uses a *selection of the data*. Our atomic age has seen that this selection has only negative significance to the human situation, the human data. Einstein wrote: 'Perception of this world by thought, leaving out everything subjective, became partly consciously, partly unconsciously, my supreme aim.' Another direction of mind might very well not have brought such encouragement to the generals.

Other selections of scientific data are verifiable too, and may be full of the energy of subjective, human meaning, as well as the energy of the objective universe, rather than the detachment and vacuousness of the thought-experiments of relativistic travels through the cosmic vacuum at the speed of light.

For instance, there is the fact that the sun, a star (which it is customary to describe as working like an enormous H-bomb), gives out its light by passing hydrogen nuclei along a chain of processes. It is also true that the reactions called 'photosynthesis' in the green leaves of plants are precisely comparable to this chain reaction, but on a slower timescale. Photosynthesis in the plants, then, receives this light on the cooled sun-matter we call the earth,and turns it into human life via the whole food-chain.[2] This image from science is one worth dwelling on, and its consideration might bring better consequences than those of 'Irrelativity'. It is as though the sunlight creates the receptacle that catches and seeks to understand it. Or, to take a more homely image, it is like a baby smiling at the nipple full of milk that has created the tender folds of flesh it smiles with. And Mother smiles back.

Accepting and contemplating this image, subjectively and objectively, seeing and wondering, can lead us to know that we are part of the continuum that begins with starlight; and issues now in our attempt to feel the meaning of that starlight, here, on this page woven of star-substance. We have no reason, except Irrelativity, which is sometimes called schizoid thinking, for standing outside this complex implicated inter-relationship of everything we know.

I'm implying that the theories or mental images of human geniuses may, to our sorrow, cause working scientists who follow them to over-select data, and thus to create inventions that correspond to and perpetuate that theory or image or alienation. Because Einstein, 'partly consciously, partly un-consciously', showed that the bomb was possible, and because Einstein did not wish (according to the quotation I have given above) to turn his mathematics so far as for them to be relative to human existence, lo and behold, we have a bomb and a near-intolerable state of world. Perhaps, as Anthony Storr has suggested, Relativity was a reflection of a particular kind of failure in Einstein's personal psychology. If so, then it is a mental disorder that has spread like a virus.

Perhaps it follows that if we have a beneficent image in physics, which inspires our scientists to make discoveries of another kind, then we shall have a different world. If we have a human image, and not a mechanistic one, then we stand a better chance of living in an integrated human world; if we have a magical image (such as the amateur one I have offered about the starlight, which is pure Kabalah) then perhaps we shall have a magical world. Images, paradigms, are like tuning devices. With the right 'subjective' image to guide us, we can tune our circuits to resonate with a new, but still objectively – verifiable universe.

I have been very much impressed, particularly as a poet, from the first time I heard about it some ten years ago, with the physics built on quantum theory of David Bohm who worked with Einstein. Broadly speaking, he does indicate just such a beneficent image in physics. He proposes, and it fits the facts better than Relativity alone does, a universe of infinite *implicated* relationships, which could be called a holo-movement, and that the world we experience is like a writing, signature, or holograph of this holo-movement. A holograph is a picture which, if you take only one small piece of it, from that piece you can nevertheless still project the entire picture. This means that the image of the whole is present in every part of the holograph.

> That is to say, the form and structure of the entire object may be said to be *enfolded* within each region of the photographic record. When one shines light on any region, this form and structure are then unfolded, to give a recognisable image of the whole object once again. We proposed that a new notion of order is involved [in this image] which we called the *implicate order*....In terms of the implicate order one may say that everything is enfolded into everything. This contrasts with the *explicate order* now dominant in physics in which things are *unfolded* in the sense that each thing lies only in its own particular region...and outside the regions belonging to other things...our basic proposal was then that *what is* is the holomovement.[3]

In our ordinary world, manifested under the control of dominant images, we do not usually see how each entity is implicated with every other entity. The Buddhist Sutra which describes this would be taken by most scientists as a 'subjective fantasy': 'In the heaven of Indra there is said to be a network of jewels so arranged that if you look in one you see all the others reflected in it.' But with this fresh image proposed in quantum physics, scientists are looking for experimental verification, and finding it. For example, Alain Aspect at the Institut d'Optique Théorique et Appliquée seems to have demonstrated what is called technically instantaneous 'action-at-a-distance'. This appears to mean that if distant particles somehow 'know' or instantaneously resonate to what is happening to each other, then some signals can travel faster than the speed of light, which Relativity says cannot be so. So in the important case of 'action-at-a-distance', which Einstein found 'ghostly and absurd', too subjective and mystical, he appears to have been wrong.

The work has gone further than this. We have been speaking so far about the apparently outward world of theoretical physics, which for years has been taking on a more and more 'mental' aspect, open to the layman such as myself in such books as Fritjof Capra's *Tao of Physics* (Wildwood House, 1975), or the older and much more powerful *Symphony of Life* by Donald Hatch Andrews (Unity Books, 1966). In a recent book, *The Holographic Paradigm* (ed. Ken Wilber; Shambhala, 1982) Bohm in interviews speaks most powerfully about these matters, and amusingly about the jumps of dislocated thought scientists make to avoid integrations beyond the fractured physics they have inherited.

However, as I've suggested, Bohm's image of the universe as an implicated order of interacting fields and vibrations gives us permission to seek out new matters, which implicate in their holo-movement the whole human being. In atomised physics and nuclear strategy, the human being is merely a megakill number. Human beings and their subjectivity are not relevant to military science or to ordinary physical science: in this the scientists bear equal responsibility with the generals. In science, as in war, subjectivity is closed off. But what if this subjectivity, the inner world, is also seen as part of the implicate order, and as arising from it?

Here the neurosurgeon Karl Pribram has found a great deal

of evidence that the human brain works as a holograph too, resonating to the universe as a tuned circuit resonates to radio waves. This must mean that subjective experience (as opposed to observations or measurements obtained from external instruments) is a mode of knowledge too, or can be. In Bohm's words again: 'In the implicate order we have to say that mind enfolds matter in general and therefore the body in particular. Similarly the body enfolds not only the mind but also in some sense the entire material universe '[4], and 'In the old physics, matter (which was the only reality) was completely mechanical, leaving no room for mind. But if, according to the new physics, everything is enfolded in everything else, then there is no real separation of domains.'[5] Or, as William Blake had it: 'If the doors of perception were cleansed, then everything would appear as it is, infinite.', and 'Every man and every woman is a Star.'

Unfortunately, even though the bomb arises from a partial truth and a crudely mechanised physics, no concept, however magical or complete, will automatically switch off that mechanism once it starts ticking. But if we are lucky, and work aright, the deep and shared subjectivity of right feeling can make that bomb's use inconceivable, in a world of verified wonders. We are all working scientists, who follow, with our life-experiments, the images that the geniuses of our culture give us to work with: '*Weber*: Life is then a continuum; everything is alive? *Bohm*: Everything is alive.'[6]

NOTES

1 David Bohm, *Wholeness and the Implicate Order* (Routledge & Kegan Paul, 1980) pp. 174, 176.
2 George Wald, 'Stars and Living Organisms: a Metabolic Connexion', Penguin Science Survey 1968.
3 Bohm, *Wholeness*, pp. 177–8.
4 ibid., p. 209.
5 *The Holographic Paradigm* p. 194.
6 ibid., p. 195.

Our Shy Masters

ROBERT SIMPSON

Hope of escaping a nuclear holocaust could seem to hang on the inconvenience of such a catastrophe to the multi-national corporations which, as they grow bigger and fewer, seek to dominate and eventually control the world economy. They are still too diverse to have formed a coherent strategy, but their achievements are already alarmingly impressive, certainly more potent than most people understand. It is plainly in their interests to unify; this process is probably inevitable, and will entail the ruthless sacrifice of humanitarian considerations as well as the ambitions of many individuals within the corporations. Compunction will not be one of the salient virtues engendered in the process. The multinationals are even now deeply influential in the East as well as the West (a matter meticulously examined by Charles Levinson in his courageous book *Vodka-Cola* (1980); they work systematically to gain economic power in repressive regimes of both Right and Left, where they are assured of cheap, strike-free labour, enabling them to create convenient large-scale unemployment (in order to keep down wages) in the more advanced industrial countries. To this end they are much assisted by interested governments, including our own. Total destruction of these happy hunting grounds would clearly not be to their advantage; they will not be disposed to bring this about, though as will be seen they are not afraid to take risks in the pursuit of power. Moreover, by concealed infiltration of the political arena they are rendering national politics parochial, pliant and obsolescent, even in the largest and strongest states. This is a further method of safeguarding the gradually maturing strategy.

As the multinationals fuse together and concentrate themselves, increasingly able to circumvent contradictory national laws and regulations, they must be expected to form a faceless, clandestine world government, dedicated to its own power and profit. There are no strongly constituted, international monopoly commissions capable of preventing this. Many communication media, significant banking systems (including the International Monetary Fund), and most very large industries producing fuel, food, drugs, arms, machinery and advanced technology of all kinds, with research and development facilities, are already a part of this rapidly expanding organism. Giant entities tend to breed ingrowing inefficiency and possibly this one might at length break down, but not during the present dynamic formative stage or before it has become economically invincible.

This growing force obviously needs to avoid a nuclear world war, and although it is not yet fully able to dictate the course of events, it has a better chance of doing so than any other grouping. This does not mean that it is pacific. Its interests are effectively served by a constant and widespread succession of wars, large and small, in which some 30 million persons have been killed since the Second World War, conflagrations stoked by the arms trade, for which they are valuable proving grounds. The $17,000 million spent on arms every two weeks would provide decent housing, food, education and health services for the world population in the same period (quoted by COPAT, Committee on Poverty and the Arms Trade). Most of the large-scale commerce in arms involves massively the corporations. By their activities and those of the US, USSR, French and British governments (the largest national participants) the Third World has been steadily made poorer and its regimes more oppressive, usually rich militaristic elites sustained by organisations into whose debt they have been manoeuvred. Their need to suppress protest means the purchase of more and better weapons, incurring greater debt, with increased subservience to the bodies that either initiated the process or simply exploited an existing situation.

So it is not advantageous to the corporations to expunge war; they benefit immensely from maintaining world tension. Their own extinction, however, is another matter; that would be involved with everyone else's in a nuclear conflict. But nuclear productivity is very much their business, and since (being still too many and too competitive) they are not yet able to control all the consequences of their activities, we cannot be completely hopeful that they will succeed in preventing disaster, precipitated by accident or by panic. Yet the spectacular arms race is at this stage necessary to them, and in fostering it they cannot be guiltless of inspiring the politicians, though they cannot stop some of these from uttering inanities that could never be ascribed to the cold rationalities of the calculating organisation man. But while political fanaticism might *seem* to father the chilling suggestion that a nuclear war could be both winnable and survivable, this may well be traced to covert industrial salesmanship aimed at governments all too willing to buy new types of 'strategic' devices. On the other hand, the terrifying *Report of the British Medical Association Board of Science and Education Inquiry into the Medical Effects of Nuclear War* (April 1983) makes it perfectly clear that the British government's proposals for 'civil defence' are cynically preposterous. Where more sophisticated theories are concerned, many politicians still have to prove their disinterestedness; in some cases proof of honesty would be a certificate of madness. The BMA's report, estimating a possible 38.6 million deaths and 4.3 million casualties in a nuclear attack on Britain, seems to display a gaunt sense of humour in stating that it does not involve politics and could be used equally to justify massive armament or unilateralism. This disclaimer might have been better omitted, leaving the facts to speak for themselves.

The multinationals have grown from the capitalist system, but the physical destruction of the so-called communist bloc is not their object. They want rather to dominate it economically. In the not very long run the Soviet Union and its satellites will be unable to withstand this insidious pressure, and there is clear evidence that it is already coercive. Nuclear war is not needed for this purpose. Patience, unremitting assiduity and sustained, highly profitable terror — these will serve admirably, and the last is efficaciously assisted by aggressive political bluster on both sides of the Iron Curtain. A number of these mouthpieces have readily identifiable multinational connections (see *Vodka-Cola*, cited above). Also helpful in this long-term cause are the predictably fruitless 'disarmament' or 'arms limitation' discussions at Geneva and elsewhere. The crazy spiral of expenditure, against a background of well-staged charades, is reaping untold profits for our shy masters, so skilled in exploiting the suspicion between rival blocs, while governments on all sides are increasingly in thrall to these unostentatious potentates.

In such a situation NATO and the Warsaw Pact are complementary. Without both, the strategy would be in some trouble — there can be no race without rivals. Capitalist the corporations may be, but they can scarcely be inclined to undermine militarily the Warsaw Pact while NATO exists. Technological 'secrets' pass to and fro — who knows by what mechanisms? These can always be shown to be various sorts of smuggling, and any accomplice whose cover is blown can always be dispensed into a handy jail by due process of law — or discreetly murdered. Khrushchev may not altogether have been joking when he asked why everyone didn't employ the same spies, since we all knew the best ones. Ownership or control of much of the world's press and broadcasting makes it possible to represent whatever is desired; in dictatorships there is no problem, while in so-called democracies dissenting views may be allowed ephemeral outlet, virtually ineffectual against insistently and often subtly nurtured prejudice.

So what of the nuclear danger? It is now being proposed (at least in the US) that sole responsibility for peace should be put in the 'hands' of a sophisticated computer, programmed to fire on warning. This final attempt at intimidation has been rightly described as 'the ultimate madness'. Effectively forbidden objectives do not loom large in the history of nuclear armaments and if such a computer were to be employed it would constitute the extremity of risk. Because a technical hitch could mean catastrophe, the device would instantly abolish all human rights on earth, even if it never actually functioned. Such an apparatus would certainly have to be ordered from one or more of the multinationals. Human rights do not interest them. But they do need a human population and could decide against the risk for amoral reasons. Rivalry between them, however, could ensure that if one group feigned altruism, another would be more 'realistic'.

Those who propose that the deterrent should be retained because it purports to have prevented a major war for thirty-five years ought to be consistent enough to express satisfaction that both sides possess this great prophylactic. They should also realise that the opposing deterrents do not constitute some kind of reassuring *status quo*. There is an arms race going on. And who is being deterred? All the information we receive in Britain about Soviet weapons and Soviet intentions comes from the US, either directly or through government channels. The man in the street cannot find out how much of this is truth, and its sheer volume is enough to soften his brain. Have no doubt about the repressiveness of the so-called communist regimes; it perfectly suits the aims of the multinational corporations which increasingly are propping them up. The economic weakness of these 'peoples' democracies' makes suspect the constant western harping on their military potential, which depends on vast loans from western banking systems owned or manipulated by the multinationals. While the political West tries to scare its poorer rival bloc into ever deeper expenditure and economic straits, the corporations pull it out of these into ever deeper debt.

This phenomenon adds significance to the fact that so far almost all talk of pre-emptive strikes or strategical nuclear devices has originated in the US. Sometimes rogue information slips embarrassingly out of America. A senior US weapons expert, Kosta Tsipis of the Massachusetts Institute of Technology, has recently revealed that US monitoring of Soviet missile tests has shown them to be 'not nearly accurate or reliable enough to destroy American missile silos in a first strike.' Tsipis estimates that Soviet missile accuracy is unlikely to improve dramatically in the foreseeable future. Unless one cynically interprets this as a green light for an American first strike, and even if one does not, it seriously compromises the persistent exaggerations of President Reagan and the Pentagon. And we should not forget that the Cruise missile is itself a first strike weapon.

The British government's film against the peace movement, *A Better Road to Peace*, insists that the nuclear deterrent has kept the peace and that 'we just have to see that we keep it that way.' The Quaker Peace Secretary, Ron Huzzard, rightly points out that 'this astonishing assertion implies an indefinite continuation of the nuclear arms race.' The 'keep it that way' mentality is creeping towards the sly totalitarianism exemplified recently by a small secret committee, permitting no public discussion, which contrived to turn Greenham Common into private land so as to be able legally to evict the Women's peace camp. This type of person is always the first to denounce the denial of human rights in the USSR (though they rarely mention Chile or South Africa).

If a nuclear war occurs between the super-powers it will be more likely by accident than by design. But the mere accumulation of such destructive power incalculably compounds the chances of an irreversible accident. It also advances the nightmare certainty of proliferation, which can hardly be forbidden or even discouraged by those clinging to their own arsenals. Advocates of the independent deterrent ignore both these perils. One cannot deter a mishap, nor can it be prevented for certain by any human or technical means. The longer this stockpile exists and waxes, the nearer looms inevitable global accident. The multinational corporations offer no plausible assurance of whatever sinister safety they have in mind for us. The sophistries that would risk the torment and annihilation of humanity cannot be defended and must be attributed to criminal intrepidity, cynical disregard or hapless gullibility.

In permitting political influences to affect its vote on the subject, the Synod of the Church of England betrayed not only its avowed faith but also the people who depend on it for moral guidance. That Jesus would have voted against the nuclear deterrent must be obvious to Christian and non-believer alike. In a letter to *The Guardian* (14 February 1983) Donald Matheson said crisply 'The Synod has voted. When do the Christians vote?' The Archbishop of Canterbury averred that the absence of a nuclear deterrent would make a terrible conventional war more probable. But it cannot logically be asserted that a war between the great powers would remain 'conventional', and if this argument is carried to its conclusion, the only sane policy is to get rid of all weapons; as a leader of Christians the Archbishop of Canterbury should have insisted on this as the only moral policy — indeed the only hope, now all guarantee has gone that the pursuit of violence will not end in our demise. The splendid and inimitable James Cameron might perhaps observe that this demise would not dismay the Christian sure of the delights of heaven, though he would no doubt wonder what could be done about the sudden overcrowding of that glorious place, and the even worse problems facing the administration in the other.

Here is the crux. For the first time in history it is possible for the human species to wipe itself out, almost at a stroke. It is not necessary to refute the thoughtless objection that there have always been bigger and better weapons, from the stone axe to the bomber, that nuclear bombs are simply worse bombs. Nor should it be necessary to point out that those insisting that it is better to be dead than red are somewhat presumptuously inviting everyone else, whatever their persuasions, to join them in oblivion. They really must include everyone else — it is no longer possible to defend what has to be destroyed in the process. If we do not wish to be a wrong turning in evolution we must determine that these Damocletian devices be dismantled before they dispose of us, by accident, by human panic or by mere technical inefficiency. This insistence will have to come from every quarter of the world if it is to have the least effect on the small number of powerful and obdurate people who have imposed the threat. Nothing would be more likely to start such a reaction than the courageous decision of one country to give up not only the most obscene option, but *all* armaments. If no other state followed this example the moral necessity would have been honoured. Whether or not there were any positive official responses, the consequent pressure from the common people of the world might well become irresistible, a possibility not less credible than the disaster that will surely follow its denial. The fact that there is now a quite large body of opinion in favour of this action is the one gleam of visible hope.

No one should believe the dissembling protestations of the present British government that it realistically serves the peace by hanging on to its own nuclear armoury and by harbouring a foreign power's offensive missiles, so rendering the UK a prime target in any conflict. Such talk serves only the arms race and those who profit by it; the arguments are fabricated and their recent intensifications reflect no more than a sneaking fear that the peace movement might become too influential in trying to save what remains of honest sanity. How much sanity does remain after the stultifying onslaughts of the media — East and West — the repressive terror in totalitarian states across the world, the unthinkable poverty, starvation, and crippling diseases in the multinationals' vast guinea pig, the Third World — all terminally menaced (not deterred!) by a giant, mindless precarious mechanism?

This is the moment in human evolution when it has become finally obligatory to give up violence as a means of settling differences. It has previously been possible to survive this flaw, at least physically; morally we have been diminished by every manifestation of it. It would be naive indeed to expect this chaotic and misdirected world to arrive at a practical solution of this or any other kind. But to relinquish violence is not only our last hope of climbing successfully out of the jungle — it is the one slim chance we have of survival. Its unlikelihood does not bar it from being the only realism; the Domesday clock ticks on remorselessly. If you are drowning there is no time for sophistical pragmatism. Can the world learn to swim so quickly? There is no lifeline in the prevarications of Church dignitaries, the sophistries of politicians, the ingenuities of diplomats, the viciousness of terrorism or the machinations in multinational boardrooms. The voice of sanity is heard but faintly through the roar of the big battalions. Are we, after all, Mother Nature's most disastrous mistake? Did Beethoven, Rembrandt and Shakespeare live for nothing? Were they no more than a fleeting glimmer of what might have been? And what about Mother Teresa and the uncountable kindnesses in the world from age to age? If all these wonders vanish, can there be any tiresome recriminations? Yes — there may still be a few of us left to gasp them out, but not for very long.

False Poles

ELIZABETH YOUNG

Why is it that public discussion of disarmament and arms control has the appearance in Britain of being violently polarised? Except at their extremes, unilateralists and multi-lateralists do not seem to differ fundamentally over their final aim: the prevention of war, including nuclear war, and the reduction of nuclear weapons; the preservation of our liberties; and these at the lowest convenient level of expenditure. The reason for polarisation does not lie there.

On the question of how to achieve this aim, there is no longer agreement, but rather an enormously wide spectrum of opinion, reflecting the complexity of the issues themselves and of the many contexts in which they have to be thought about and dealt with. The spectrum straddles Left, Right, Centre-left, Centre-right, Centre-centre; pacifists, nuclear disarmers, general and comprehensive disarmers, arms controllers, carry-on arms racers; negotiators from weakness, negotiators from parity, negotiators from strength; proponents and opponents of linkage — economic linkage, political linkage, human rights linkage....People advocating more or less the same policy often advance different diagnoses of where we are now, how we got here, where we seem to be going, who is to blame.

Yet there is an assumption, warmly embraced by the Conservative party and by some leaders of the Campaign for

Nuclear Disarmament (and reflected enthusiastically by the media) that this is, or should be, or can be, a simple either/or debate, goodies versus baddies, absolutes of this stripe here locked with those of that stripe there, in a battle which one lot might actually win. The reality is different.

Most people who would accept being called unilateralists will agree that only multilateral disarmament will make the world safe from nuclear war and, given that nuclear war almost certainly could not be limited to the mainland of Europe, will make Britain safe from nuclear war. They are in short 'first step' unilateralists, who believe that the British government can, and therefore should, push the first stone to get the multilateral avalanche moving. Meanwhile, they believe, we would probably be safer without nuclear weapons in Britain because they may provide a temptation to the Russians to use theirs, (in spite of the unwinnable nature of nuclear war, which the Russians recognise as well as anyone else). Also, any reduction anywhere is valuable.

The women in the Greenham Common and other peace camps are there 'on the side of life', to prevent the 'genocide' which they believe men, and the nuclear weapons they have so blithely invented, are bound to unleash. Yet few of them are likely to claim that stopping Cruise missiles would be enough: once again, it would be a beginning, and we would be safer.

Some specifically Christian unilateralists will say that we have a duty to trust in God for our protection. Arguing the absolutist 'ethical' point more closely, a few, a very few probably, will argue that even if Britain giving up nuclear weapons made nuclear war more likely and nuclear blackmail certain, yet these weapons are pitch, not to be touched: the very possession of them cannot but imply an already formed decision, indeed intention, to use them, which is not compatible with Christ. 'Safety' is not relevant: if it can only be bought with such evil means, it must not be bought at all, regardless of all other consequences. This way lies, one may suppose, an advocacy of state pacifism and, if necessary, state martyrdom.

On the other hand many unilateralists, in the Labour Party for instance, believe that Britain should stay in NATO but, despite their general distaste for President Reagan, leave nuclear weapons within the alliance exclusively in the hands of the United States, (and presumably in France's). Conventional weapons might or might not have to be increased, and defence budgets with them. Others believe that a build-up of conventional weapons by Britain could allow a withdrawal, partial or complete, from NATO: Britain to become like Norway or Sweden. Yet others think a position like Finland's, though never quite Poland's, would suit.

In each of these positions the defence needs which the proponents envisage mirror his or her judgement and picture of the Soviet Union's intentions and nature: national security is recognised as a proper aim, indeed as a responsibility, of any government.

The European Nuclear Disarmament Movement (END) have found that the suppression of human rights as in Eastern Europe, particularly the right to monitor the operation of the Helsinki agreements and the right to discuss disarmament matters with western disarmament groups, is an element in the militarisation of those societies; their conclusion is that the protection of these particular rights cannot but be part-and-parcel of disarmament itself.

To judge from public opinion polls, it seems likely that most people — that is, those grouped round the political centre — are well aware of the horrors and unwinnableness of nuclear war; but that they accept that nuclear deterrence works and that Britain's own nuclear forces and NATO's for the time being make the country less, rather than more vulnerable; and that any substantial disarmament by Britain must be proportionately matched by Soviet disarmament.

Evidently these people have to be called 'multilateralists', and it seems safe to suppose that they are making a pragmatic judgement about national security — how best to prevent nuclear war, and so on. But so, in point of fact, are most unilateralists, with the exception only of the Christian absolutists. (The Bishop of Salisbury appears to be one himself; but not all members of his working party.) If this is right, then it is most unlikely that this central group would oppose proposals, even if they involved 'unilateral' action by a British government, as long as they thought they would serve national security: there was certainly no general outcry when a British government unilaterally got rid of our chemical weapons, or abolished conscription.

And it is from the centre in Britain that calls are now coming for a reduction in NATO's early dependence on nuclear weapons by the withdrawal of forward-based nuclear weapon launchers. Such 'unilateral' action would improve deterrence by making a military response to attack more credible: any actual use of nuclear weapons has been becoming increasingly less believable, and by posing a less credible risk, they have become increasingly less effective, one must suppose, in deterring attack. NATO's Commander-in-Chief, General Rodgers, has himself been advocating an increase in conventional weapons on the central front, to allow a reduction in nuclear weapons.

It begins to look as if it is not because the unilateral nuclear disarmament of Britain would be unilateral that most people reject it as a policy. It is rather because it does not seem likely to secure those things its promoters claim: that is, improved national security for Britain (which would become open to nuclear blackmail); or movement towards multilateral disarmament (which depends on agreement between the super-powers); or restrain proliferation (none of which has been prompted by British nuclear weapons).

This political centre, straddling Left and Right (and again according to the polls), does not appear to approve the Conservative government's decision to buy Trident missiles from the United States. These would be more powerful, have more warheads and a longer range than the existing Polaris system, and the decision to buy them suggests a government belief in the desirability of Britain going beyond the minimum deterrent posture which previous governments have thought sufficient. Although the 'bargaining chip' argument is by no means as threadbare as some of its opponents suggest (in 1969, for instance, the Soviet Union waited to agree to discuss strategic arms limitations with the United States until after the United States Senate decided, by one vote, in favour of a United States ABM system; an agreement closely to restrict ABM was then reached), it is hard to see how the British Trident programme – too powerful to be ignored by the Russians, yet consisting of too few submarine 'units' to be conveniently reduced – could fit into a long-term disarmament process. Yet it seems more likely that the Thatcher government did not really consider Trident in this aspect (even though the pro-gramme would stretch into the twenty-first century) than that it had confidence in long-term arms racing. Certainly it was not unaware of economic limits to defence expenditure, as the Navy, and the maritime community it serves, have found out.

Going on going on seems to be the Conservative doctrine: as the Secretary of State for Defence Mr Heseltine put it, 'the only way to preserve freedom is to keep up our defences within the North Atlantic Alliance and to work patiently to secure real, mutual and balanced arms reductions.' Few of his fellow citizens will be content if 'patience' is the only virtue the government shows: it needs also to show imagina-tion, determination to identify and seize opportunities, and a proper sense of urgency. This no British government has done for twenty-odd years. Nor, until recently, has there been much demand that they should.

What then is it that the polarising words 'multilateral' and 'unilateral' actually distinguish?'[1] Not, evidently what their usual meanings would suggest. One alternative scale along which opinion could be measured is the sense of national sovereignty: in France, which has only its own nuclear weapons on its soil, the peace movement is weak. In Greece, not a nuclear power, Greek control within American bases is under hot discussion.

In Britain, where the good sense and general reliability of the Reagan administration is not rated very highly, most people undoubtedly want a British finger on the safety-catch of any American missile that may be based here: without it there appears to be a substantial majority against. The national sovereignty argument, which would seem to be a natural for the Conservative Party, is being played down by Mrs Thatcher and Mr Heseltine; and Trident itself is to come from the United States. It is the Social Democrat Party in the centre, which is now articulating the sovereignty view rather than either the Conservative or the Labour Parties: again, no polarisation. Which leaves us with the 'urgency' scale. And indeed it seems to answer best: Mr Heseltine's rather languid 'patience' at one end, the Greenham Common women's absolute here-and-now-ism at the other.

What then of the aetiology of the urgency pole? The patience end appeared to be inherent in Mrs Thatcher's government. At the other end several elements combine, not all equally valid; they can best be understood by looking back over events that started in 1976, when Mr Carter was elected President of the United States, on a strong disarmament platform.

One of his first actions was to send his Secretary of State, Cyrus Vance, to Moscow to propose to the Soviet government that instead of just carrying on with the SALT II negotiations, which were not about the reduction of strategic weapons, the two super-powers should negotiate 'deep cuts' in their weapons — 'even to 50 per cent'. The Soviet government was just beginning to recognise in the prevailing discomfiture of the United States (its ignominious withdrawal from Vietnam, the Watergate *débacle*, its growing inferiority in strategic weapons relative to the Soviet Union) just that change in 'the correlation of forces' that Lenin had forecast could provide victory without war: deep cuts it did not want, and rejected out of hand as no less than insulting.

The Carter administration had not at all prepared them for this, at the time, amazing, *démarche* and neither allies nor public were alerted, let alone galvanised, to back it.

Disarmament was politically and for the media, a dead issue, and the Carter 'deep cuts' sank almost without trace.

The Soviet government continued for a couple of months to denounce the Carter 'insult' and then, seizing an unforeseen opportunity, latched on to American plans to produce what came to be called 'the neutron bomb', which proved a highly effective stick with which to beat President Carter. 'The capitalist weapon that kills people and leaves buildings standing' was a bolt that smashed general complacency and triggered all the fiery images the Christian and post-Christian mind holds of hell. What had indeed begun as a Soviet propaganda campaign turned into something quite different: first President Carter, rebuffed, switched American policy from the disarmament he had hoped and campaigned for to a renewed military build-up (which President Reagan has continued), putting paid to Soviet illusions about any permanent change in 'the correlation of forces'; and, second, a new constituency emerged, horrified at the prospect of 'Hell on Earth', distrustful of those who had tolerated the possibility for so long, and particularly impatient of any call for patience. Propagandists of East and West have egged them on by claiming the other side is only waiting for a few more weapons before initiating nuclear war and exterminating us all, and life on earth with us.

Not surprisingly, they saw nuclear disarmament as an immediate single issue, and the nuclear weapons nearest to them as the first to roll away and disown. The 1979 NATO double-track decision, yoking the deployment in Western Europe of Cruise and Pershing missiles under sole American control to a negotiating failure that either side could only too easily secure, could and did exacerbate feelings too bitter to be assuaged by historical or geo-political analysis.

Time passing, without Armageddon encompassing us, is beginning to show those, whose first reaction was that this is the single issue above all others, that, single though it may be in importance, it has essential intercommunications with and ramifications for other issues. As END has found that the right of East Europeans to engage in 'peace talks' is of the essence of demilitarisation, so others have found that 'confidence-building measures' and the need for 'verification' are central to the substance of disarmament and arms control, and indeed to that minimum of mutual trust on which negotiation depends. Yet these are all matters fundamental to the political, as well as to the military, structures of the Soviet Union, and linkage immediately reintroduces itself.

The realisation is slowly emerging among some of those only recently alerted to the nature and scale of the threat of nuclear war, that the safety of us all does not depend only on the actions of a British government: that disarmament by Britain alone would change little if anything for the better, simply because 'nuclear-free' does not, in a world of nuclear weapons, mean 'nuclear safe'. Those whose sense of urgency is most single-minded, who have an urge to do something, to do almost anything rather than nothing, have so far harnessed their energies mainly to short term objectives. For various reasons, one of which is the coincidence of some of those objectives with Soviet objectives, they have achieved little as far as influencing the British government is concerned; and the result is frustration, both for them, and also for the government whose anachronistic watchword is 'patience'.

This is where the polarisation comes from: the polarisation of mutual, and fundamentally irrelevant, frustration. The general and comprehensive disarmament the world needs remains to be worked and campaigned for.

NOTES

1   Like other words in this debate these two have become encrusted and anachronistic: 'the bomb', as in 'ban the bomb', survives from the 1950s when just that was not impossible. 'Peace', as in the 'World Peace Council', or 'the peace policy of the Soviet Union', means the victory of communism without war (and what leads to it is 'the build-up of the military and economic might of the Soviet Union'.) 'Moral', as used by members of the Reagan administration,

means what the President thinks well of as in 'moral majority' and the zero–zero option. 'Deterrence', in some circles, means 'the decision to use nuclear weapons has already been taken and therefore amounts to genocide.' Myths too abound: 'Arms races always end in war.' Blame is misplaced: United States administrations are castigated for not getting the facts about Soviet weapons and policies right, when it is the Soviet Union's paranoid secrecy which is responsible. 'We have been lied to, we haven't been told' usually is a cover-up for 'We couldn't be bothered until the subject hit the headlines.'

Armageddon Now?
Images of the end in prophecy and contemporary arts

PETER MULLEN

It is almost thirty years since, as a boy, I went to hear a radio relay of Billy Graham's Edinburgh crusade. The sermon was based on Nebuchadnezzar's vision of the writing on the wall: 'Thou art weighed in the balances and found wanting' (Daniel 5:27). We were told that the writing was on the wall for us as well. As sinners we stood under God's judgement. And did not the H-bomb tests so recently carried out in the South Pacific warn us that the apocalyptic vials would not be long delayed? We were living in the last days; soon Armageddon would erupt. After that, Christ would appear on the clouds of heaven and those who were saved would be caught up to meet him in the air, while the damned would be consigned to the lake of fire.

Such use of the Bible's apocalyptic literature seemed entirely justified to a thirteen-year-old boy haunted by the vague and nameless guilts of adolescence; of course, God who had made the world would one day end it, and then gross sinners like myself would be despatched to the perdition prepared for us from the beginning. All the authority of Scripture and the Church was behind this interpretation, and any attempt to rationalise the Book of Revelation by

consigning it to the categories of myth or symbol was to
blaspheme the pure word of God.

Sophistication came later with a reading of Rudolf Bultmann and others who taught that the apocalyptic writings
pertain to their own times and not to ours; that they are
codified accounts of God's displeasure at the heathen,
Babylon or Rome. It was not until I read C. G. Jung's *Answer
to Job* that I began to wonder whether this liberal view told
the whole story.

Jung writes, 'The four sinister horsemen, the threatening
tumult of trumpets, and the brimming vials of wrath are
still waiting; already the atom bomb hangs over us like the
sword of Damocles.' And again, 'Could anyone in his right
senses deny that John correctly foresaw at least some of
the possibilities which threaten our world in the final phase
of the Christian aeon?' For modern man, whose fear of
fundamentalism is greater than his horror of hell, such an
interpretation is never seriously considered. The devices of
literary and historical criticism have taught us that prophecy
is not the same thing as prediction and that the mythological
world-view of the first century is no longer tenable in an
age of what Bultmann used to call 'electric light and the
wireless'.

And yet there is the suspicion that the doctrines of
enlightened liberalism might turn out to contain more than a
whiff of prejudice. For close attention to the text of the
Book of Revelation does seem to reveal images of an
apocalypse of just the sort that would be loosed upon us
by worldwide nuclear war. 'Men scorched with fire' (16:8),
'the lake of fire and brimstone' (20:10), 'war in heaven'
(12:7), 'men seeking death and not finding it' (9:6), 'the
sun black as sackcloth and the moon as blood' (6:12) –
all these are images of the final holocaust. I do not think
that their application to our own time commits us to the
irrational excesses of fundamentalism, but contemporary
techniques in literary criticism show that a text can be
interpreted on many different levels. In fact, the structuralist

methodology is a refinement in the scientific jargon of
linguistics of allegorical techniques in interpretation that
were common enough in the middle ages. Dante's circles of
despair in the Inferno have as much to do with the inner
torments of the soul or psyche as they have with speculative
metaphysics.

The 'new' or rediscovered style of criticism — which might
aptly enough be styled 'multilateral' — avoids the one-sidedness
of earlier interpretations. Both Dr Graham and Professor
Bultmann are reductionists: Graham reduces the text of
Revelation to a bland historical discourse; Bultmann reduces
it to the level of irrelevant myth. If we regard the text as a
good example of visionary poetry we shall see that it refers
successfully in many different categories of language. Its
immediate meaning for the original Christian readers was
the codified reference to the persecuting Roman empire as
'Babylon', and its downfall at the Second Coming of Christ,
which was thought to be imminent. Medieval interpreters
saw the book as the theological antidote to the original rebellion of Satan which led to the Fall of Man. The alchemists
saw it as one pole in the *coniunctio appositorum* in which
all the parts of the cosmic whole become one. Jung saw it
as a description of the stage reached in the development of
the psyche in this final phase of the Christian aeon. A non-
reductionist view does not find it necessary to select any
particular interpretation as true at the expense of all the
others; visionary poetry is always true in many senses.

In Jung's opinion, these many senses can sometimes
usefully cross-refer so that symbols and myths can be put
to very practical use. This is, of course, only an extension
of the technique developed by Freud for curing psycho-
neurosis by invoking the language of the Oedipus story.
But Jung went much further than Freud and, in his analysis
of the doctrine of the collective unconscious, created a
method by which the archetypal symbols and myths can be
applied to psychological processes and conflicts and to the
way we project these onto the world. For instance, in his

book *Flying Saucers* he interprets the reported sightings of these objects as a modern manifestation of man's desire for salvation or wholeness as the gift of supernatural agency. Modern man has lost his belief in the supernatural realm, and the energies which he once devoted to the religious enterprise are now expended on technology. Science has replaced faith. What is more natural then but that technological man should picture extra-terrestrial redeemers in the guise of advanced visitors from outer space? Thus the old stories about supernatural redeemers are not discarded but retold in the language of the present age.

For Jung, the prophetic symbolism of the Book of Revelation applies directly to our own time. *Answer to Job* is a careful analysis of Revelation 12 in which during the last days a mysterious woman gives birth to a miraculous child who is caught up by God into the safety of heaven:

> Everything now depends on man: immense power of destruction is given into his hand, and the question is whether he can resist the will to use it, and can temper his will with the spirit of love and wisdom. He will hardly be capable of doing so on his own unaided resources. He needs the help of an 'advocate' in heaven, that is of the child caught up to God and who brings the 'healing' and making whole of the fragmentary man.

Man is fragmented, as Jung says, because he has not learnt how to integrate into his whole personality his own irrational or emotional tendencies. So these are out of control — in effect demonic — and as such they threaten to destroy mankind. This is the meaning of Revelation's 'war in heaven'; it finds its present reality in the threat of nuclear destruction. But, according to Jung, there is hope; for the woman who gives birth to the miraculous child is herself fed and protected by God. This woman 'clothed with the sun, and the moon under her feet, and upon her head a crown of twelve stars' (Revelation 12:1) is the symbolic representation of man's intuitive wisdom and his emotions redeemed. Like the Old Testament prophets who always seemed to be saying that there was just the chance a remnant would escape the doom of God's wrath, so Jung argues that the symbolism of Revelation suggests to our age that the nuclear holocaust might be avoided if man is able to integrate his irrational aspect in time. It is something like the call to repentance. Moreover, Jung identifies the necessary integration of the intuitive, irrational aspects with the Papal promulgation of 1950 'Munificentissimus Deus', in which the Assumption of the Blessed Virgin Mary into heaven was defined as an article of faith.

All this is a stumbling-block to literal-minded Protestants who follow Dr Graham's historicising interpretation of Scripture and who consequently regard all attempts to make psychological sense out of the words of the Bible as a faithless watering-down of God's definitive revelation. And it is foolishness to liberals of Bultmann's tradition who seek to imprison Revelation within one very limited cultural context which has nothing to do with our age of 'electric light and the wireless'.

We no longer live in an age of explicit religious writing of the kind that created normative religious texts like the Bible, but, even if theologians of many hues have given up the prophetic task, the writers and artists of the twentieth century certainly have not. I would like to end by giving a few examples from what is a huge catalogue.

Gustav Mahler's music is full of apocalyptic references, most famous among which are the second and the eighth symphonies. In the last movement of the second, 'The Resurrection', the programme notes written by Mahler himself tell of a nightingale singing above the devastated earth before the final procession to judgement of the quick and the dead. The eighth is a musical commentary on the last section of that other visionary poem, Goethe's *Faust*, in which the soul of man is borne to heaven by the power of Das Ewig-Weibliche — precisely the Eternal Feminine which

Jung equates with the intuitive aspect of the psyche, that which we must recover and integrate if we are to survive. Just as there are scholars who would limit the meaning and significance of the Book of Revelation to the time of St John, so there are students of music who restrict Mahler's influence to that period of artistic brooding and dread which preceded the outbreak of the First World War: but the inspiration and genius of great creative works cannot be limited in this way. Only listen to the music and see if you do not feel even more forcibly in our own time the words of Mahler's contemporary Egon Wellesz who said, 'We all knew we were living at the end of an era.' Much of the same apocalyptic strain can be seen in the work of Picasso and Braque and in the disordered expressionism of Schoenberg in his middle period, and in the radical dissociation of Dadaism.

In the 1980s the critically acclaimed writer Russell Hoban has written a novel, *Riddley Walker*, about human society after the nuclear holocaust. In this book, Hoban has accomplished what for T. S. Eliot was one of the main functions of poetry — 'to purify the language of the tribe'. The language of *Riddley Walker* is a post-modern mixture of standard English and computer jargon. The impressive result is irresistibly of our own time and it adds to the authenticity of Hoban's prophetic text. Much other modern fiction from Martin Amis to Ian McEwan seems to be written against a background of universal horror in which there has occurred a final collapse of the moral order. If morals be dead can nature's death be long delayed?

Is it fanciful to judge prophecies authentic before the event? Perhaps not when one of the most influential of all modern composers, Karlheinz Stockhausen has said that he is 'composing music for after the apocalypse'. And then there is Gyorgy Ligeti's evocative choral work *Lux Aeterna* in which the image of eternal light is cast onto the derelict landscape which would follow the devastation of the bombs.

I have omitted all reference to the appearance of apocalyptic imagery in the pervasive popular culture because that aspect is covered elsewhere in this volume by Bernice Martin; sufficient to say that intimations of our nuclear mortality are well represented in that genre. It has become fashionable in fiction to write alternative endings to novels, and what I have attempted to show is that prophecies about the end or how it might be avoided abound in serious contemporary art. The prototype — Jung would say archetype — for all these prophecies is to be found in the Book of Revelation. If from a view of the Bible based on naive literalism or one derived from demythologising sophistication we reject these prophecies, well, we can hardly say we were not warned.

The Church and the Bomb

BASIL MITCHELL

We owe a debt of gratitude to the authors of the Church's working party's report *The Church and the Bomb*. Anyone who sets out to criticise it must acknowledge at the start that it sets high standards of clarity and sustained argument. It is a worthy contribution by the Church of England to the public debate on a question of urgent moral and political importance.

The report falls into two parts of which the first, consisting of six chapters, is very much longer than the second. The first part argues to the conclusion that there are fundamental objections of ethics and faith both to the use of nuclear weapons and to the conditional intention to use them. The second, consisting of two chapters, puts forward practical recommendations, the most important of which is that the UK should, while remaining in the NATO alliance, give up its own nuclear weapons in the expectation that this would make a general reduction in nuclear armaments more likely.

The crucial problem for the interpretation of the report is that of the relationship between these two parts, and it *is* a problem because comparatively little is said about it. The conclusion of the ethical argument is, quite unambiguously, that it is wrong, absolutely and intrinsically, for a nation to use nuclear weapons, and equally wrong for it to threaten to use them, even if it does so in the hope and expectation that the threat itself will render use unnecessary. The ethical case against the use of nuclear weapons is developed in terms of the just war tradition, and I find myself in substantial agreement with it. Such weapons are inherently indiscriminate and the consequences of their use are incalculable. The report does not, however, persuade me that it is in the same sense absolutely wrong to threaten to use the bomb with the intention of deterring a potential adversary from its use, given that there is a reasonable expectation of so deterring him, although I would not deny (and this question will be returned to later) that there are, as the report urges, serious moral ambiguities involved in this deterrent posture.

Its ethical and theological arguments would thus seem to lead inexorably to one policy only as morally acceptable: the unilateral renunciation of all nuclear weapons by one of the alliances, no matter what the consequences. This is not, however, the policy recommended in the report and two sentences only (p. 134) are devoted to explaining why not. These are: 'Total abandonment of nuclear weapons by one of the alliances in the international line-up could undoubtedly have serious destabilising effects. As a policy option, however, it lies in the realm of fantasy as things are at present.' The next reads: 'What is not mere fantasy is the possibility of a unilateral renunciation by the UK of direct association with nuclear weapons'; and it is this option which is then developed.

What, then, is the report saying at this crucial point? We need to be clear what is the status of the policy actually recommended. It could be either second-best, put forward as a step in the right direction in recognition of the fact that the right policy has no chance of being adopted; or the best possible resolution, in all the circumstances of the case, of the dilemma presented by the present state of affairs, involving as little compromise with moral principle as the nature of the case allows.

The first interpretation implies that, were there a realistic hope of electing an all-out unilateralist government, this should be striven for; and were the authors of the report in power themselves, they would not compromise their principles in the way they now propose. The second interpretation implies that a government is bound to take into account the consequences of its policies even at some cost of principle, and that the authors of the Report, if in power themselves, would be prepared to do so.

The alternatives may be illustrated by an analogy — the morality of capital punishment. There are those who would argue that it is wrong, absolutely and intrinsically wrong, to take human life as a means of punishment, because it is totally irreversible, and degrades those who have to authorise and carry it out. Suppose, now, that a situation were to develop in which acts of terrorism threatened the stability of society and there was good reason to believe that the reintroduction of capital punishment was the only effective deterrent. Some opponents of capital punishment would continue to reject its use, whatever the consequences. Others would find themselves in a moral dilemma. Faced by the imminent breakdown of society and believing that the wave of terrorism could be halted by the threat of the death penalty, they would, albeit with the greatest reluctance and compunction, be prepared to support the measure as one which they would themselves enact if they were the government. Yet others, while unable themselves to countenance this step, but recognising that most of their fellow citizens did not share their conscientious convictions, might lend support to the measure as the best course available in all the circumstances of the case. They would all be adopting a fundamentally different attitude from people who have no moral objection to capital punishment as such, and for whom the only question is whether it operates as an effective deterrent.

In this example the difference between the latter and all the others is clear enough both in theory and in practice. Those who judge by consequences only are likely to introduce the death penalty at a significantly earlier stage than the others; for them it is not a matter of last resort.

In principle at least, there is a similar difference between those who are out and out 'consequentialists', and do not regard nuclear weapons as posing a moral problem that is at all unique, and for whom the sole question is: What practical policy is best calculated to prevent the outbreak of nuclear war? and any of the following: those who, regarding the use of nuclear weapons — and the threat to use them — as intrinsically wrong, refuse to assent to any policy that involves either; those who, while themselves holding nuclear weapons to be intrinsically wrong, nevertheless are prepared to assent to the maintenance, by a government which is not unilateralist, of a nuclear strategy which reduces the reliance on nuclear weapons to the minimum extent judged practicable; or those who, while sharing this view of the morality of nuclear weapons, would themselves be prepared, if they formed the government, to adopt a policy based on nuclear deterrence as the least objectionable of the unsatisfactory options open to them.

The consequentialists will rely without hesitation on the threat to use nuclear weapons and will, in general, make the sole criterion for their policy whether it will make nuclear war less likely. The other three groups will not make this the sole criterion, for they will be bound to strike a balance of some sort between this aim of policy and the 'moral cost' of reliance on the nuclear threat. But it will nevertheless come into their reckoning, even if they make their predominant aim the abolition of nuclear weapons, so long as they want this goal to be pursued in a politically realistic fashion. For, in pursuing this ultimate goal, they will wish, so far as possible, to avoid making nuclear war more likely. I say in principle because in practice, as we shall see, things may be somewhat different.

Having established that prudential considerations play a part in the argument of the report, we need now to ask its authors just how much importance they attach to preventing the outbreak of nuclear war. We are entitled to ask them: 'Suppose you were persuaded that the option you at present favour (i.e., unilateral abandonment of nuclear weapons by the UK only) was more likely than a policy of deterrence to increase the risk of nuclear war, what line would you then take? Would you say that, even so, your original recommendation should stand, because it involves less compromise? Or would you regard the need to prevent nuclear war as paramount? It is essential to note that the kind of moral dilemma which this question poses is not peculiar to them, but affects anyone who shares, as I do, their view of the intrinsic wrong of nuclear weapons. It is of the same order as the dilemma which faces those of their critics who are not out-and-out consequentialists. We are all in the same boat — and a desperately uncomfortable one it is. So long as unilateralists are prepared to be wholly uncompromising they can escape from this particular dilemma. However, as soon as the need to prevent nuclear war is brought into the reckoning, the question arises what degree of priority it ought to have; and it seems to me — and here I diverge from the report — that once it has been brought into the reckoning, it can scarcely fail to become the overriding consideration, so incalculably destructive and so morally abhorrent would that war be. Hence, although in theory the various positions can be distinguished, as was illustrated in the case of the death penalty, in practice they are almost bound to collapse into one another. It would be well-nigh impossible to justify a political policy, however morally preferable it might be when abstractly considered, if it would in practice make nuclear war more likely. And this means that the policy which the report puts forward must be judged in terms of its probable political consequences. Many, if not most, of those who differ from the conclusion of the report are in agreement with its authors that both normative and prudential considerations are involved; they differ from them in their assessment of the latter.

This means, as I see it, that we confront a serious — indeed tragic — moral dilemma. The moral costs of deterrence to which the report draws attention are real. It is not possible for a nation state to bluff, in the way that an individual can, with no intention of doing what it threatens to do. There must be those who are now prepared to do, if ordered, what it is intrinsically wrong to do — to cause death and injury on an incalculable scale to innocent people. But, on the other hand, to refuse on grounds of morality to undertake political measures which are designed and may reasonably be expected to prevent the situation ever arising in which (by one side or the other, or by both) that moral evil is actually committed, is not in itself a morally secure position. This can be seen most clearly if, for the sake of argument, we suppose it to be certain that deterrence will work. There would still be a moral taint (albeit a lesser one) attaching to the possession of nuclear weapons and the threat to use them, even if one was sure that they would never have to be used: yet it would surely be irresponsible for a government to refuse to avail itself of this method of preventing so great an evil in order to be free of this moral taint. Our actual situation is less clear cut than that, but if there is only an excellent chance that nuclear war will be prevented by a policy of deterrence, that aim would seem still to have an overriding claim upon a responsible government, notwithstanding its inevitable moral costs.

But, it may be argued (although not in the report) that we have it in our power to prevent a nuclear war by other and morally preferable means, viz. by abandoning our nuclear weapons altogether and urging our allies to do so, and exposing ourselves and them to whatever risks there might be of domination by an alien and oppressive regime. Even if, to assume the worst (and somewhat improbable) outcome, this entailed an immediate Soviet conquest of this and other western countries, it would be a lesser evil than nuclear war and would relieve us of the moral guilt of readiness to use nuclear weapons. We should not have that on our conscience.

Since it is the essence of the argument that by surrender of whatever political aims might provoke an aggressor, we have it in our own power to prevent a nuclear war, the policy can be sure of achieving its purpose only if undertaken by one of the super-powers. Renunciation by the UK alone of nuclear weapons would, at best, bring about some temporary relaxation of tension, and could not, of itself, guarantee that nuclear war would not, after all, occur. And the attempt to persuade either the Soviet Union or the United States to accept a policy of unilateral nuclear disarmament has little chance of success. It is, as the report says, 'in the realm of fantasy'.

Nevertheless, as I began by noting, it is this policy which the earlier chapters of the report seem inexorably to point to, and the argument for it is a powerful one; and deserves to be considered in its own right. Is it not better to refrain from doing wrong and suffer the consequences, whatever they may be, than to seek to prevent an evil, however, grievous, by means that are intrinsically wrong? And I am agreeing that to possess and to threaten the use of nuclear weapons is intrinsically wrong. We have still, I think, to consider what the consequences would actually be. Among the consequences would (or, might) be the extinction of hope among enormous numbers who now suffer the reality or the threat of imprisonment, and the insidious terror that goes with it; and the extension of this to countries which are at present free of it. Not much can be done as things are for the cause of human rights in Eastern Europe, but at least there is a pattern, not perfect but precious nevertheless, which exists and whose existence affords some mitigation of suffering and a model of what can be. One cannot be morally indifferent to the spread of such suffering or the intensification of it where it is now experienced. But it is not a matter of suffering alone. With this suffering, and inextricable from it, goes an enormous burden of moral evil, and that too must be brought into the reckoning. Where such an oppressive system prevails, innumerable dilemmas are daily posed to individuals and to institutions of just the same kind as we have been exploring in relation to nuclear weapons. Whether the regime to be placated is that of a powerful neighbour only, or of a satellite government actually installed in one's own country, there are agonising choices to be made — whether to stand by principle come what may and let others suffer and be, perhaps, corrupted, or to accept a more or less unsatisfactory compromise; where men and women strive to do the best that their situation allows, but where the best that they can do is a choice between evils, because to do what is unequivocally good is not permitted to them.

It would be worth sacrificing much to prevent these evils spreading, and if we are persuaded that, in present circumstances, in order to prevent it, it is necessary to maintain the nuclear threat, with all the risks and moral ambiguities that involves, can we in good conscience refuse to do it?

The great value of the report, it seems to me, is that we can discover in it the true character of our dilemma — one of which there is no resolution possible that is altogether free of risk or moral cost. No one who reads it can espouse any of the options open to us with an easy conscience. To make the right choice demands a combination of moral sensitivity with political judgement, and the two must not be separated. The danger in the highly polarised way the debate is sometimes conducted (but not by the authors of this report) is that sensitive people may be led to think they need not be responsible and, worse still, that responsible people may feel they need not be sensitive.

Resolutions Passed by The General Synod of the Church of England concerning *The Church and the Bomb*

1 This Synod recognising:

(a) the urgency of the task of making and preserving peace;

(b) the extreme seriousness of the threat made to the world by contemporary nuclear weapons and the dangers in the present international situation; and

(c) that it is not the task of the Church to determine defence strategy but rather to give a moral lead to the nation;

    (i) affirms that it is the duty of Her Majesty's government and her allies to maintain adequate forces to guard against nuclear blackmail and to deter nuclear and non-nuclear aggressors;

    (ii) asserts that the tactics and strategies of this country and her NATO allies should be seen to be unmistakeably defensive in respect of the countries of the Warsaw Pact;

    (iii) judges that even a small scale first use of nuclear weapons could never be morally justified in view of the high risk that this would lead to full-scale nuclear warfare;

    (iv) believes that there is a moral obligation on all countries (including the members of NATO) publicly to forswear the first use of nuclear weapons in any form;

    (v) bearing in mind that many in Europe live in fear of nuclear catastrophe and that nuclear parity is not essential to deterrence, calls on Her Majesty's government to take immediate steps in conjunction with her allies to further the principles embodied in this motion so as to reduce progressively NATO's dependence on nuclear weapons and to decrease nuclear arsenals throughout the world.

2   This Synod believes that indiscriminate mass destruction in war cannot be justified in the light of Christian teaching and calls upon the dioceses to study and pray about the issues raised in the report *The Church and the Bomb*, and in particular the theological and moral issues, so as to enable Christian people to make a more informed and committed contribution to the making and preserving of peace and to the search for ways of resolving conflicts other than by war.

The Morality of Nuclear Deterrence

GRAHAM LEONARD

I begin this brief consideration of an issue which has such grave implications for mankind, with three quotations. The first is from the Government White Paper, *Statement on the Defence Estimates 1981*, Command 8212 published in 1981:

> Nuclear weapons have transformed our view of war. Though they have been used only twice, half a lifetime ago, the terrible experience of Hiroshima and Nagasaki must always be in our minds. But the scale of that horror makes it all the more necessary that revulsion be partnered by clear thinking. If it is not, we may find ourselves having to learn again, in the appalling school of practical experience, that abhorrence of war is no substitute for realistic plans to prevent it.

The second quotation is from the end of chapter 2 of the report of the working party appointed by the General Synod Board for Social Responsibility, *The Church and the Bomb*, and reads as follows:

> There are, however, no simple solutions to the problems created by nuclear weapons, no risk-free policies, no courses of action that allow us to escape from ethical dilemmas. Even if it were possible to dismantle all the

nuclear weapons that now exist, people would still have to live for all time with the knowledge of how to make them. History cannot be reversed and nuclear weapons cannot now be disinvented.

The third quotation comes from an essay by Sir Arthur Hockaday entitled 'In Defence of Deliverance' included in a book of essays recently published under the title *Ethics and Nuclear Deterrence*. Sir Arthur, who is Second Permanent Under-Secretary of State in the Ministry of Defence, says that:

> The two Christian convictions...reflected in the tradition of Christian pacifism and in the search for a Christian definition of the just war, may be respectively characterised, in a world in which power has repeatedly been rampant, as concepts of abdications from power and management of power....But, however much these two traditions may have diverged in the past, we must recognise that in the late twentieth century when we have seen not only conventional warfare on an unprecedented scale but also the invention of nuclear weapons, the objectives of the Christian pacifist and of the Christian managers of power must be the same — the prevention of destruction and the preservation of peace. The questions at issue between them relate to the means of achieving those objectives and the nature of the price that must be paid.

I begin with these quotations because they make it clear that those who try to think deeply and to care deeply about these issues have a degree of common ground. It is not conducive to that clear thinking which is essential, nor is it of ultimate benefit to mankind to polarise the issue and see it as a conflict between 'warmongers' on the one hand and 'peacemakers' on the other — between hawks and doves. However mistaken we may believe the other side to be, there must be a mutual recognition of integrity, accepting that both sides desire the best for mankind.

I propose to limit what I have to say to trying to answer one question which is implicit in the title I have been given: 'Can a policy of nuclear deterrence be morally acceptable?' This is, I believe, the fundamental question, and I do not believe that secondary questions dealing with such matters as what forms of deterrence are acceptable or right, or whether Great Britain should act unilaterally, can be considered properly without prior consideration of this fundamental question.

The authors of the report have no doubt as to the answer, which they put in stark terms, and I quote: 'The ethics of deterrence are the ethics of threatening to do something which one believes would be immoral, which one intends to do only in circumstances which will not arise because of the conditional threat.' I cannot be sure, even from this context, whether the statement is intended to apply to any policy of deterrence, even for example, as pursued by someone in the USA who lets it be known that he or she has a gun or offensive spray as a deterrent against muggers, burglars or rapists, or whether it only applies in the case of nuclear weapons. My uncertainty is now resolved by the fact that at the end of the report, the working party refers with approval to the possible beneficial effect of the existence of nuclear weapons as deterrent. Having reaffirmed that nuclear weapons cannot be disinvented and said that the monster can only be locked up in prison, it continues 'But from its prison, it would for this very reason have a salutary effect. The irreversible possibility of nuclear weapons could be potent to warn simple and stupid humanity away from all war as a means of settling international dispute.' However, for my purpose, I shall assume that the definition of deterrence applies only to nuclear weapons, and will not spend time arguing for the moral justification of deterrence in principle.

I return to the fundamental question, 'Is a policy of nuclear deterrence morally acceptable?' Consideration of the question demands, I believe, examination of three underlying matters: the distinction between the morally acceptable and the morally good, and its significance for moral judgements; the place of power in international diplomacy and its relation to the pursuit of justice; and the criteria by which the morality of the actions of governments and nations should be determined as compared with that determining the morality of the actions of individuals.

On the first of these I want to make two points. First, we must accept that we do not live in an ideal world, in which the choices before us all involve acts which are morally good. Frequently, we find ourselves in situations in which none of the options open to us is wholly good and all have elements within them which we would deplore. How, in such situations, are we able to act in a way which does not do violence to our moral nature? We may well not be able to opt out of the decision we have to make, as is often the case with those who are in positions of responsibility. To do nothing can represent the abdication of our moral responsibility to an even greater extent than to make a choice between decisions with none of which we are happy. What we have to do is to consider the various courses open to us. We then have to judge that one course of action, even though it may involve consequences which we would deplore, which we would certainly not describe as good and which we would certainly not intend, is that which we are under an obligation to pursue. Our moral nature has been expressed in our assessment of all the actions open and by our acceptance of our obligation to decide and to act. Having decided that the particular course contains less of what is undesirable than the others, we have a further obligation to minimise the possible bad consequences as well as to try to maximise the good. The course for which we have decided can, I believe, be described as morally acceptable, though not as morally good. The distinction which I have drawn is the same as that between the right and the good which dates back to pre-Christian philosophers. I have avoided that terminology because, particularly in recent years, the distinction is increasingly blurred. In popular speech the right and the good are frequently identified. It is for this reason that I have phrased my fundamental question as 'Can a policy of nuclear deterrence be morally acceptable?' rather than 'Can it be right?' which would almost certainly be taken to mean asking whether it could be good.

Another way of putting this vital distinction might be to speak of moral values which describe what is good, and moral obligations which describe what it is our duty to do in particular situations. You will also notice that I have phrased the question 'Can it be...' rather than 'Is it...'. If we decide that an action is morally acceptable but not good, we have to decide on the circumstance in which it would be proper to act.

I come now to the second point I want to make under this heading. During the last few decades, it has been increasingly maintained that there are very few absolute moral prescriptions or rules which must be obeyed always without qualification, whatever other moral demands may be present in the situation. While this development may have had undesirable results in society as a whole in encouraging people to discount moral standards and feel justified in doing that which seems right in their own eyes, it has not arisen simply from moral relativism. Rather it has arisen from a desire to take more seriously the moral nature of man and the responsibility which he has for making moral judgements and for assessing the diverse moral claims which are made upon him.

Such judgement as I quoted from *The Church and the Bomb* about the use of nuclear weapons for deterrence elevates the question of the possesssion or use of nuclear weapons to one in which a moral prescription is made which admits of no qualifications. In so doing, it removes the necessity to consider the moral demands made by many other issues, such as those of the preservation of liberty, truth and human dignity. It is, I believe, not consistent with the moral nature of man to proclaim one principle of such moral rigidity that these other fundamental moral issues become secondary. Nor do I believe that for a Christian who believes that man is made for eternal communion with the living God who is just and holy can the principle of survival take precedence over all other moral claims.

Turning to my second underlying issue, the place of power in international diplomacy, I want to quote from a lecture I gave in November 1981 in St James's, Piccadilly on 'The Politics of Forgiveness — Towards a Theology of International Security'. 'It is often assumed', I said, 'that there are basically two ways of settling conflicts. One is by the way of power or force. The other is by means of the negotiating table in which the parties sit down to resolve the situation by reasonable discussions. Such a view is un-realistic and does not reflect the actual situation. In the first place, it does not take account of the limited extent to which any objective can be achieved by force. Second, it fails to take account of the extent to which power is an integral element in any process of negotiations.' I developed the second point as follows:

If there was ever a time in international relations when an academic discussion could settle a matter on the basis of, say, the interpretation of the law alone, that time has passed. Any international problem now has such worldwide implications that no party, no single nation, can adopt a wholly disinterested position. In any form of negotiation, whether in international affairs or in an industrial dispute, there is a conflict of wills — not merely a difference of opinion to be settled by an expert judgement, though the parties may *will* that their differences should be settled by acceptance of such a judgement. Second, it represents a willingness for this power, which is possessed by the interested parties and which continues to be theirs during the negotiations to be exercised not by direct actions but in the context of a resolve to settle the dispute by the intelligent exercise of the will, taking into account the moral good. The power which resides in the negotiators is transformed into a kind of bargaining power — a 'pull in negotiations'. As Professor Herbert Butterfield put it: 'Men under this system make their decisions after doing a piece of mental arithmetic — after making a calculation of forces and chances — instead of enacting the full tale of violence, with the forces actually colliding and everything really consigned to the hazards of war.'

Not only does the power remain, even if hid in the velvet glove. It may be that negotiation has only become possible because the existence of that power has previously been made evident in an exemplary and limited way. Diplomacy is always, in a certain sense, a trial of strength — strength which need not be the strength of mere power and might [but can include the strength of will that a solution should be found by peaceful means.] The power in diplomatic relations is not, of course confined to military power. It can also be economic or industrial and its significance must not be underestimated. It is partly for this reason that the mere absence of armaments must not be supposed to remove conflicts of interest between nations.

My argument is that, human nature being what it is and, as we shall see, the responsibility of governments being what it is, a balance of power can be more than a deterrent, valuable though it is as such. A balance of power, unlike an ability for over-kill, can be a very effective force in bringing governments to the negotiating table and in strengthening their resolve to settle disputes by means other than war. For one party to remove or weaken its power to deter and thereby to give another nation the ability for over-kill can positively encourage the stronger party to resort to force to remove its fears or to achieve its aims. I say remove its fears or achieve its aims because, though fear is a most powerful element in the force leading to the escalation of arms, I do not believe that it is the only one. As has been evident in Africa for example, force, in the shape of military action on a comparatively minor and non-nuclear level, has been used to secure justice, remove tyranny and oppression and achieve self-determination. There is not time for me to consider the likely reaction of the USSR to a repudiation of nuclear weapons by another nation. I would only say that on the basis of the clearly stated aims of its government, it would not hesitate to take the fullest advantage of the situation, certainly at diplomatic levels, and would be entirely logical in doing so; and I believe it would be folly to suppose otherwise.

I come now to the third of my underlying issues: namely, the criteria by which the morality of the actions of governments should be determined, as compared with those determining the morality of the actions of individuals. The distinction must at first appear to reside simply in the fact that a government has to exercise a responsibility for the people as a whole and cannot therefore take account of the needs of the individual. In the matter of justice, for example, it is often said that whereas the individual when acting in accordance with justice has to take into account the needs of the particular person towards whom he is acting, the best that the government can do is to provide a framework in which the maximum degree of justice is available for everyone. This inevitably means that there will be a degree of injustice towards many, even though the government may have acted in the best way possible. But this distinction will not hold, for the same applies to a lesser or greater degree to anyone who is responsible for the welfare of any social group, if only that of the family of which he or she is a part. It is sometimes argued that the distinction lies in the fact that it is the duty of the state to create conditions and possess the power to enable a man or woman to live in security, to have an adequate wage, to be free from attack by others, and to be free to express his or her beliefs, and so on. But, these things are again in varying measure with consequent degree of responsibility to be found at every level of corporate responsibility albeit with an increasing degree of tension between the needs of each individual and the needs of the corporate body which will affect the moral judgement which individuals have to make.

The real distinction lies in the fact that the primary duty of those in government is to ensure that the state survives *and* to retain the powers to protect its members and provide the conditions for a good life. Ideally, this would be the responsibility of an international authority but we live in a world in which international law, to quote Professor Michael Howard, 'remains a system of agreements and conventions based on mutual convenience, without mandatory powers.' It is necessary for the state to be able to defend its members in order that they shall be able to live in accordance with the moral instincts of man. Such defence may have to be against the age-long threats of tyranny, oppression or against the expansionist aims of a regime, such as that in Nazi Germany, based on an ideology which we would in many aspects regard as immoral. If the state willingly acquiesces in the face of such threats, it treats the attitude on which they are based as morally acceptable or as a matter of indifference. Further, a government which is morally indifferent to such attitudes is very unlikely to be party to any form of international order. I would therefore maintain that not only has the state a duty to defend its members in the sense of enabling them to survive. That duty also carries with it the duty of bearing witness to the moral basis of a free society.

I do not believe that it is right for the state to preserve its members at the expense of that witness. It is, in my judgement, irrelevant to say that people can survive under the most tyrannical situations. What matters in this context is the public and corporate witness to the moral values, which even if the state abdicates its responsibilities, they then continue to try and maintain. Our Lord said that He came not to destroy the law, but to fulfil it and the purpose of the Gospel is to enable us to do that out of love for God. We cannot fulfil the law unless it exists, which is why our first duty and the duties of governments is to stand for the moral values which give liberty, justice and human dignity.

I must at this point enter a caveat. I do not mean to imply that this involves an uncritical acceptance of the *status quo* which is to be preserved at all costs. On the contrary, what I have said about the responsibility of the state involves the acceptance of moral standards which are not the creation of the state and by which the life of the state and the actions of government are to be judged. In this respect, what I have said is in sharp contrast to the Marxist—Leninist tradition which believes that the state creates its own ethical values, and, it must be added, believes that it is justified in propagating these values wherever they can and extending their implementation whenever opportunity occurs. Whereas I endorse what *The Church and the Bomb* says about the danger of identifying a people with its government and of dehumanising them, I do not believe that it takes sufficient account of the ideology which inspires the rulers of the USSR.

Under this heading, I want to say a word about the position of those who have to exercise responsibility in government, for whom Christians in particular should demonstrate understanding and concern. On this point I cannot do better than quote what Professor Michael Howard has written. He begins by quoting the Dutch Augustinian priest, Father Robert Adolfs, who wrote: 'the Church which is coming to be is one which will view the whole history of the Christian Church from the fourth century (that is after the recognition of Christianity by Constantine) as a kind of collective experience of the far country in which the prodigal spent his inheritance with harlots.' Professor Howard then continues:

Yet if the Church were to return to the catacombs, what happens to the unfortunate harlots — the statesmen who have to go on doing their job, and who may be members of the Church as well? Do they incur excommunication by continuing to do what is, by any standards, necessary work? They can of course always escape from their dilemmas by resigning; admitting that a certain action may be necessary in the context of the power situation in which they find themselves, but being unable to square it with their ethical principles, and regarding the latter as overriding. Few do. The cynic will attribute this to simple lust for power, but the explanation is seldom as easy as that. The statesman knows that somebody has to take the decision, and to refuse to do so is an abdication of responsibilities deliberately assumed. Pontius Pilate is an unattractive figure for Christians, not because he did his duty and firmly took a disagreeable decision, but because he failed to do so; taking water and washing his hands saying: 'I am innocent of the blood of this just person; see ye to it.' President Truman, staunchly accepting responsibility for decisions of unimaginable consequence, is likely to occupy a more comfortable part even of the Christian Purgatory.

We may not envy the position of the statesman and we may not always agree with decisions made but we cannot, if we are seeking to exercise our moral responsibility, condemn him for being willing to accept it.

While recognising the utterly appalling prospect of the use of nuclear weapons, I believe that their possession and use can be morally acceptable as a way of exercising our moral responsibility in a fallen world. I do not believe that we can ever say that their possession or use can be morally good. At best, we can say that they may be morally acceptable.

I believe that in a fallen world in which power is the major factor in international diplomacy, the preservation of peace and the acceptance of limitations on nations, are most likely to be achieved by the maintenance of a balance of power.

I believe that the duty of government is both to ensure the survival of the state and to bear witness to the moral basis which is necessary for a free society.

However I want to end on a positive note, and I want to make four points about the way forward.

First, and somewhat ironically, there must be a common acceptance of conflict as part of the international situation. By that I do not mean conflict in the military sense. I mean conflict in the sense of conflicting interests and ideologies. Such acceptance is not cynical but realistic, and is necessary if nations are to acquire the will to resolve conflicts in a non-military way. By acceptance of conflict, I do not mean endorsement of it as a good thing. Few things are more mischievous than the stirring up and fuelling of conflict for the fun of it. I mean the acceptance of it *as a fact* in the situation which is to be redeemed.

Second, there must, I believe, be a recognition of the power which the various parties possess. It is folly to deny this, whether it be military, economic or industrial power. It inevitably provides the starting-point for any negotiations, and this must be openly without facing other forms of power, is to create an unstable situation which, sooner or later, will express itself again in a military way.

Third, there must be a common resolve to exercise such power in a non-military way — in other words, a determination to solve problems other than by killing and subjugation. As I have said, I am not attempting to deal with the particular issue of nuclear warfare, but I would say at this point that the appalling consequences of nuclear warfare may possibly be used to give mankind the will to transmute this exercise of power. This, I believe, will happen only if pressure to reduce nuclear weapons is not seen as an end in itself but is accompanied by a determination to resolve conflict in a non-military way.

Fourth, I believe we have to recognise the nature of peace.

It is not a negative condition — the mere absence of war — a condition which would automatically come if no aggressors were about. Our Lord, in the Beatitudes, spoke of the peace-makers — and peace is the result of a continuing process. Its creation and maintenance require continuing effort and there can never be a situation in which we can reside without working for the future, recognising the forces which are always at work for its destruction.

The way forward is, I believe, not simply by attempts to secure nuclear disarmament or reductions in nuclear weapons, valuable and essential though such attempts are. To pursue that aim alone, while failing to examine the ways in which the conflict of interest arises, is inadequate and unlikely to be of lasting effect. What is needed is for the nations to examine how conflicts of interest are to be resolved, with a common determination that this be achieved without military force. If this is to happen, we need not merely leaders dedicated to this end but the constant and sharp pressure of the will of people — and we can begin with ourselves.

Dr Conor Cruise O'Brien, at the end of his two articles in *The Observer*, asked the question 'What does God expect His destructive species to do with His destructive power?' My answer to that — and I am not sure if it is what Dr O'Brien expects — is that God expects His destructive species to be true to his moral nature and to use his moral instincts to control the destructive power which he possesses, and not to deny them by capitulation to it.

A naval chaplain has written:

Our universal situation contains, within itself, a judge-ment upon the individual, the nation, and upon humanity collectively, as it demonstrates man's rejec-tion of the divine pattern for human life. To condemn nuclear weapons, as though we could disentangle both them and ourselves from the whole human condition is in some ways a comfortable position. It is harder, but more in keeping with the Christian prophetic tradition, to recognise and declare the judgement which is present in the whole of our social life (of which the prophet himself is part) — not only in our possession of nuclear weapons. We have brought this judgement upon ourselves by our common failure to obey God.

The response to that judgement must be a recovery of our moral sense and that begins with repentance in every aspect of our life and not simply with the repudiation of one result of our sinful condition.

'. . . but I say unto You'

PAUL OESTREICHER

For centuries, in village churches and cathedrals, members of the Church of England have sung at Evening Prayer: 'Give peace in our time, O Lord, because there is none other that fighteth for us.' The many memorials to Britain's fallen warriors in those same places of worship attest to the fact that the Church's first line of defence has *not* been the Lord. The Thirty-nine Articles of Religion saw the need to spell out that Christians were entitled, at the behest of the state, to take part in the wars of the realm. The Latin version spoke of *iusta bella*, *just* wars. In the Prayer Book version, the word 'just' somehow got lost.

Augustine was the first major theologian to dismantle what Christians had believed for the first three centuries of their history, that war was incompatible with Christian discipleship. Few theologians have tried to deny that to engage in armed conflict is hard to reconcile with the ethics of Jesus. But it is widely held that that ethic was only relevant to a small alien religious community in a hostile Roman world, or alternatively that it was only a short-term interim ethic propounded on the assumption that the *parousia*, the end of the world, would come within a generation.

From the moment the Roman Emperor became a Christian, everything changed. Since then, Christians have been encouraged to engage in war either as a necessary evil (the just war doctrine) or more often as a sacred duty (the doctrine of the crusade). Most Christians still waver between these two positions. The theologians have generally given precedence to some version of the just war doctrine, a position that does not glorify war but regards it as the lesser of two evils in certain circumstances. These circumstances were so strictly defined (for example, by St Thomas Aquinas and a whole school of medieval lawyers) that very few wars have, in these terms, been 'just'. As most wars in Europe have been fought between Christians, it follows that, objectively, the warring sides could not both have had a just cause. Yet both sides have always thought so, right up to the Falklands/Malvinas War.

In practice, once a war has started it has nearly always been fought as though it were a holy war, a sacred duty. The Germans in the First World War had the words 'God with Us' inscribed on their belt buckles; the Americans spell out their trust in God on their most sacred possession, their coinage; the British tend to take all that for granted. The just war doctrine is largely about the need for restraint in war, the need to minimise its evil effect. But once war is under way that can be a considerable hindrance on the road to victory. A crusade imposes no such restraints. If God is commander-in-chief, victory at all costs becomes essential. In some Catholic countries that honorary role was apportioned to Mary, Virgin Queen of Heaven.

The Jesus tradition of the first centuries was almost totally obscured. It was not held to be relevant in a fallen world. According to one Catholic school of thought the priesthood alone was to be kept from shedding blood. As it was holier to be celibate than to marry, so it was holier to pray than to fight. This made pacifism a priestly vocation but clearly one unsuited to normal life. That did not stop medieval prince—bishops from having high military rank and, on occasion, leading troops into battle. For the protestant heirs of the just war doctrine there was no nonsense about one ethic for the clergy and another for the rest. Luther, Calvin, Cromwell

— they were in no doubt that there were many occasions when the sword had to be wielded in the cause of right, and so of God. Historically, Christians went much further than to abandon pacifism: they made war wholly acceptable. At times they were uneasy about killing fellow Christians. That problem was solved by calling the other side heretics. And if they were not heretics, devotion to the nation was reason enough to go out and kill its foes.

Yet the injunction of Jesus to love enemies will not go away. He did not just preach it; he lived it as a new way of life. There was no shame in dying or in suffering oppression. Indeed that is what Jesus predicted for his Church. But killing was ruled out. He did not see pacifism as a special vocation for the Son of Man but as a way of life for the Body of Christ. There have always been Christians who have accepted that way of life. It never was surrender in the face of evil. Quite the opposite: it was to challenge evil at its very root. It was declaring that it is impossible to drive the Devil out with Beelzebub. It was struggle by other means. It was not even the rejection of all forms of force — provided that force was compatible with loving those on the other side. The cleansing of the Temple (often cited to suggest that Jesus was no pacifist) threatened no one's life. There was nothing passive about Jesus. The fatalism of Buddhism is no part of the activist prophetic tradition to which he was heir. Christianity is not about 'leaving everything to God'. It is about the warfare of the Spirit which is concerned with every part of life. That is why Christian discipleship is always both personal and political.

Pacifism, Christian peacemaking, is about the defeat of evil through active love. Its advocates, like Jesus himself, have often been rejected either as harmless fools or as threatening revolutionaries. They have often been treated as traitors because their first allegiance has never been to one human community, set against another. Pacifism has, nevertheless, never been declared a heresy; that would be too difficult. Yet pacifists have often been treated like heretics.

Pacifism is often wrongly held to be a kind of fundamentalism based on selected scriptural texts. There are, of
course, more texts in the New Testament suited to that
end than to the other side of the argument, but none is
conclusive. Christian pacifism is based on an understanding
of the divine nature and of the whole redemptive process. In
the framework of that christology, pacifism is not some kind
of optional extra derived from the Christian faith. It is
inherent in the faith itself. It is certainly not a personal
vocation for a holy minority. It is simply an aspect of the
divine nature which the Church is called to reflect. It is
integral to the Kingdom of God.

I came to that conviction at the age of eighteen when I had
to decide whether or not to perform military service. Ever
since, I have had to learn to live as one of a small minority
in the Church, respected but, in the event, rejected. For
more than thirty years I have lived in the same Church with
Christians who have no difficulty whatever with the military
systems that are taken for granted in all nations. Even Christians in communist nations who radically reject the political
system under which they live have little or no difficulty in
accepting military service. The Church may not like the
system, but whatever the system — under Hitler, under
Stalin — it is patriotic. Franz Jägerstetter was a simple
peasant. He said 'No' to Hitler's war. His Catholic Bishop told
him not to be so infernally proud. Who was he to set his
conscience up above the interests of the nation? His conscience
prevailed, and in 1943 he was beheaded by the Gestapo. The
peasant was right; the Church wrong.

I re-state all this now, because I believe that the Church
and the world are entering a new phase of history. More and
more young Christians — some in South Africa, many in
America during the Vietnam War, and others now in every
nation with nuclear arms — are developing a totally new
attitude to nationalism and to war. It may just be that the
period of history from the fourth to the twentieth century
has been one in which the Church was not spiritually capable

of accepting the full implications of the Gospel. It is just possible that the ethic of the just war – as an interim ethic – is only now beginning to be wholly refutable, even bearing in mind that liberation theology still wholeheartedly embraces that doctrine. Conservative and radical theologians often still differ only in defining which wars are just. By analogy: until the mid-nineteenth century Christians only argued about *what kind* of slavery was acceptable, and about whether slaves were truly human. The question now becomes whether it has taken the advent of war technologies which threaten not only people and nations but human survival, to make it possible to grasp an ethic which rejects the very possibility of war.

The passage in St John's Gospel in which Jesus states that the Spirit will lead the Church into all truth because there are some things the Church cannot yet understand, suggests to me that the moment when Christians (and not only Christians) come to understand that war is unacceptable may only now be close at hand. Hitherto, pacifism has, at best, been held to be a counsel of perfection, an unrealistic kind of idealism that fails to take account of human sin. Increasingly I feel that we are moving into a phase of history when pacifism (i.e., the refusal to contemplate war as a last resort in resolving conflict) may become the only practical way to assure human survival. Of course the Apocalypse may come. But that is for God to decide. The world remains in human hands, committed to our care. War, whether nuclear or bacteriological, can now end organic life on earth. That calls for a radical transformation of human consciousness. The threat to humanity lies in the declared readiness of governments to go to war. That is what deterrence means. Pacifists have always rejected the idea that peace is best maintained by preparing for war. On the evidence of history it is simply not true. Truth is much more complex. Why has Europe had a kind of peace since 1945? It *is* possible that the horrific consequences of a war between East and West have, over the last generation, made war less likely. But there is the simpler explanation that, despite the imperialist aspirations of both the USA and the USSR, neither has at any time since the Second World War contemplated attacking the other. That is the considered judgement of Ambassador George Kennan, the diplomat and historian who probably knows Soviet Russia better than any other American.

The present tragic reality is that although the great powers know that the price of even a so-called conventional war would be unacceptably high, their mutual fear commits them, given certain circumstances, to fighting a nuclear war which would be both genocidal and suicidal. I no longer believe that conventional wisdom can save the world from such unintended disaster. Diplomatic miscalculation or technological error — and neither is improbable — would be enough to set off a chain-reaction which might not be reversible. Could it be that in these circumstances pacifist discipleship might now go hand in hand with a pacifism of prudence with or without a Christian label? Might the moment have come when nations begin to acknowledge that neither the 'maintenance of freedom' nor the 'defence of socialism' warrant risking a holocaust which would turn our earth into a radioactive desert?

This is, in effect, to say that the time has come for the parties to the Cold War to relativise the value of the way of life they claim to hold dear. Neither liberal-democracy nor Marxism—Leninism are of such infinite value to man that their preservation merits putting the whole population of our planet at risk. The people of the Soviet Union, who have known war, would readily assent to that proposition, but they will not be asked. The American people might agree somewhat less readily: they have no comparable memories of war. But regardless of what the people think, both power blocs are firmly in the grip of militarism. It was no pacifist, but President Eisenhower who warned the American people of the dangers of the industrial—military complex.

How can the radical reorientation of thinking take place

that might ensure an era of peace? I recognise the strength of the argument that the best is often the enemy of the good. To suggest that pacifism's day may at last have come *and to be satisfied with nothing less* may mean that we shall not even get arms control, let alone disarmament. Even now I am convinced that 'interim ethics' remains important. Arms control agreements matter because they improve the political climate and lower the threshold of fear. Negotiated multilateral disarmament is of great importance. It really would reduce the danger of war. But in times of high tension, like the present, the possibility of war will remain until nations solemnly, and whatever the risk, renounce their readiness to go to war.

However prudential pacifism may have become, I concede that it cannot guarantee national security. The time therefore has come to begin to implement alternative defence strategies which are prepared, as a last resort, to accept defeat as preferable to war and annihilation. For the West that does not mean the ready acceptance of Soviet domination. But in the event of such domination (which *is* preferable to annihilation) whole populations should be trained in forms of resistance which, in the long run, could defeat any alien regime. In any case, no tyranny, however cruel, lasts for ever. Even if they last a century, all earthly empires are transient; but a nuclear desert is permanent. This argument is, of course, based on the common western assumption that, given a marked imbalance of power, the Soviet Union would march westward. Soviet orthodoxy contends that the opposite is true, that it is the West that would attack. Both fears are neither wholly unfounded nor totally foolish. Nevertheless, the great weight of evidence suggests that neither is true. Principles apart (and that is what I mean by *prudential* pacifism), the risks involved in planning for nuclear war, in the hope of thus avoiding it, are now much greater than the risks of renouncing war, in the hope of achieving some kind of genuine international accord. Clearly, no course of action or inaction is fail-safe.

A pacifist response may persuade potential enemies, out

of enlightened self-interest, to respond in kind. At worst, the potential enemy will prove to be a real enemy and exploit superior power. Even this worst-case scenario is preferable to a continuation of a balance of terror which is likely to end in both genocide and suicide.

All this is made necessary by the technologies of ultimate destruction. Even a conventional war between nuclear powers is likely to end as a nuclear war. No first use declarations, related to nuclear weapons, are better than nothing. But will the losing side ever be able to keep that kind of promise? Such risks are not worth taking.

In a nut-shell; the *kairos*, God's moment, for pacifism has perhaps come. Perhaps, as the twentieth century ends, the Church which on this question has for so long been in error, an apostate church, may be given the insight to move from an Old Testament to a New Testament ethic. To say that is not to despise the Old Testament readiness, in the name of justice, to go to war. But now the Church may be prepared to listen to Jesus saying '…but I say unto you' as he expounds the need to love our enemies. In the past that need could only be spiritually argued. Today the enlightened pagan should be able to recognise that need, together with the believing Christian.

The transition will not be easy. The emotional power of nationalism, of all that Remembrance Sunday stands for, of all that the red poppy symbolises, goes very deep in the human and the Christian psyche. And it remains true — glancing at South Africa and El Salvador — that fighting for a just cause remains a perceived duty for many Christians who are far removed from the computers that control the world's nuclear arsenals.

Spiritually, Gandhi, the Hindu prophet and politician, has helped me as a Christian pacifist to live with and respect the non-pacifist position. It was the Mahatma's conviction that to see evil and not to oppose it, was to surrender one's humanity. To see evil and to oppose it with the weapons of the evil-doer, was to enter into one's humanity. To see evil and to oppose it with the weapons of God was to enter into one's divinity. Here was Gandhi, pacifist that he was, saying that to go to war against evil was better than to do nothing. It was his way of paying homage to what I have called the Old Testament ethic. But Gandhi recognised that there is a better way still. He practised it. The India he left behind did not. Jesus practised it. The Church he left behind did not either, for long. There is no Christian case for non-resistance to evil. Even now there is a case for the upright soldier, prepared to fight for justice and also prepared to disobey an unjust order. There is room in the Church for the soldier as well as for the pacifist, just as, until slavery was abolished, there was room for the slave and the 'just' slave-owner.

I suggest that in the nuclear age before us, a new consensus must emerge which will make the soldier — Christian or pagan — as much of an anachronism as the slave-owner. If it does not, the human race may come to be an anachronism on a barren planet.

Conventional Killing or
Nuclear Stalemate?

RICHARD HARRIES

Our attitude to nuclear weapons and what ought to be done about them depends on our whole understanding of human nature and human society. Before focusing more sharply on the nuclear dilemma I shall put forward a series of propositions which, I believe, would receive widespread assent.

The search for peace should not be isolated from the search for justice. In the summer of 1982 I was in Johannesburg at the invitation of St Mary's Anglican Cathedral. In the Cathedral we heard prayers for peace on our borders. I could not help reflecting on what the sons of some of the Cathedral congregation would be thinking. For they would have been on the other side of the border, concerned for peace, yes, but a just peace; and towards that goal actually fighting for justice. Sometimes in the Church we pray too easily for peace. When Martin Luther King was imprisoned for his part in the struggle for civil rights in the Southern States of America he received a letter from twenty white clergymen telling him to be more patient, to stop being so militant, and so on. The letter in reply contained the phrase 'Peace is not the absence of tension but the presence of justice.' This understanding of peace exactly captures the sense of the great Old Testament word *Shalom*. Peace in the Old Testament is not exclusively something inward, spiritual and tranquil, which is what many Christians mean by the word. *Shalom*, the peace which God wills for human society, refers to the whole of human life, in all its aspects, flourishing as it was meant to. It includes all that we mean by justice.

The search for peace should not be isolated from the search for liberty. In the fourth century, Christians argued that the prophecies of a universal reign of peace in the Old Testament had been fulfilled in the *Pax Romana*. It did not seem very much like that to the Donatists, the North African liberation movement struggling against imperialism. It did not seem very much like that to our ancestors in these islands as they sought to penetrate the defences round Hadrian's Wall. Many people in this country thought that the *Pax Britannica* was similarly blessed by God. But it did not seem like that to those being subjugated in Africa and India. There is plenty of peace around, but it is a question of what form of peace and on what terms. One very effective form of peace is called imperialism. Imperialists are often amongst those who talk most about peace. They ask nothing more than to be able to walk into other countries and annex them peacefully. It is those who don't like imperialism who are forced to talk of war, for they value liberty both for individuals and for states. And liberty is inseparable from conflict. This does not always, or even often, necessitate armed conflict. But it does mean struggle. As Professor Dahrendorf has put it: 'Conflict is liberty, because by conflict alone the multitude and incompatibility of human interests and desires find adequate expression in a world of notorious uncertainty.'

Whether through blindness, weakness or malevolence human beings are capable of great wickedness. Since the Second World War few would deny that *Lord of the Flies* is an apt parable of human life. A group of cherubic-faced choirboys are placed in idyllic conditions on a paradise island. Within a few days they have split into rival gangs and have begun to kill one another. William Golding wrote this novel, as he has written many of his others, to challenge the facile notion that human beings are somehow better than they were. Asked in a rare television interview how he came to this sombre view of human existence he said that it was during the Second World War when he was fighting the Nazis in the Royal Navy. He came to see that we all have a Nazi inside us. In short, we cannot say that another Hitler or Stalin will never arise again, or that if they do they would never get a whole people in thrall, as did Hitler in Germany. Almost daily in the newspapers we read of almost unspeakable horrors on a smaller scale, of which the massacres in Beirut and in Assam are only the two most recent at the time of writing.

As long as finite life continues there will continue to be fundamental differences of perception and interest. If I had been born and brought up on a kibbutz I have little doubt that I would be fully committed to the cause of Israel. Nurtured on the stories of the Old Testament and the vicious history of anti-Semitism I would have an Israeli perception on existence and my paramount interest would be the survival of Israel. If, on the other hand, I had been born and brought up in a Palestinian refugee camp, nurtured on stories about the old family home in Tel Aviv from which my grandfather had been so rudely expelled, my sympathies would be with the PLO. If I had been brought up in Argentina I, like 99.9 per cent of the population would regard the Falkland Islands as belonging to Argentina, and so on. It is the very nature of finite existence to have radical differences of perception and interest. Sometimes these concern religion, sometimes ideology, sometimes territory, sometimes honour, but the differences are always there and as often as not they have to do with what matters most to people; they have to do with what people live for and are prepared to die for.

In relationships between organised groupings, whether at a national or an international level, the power factor cannot be ignored. There is a tendency amongst liberal-minded people to be blind to the power factor in human affairs. This is partly because being nice liberal-minded people they conduct their personal relationships, even with subordinates, in such a way that the element of domination is minimised. They like to relate to everyone on terms approaching equality, and regard it as bad form to imply to anyone that one person in the relationship is, through wealth, status or position, superior to or in any position to control the other. It is partly too because many liberal-minded people are themselves beneficiaries of a system in which some dominate and others are dominated. This comes out well in Nadine Gordimer's novel *July's People*. Johannesburg had been taken over by black liberation forces and a white, liberal family have been rescued by their houseboy, July, and taken to his home village. The novel explores the feelings of this very decent white family as they suddenly find themselves totally dependent on someone who for the previous fifteen years has been totally dependent on them. Their new vulnerability is focused in the details of their life. For example, who should keep the keys of the Landrover with which they fled from the city, July's people, or July to whom they owe all they have including their lives? For that matter, who now owns the Landrover?

At an individual level the struggle to dominate or avoid domination can to some extent be overcome. In the social struggle, for example in the attempts by unions to achieve basic rights, or by women to overcome millennia of male domination, the power factor is very much in evidence. In the international order it is the most obvious element in relationships between states. We can urge reason, persuasion, justice — we can and must urge such considerations — but students of international affairs seem to find the clue to what is going on in the attempt by one power after another to be dominant in the international order and the attempts of other powers to avert this.

States have an ineluctable tendency to pursue their own interests. Individuals also pursue their own interests and they are, within the limits imposed by the legitimate claims of others, right to do so. But individuals can forgo their own interests if they so wish, or take risks. They can, for example, decide to dive into the sea to try and rescue someone from drowning even though it might be dangerous to do so. Nations do not and cannot take such risks. For their people elect to government (in the case of democracies) politicians whom they judge will best serve the interests of the country. They do not elect politicians who will give away the assets of the country or those who, in a hostile world, are unconcerned about defence matters.

As with individuals there is nothing wrong in itself in states pursuing their own interests. The trouble, of course, arises from the differing perceptions of what these interests are, particularly when they concern the vital matter of survival. Israel, to survive, believes it needs certain essential pieces of territory like the Golan Heights and land to the north and land to the west and a little land to the south. To others, looking from the outside, it looks like expansion. The Soviet Union, for its security, needs to ensure its influence in its satellite states, hence the oppression in Poland, Hungary, Czechoslovakia, and East Germany. The United States, for its security, is concerned that countries in Central and South America do not have Marxist regimes, hence its intervention in those areas. In all major powers there is an incipient expansionism born of legitimate security interests, fear and the will-to-power. There is a defensive/aggressive mentality that first makes borders secure and then inches those borders outwards. Nor is this the only way in which states pursue their goals. They do so through trade, and especially at the present time through the arms trade. Three-quarters of the arms in the world go to developing countries, and over 90 per cent of these arms are sold by the United States or the Soviet Union. They are inhibited from pursuing their interests by territorial conquest, and having bases abroad is more difficult than it was. But arms sales are a way of obtaining leverage in the developing world — a way that is still open.

The possibility of nuclear war will remain until the end of

time. It is a truism that nuclear weapons can never be disinvented. We cannot pretend that we do not know what we do in fact know. So even if all nuclear stockpiles were destroyed the knowledge of how to make nuclear weapons would remain. If a war broke out both sides would rush to their nuclear drawing boards and strive to be the first to make a bomb. Furthermore, the side that produced the first bomb might have no restraints on using it if the other side had not yet produced one. So it is just possible that dismantling nuclear weapons would make it more likely, not less likely, that in a future conflict nuclear weapons would be used.

Nuclear weapons cannot be disinvented nor is it cynical to suggest that it is highly unlikely that all weapons will ever be dismantled except, God forbid, after their use and the reduction of human life to the stone age again. And whatever scenario one likes to play, the threat of nuclear war remains. Suppose the West unilaterally renounced all its nuclear weapons and in due course became part of the Soviet empire? This would by no means rule out the possibility of nuclear war for we could be caught up in a great civil war, using nuclear weapons, within the Soviet empire itself.

In ethical matters, where assumptions vary so much, we can at least ask consistency of one another. In the debate on the nuclear dilemma there appear to be a number of inconsistencies. First, there are those who emphasise the value of justice and liberty in the social struggle and who will often place these above the value of peace, but who seem reluctant to give them the same importance in the international sphere. They urge the necessity of achieving peace based on justice against a tyrannical regime within a country, but sometimes do not see the necessity of achieving a similar peace based on justice against a tyrant in the international order. Reinhold Niebuhr was at one time President of the major pacifist society in America. It was when he was working as a pastor in Detroit and much involved in the struggle to get labour unionised that he became aware that justice is not achieved by relying on persuasion and goodwill. He saw that the power of capital could only be made to modify its ways if it was met by a countervailing power in the form of organised labour; as he said, 'I cut my front teeth fighting Ford.' It was this which alerted him almost before any other American to the necessity of the United States entering the war and opposing Hitler by force. The one-time pacifist became one of the leading spokesmen against American isolationism.

It is unfortunate and misleading that the debate on nuclear weapons in Britain has become polarised in political terms. There is no good reason why the Left should be unilateralist. In France it isn't. President Mitterand and the socialists, and also the Communist Party, are defenders of a policy of nuclear deterrence and supporters of an independent French system. Indeed in history it is the Left who have been most aware of the power factor in human affairs, who know that bosses don't yield just by nice talk. Consistency demands a similar awareness of the role of power in the international field and the necessity of coercion to ensure that justice is safeguarded or fostered.

The question then is, what kind of peace is possible and how is it to be attained in *this* world? That is, a world in which we seek justice and liberty as well as peace; a world in which wicked men can arise and lead whole peoples astray; a world in which there will always be radical differences of perception and interest; a world in which the power factor is always present and in which in relationships between states it is predominant; a world in which states pursue their own interests and where, we can add, there is no supra-national authority at the moment strong enough to enforce its decrees on nations which choose to flout it. How in this world, rather than in any make-believe world, this world of sovereign and suspicious states, is some kind of peace to be achieved? The Old Testament has a great longing for an age of peace, but no less does it warn its readers against a false peace. There are many reminders that people are prone to cry 'peace, peace' where there is no peace.

It would be easy to devise a form of peace for an ideal world, a world, say, in which the knowledge of how to make nuclear weapons had been conveniently forgotten. But the question we have to press is how in this real world, beautiful and brutal, recalcitrant, ruthless, yet shot through with hope, can war be avoided? We need help even to discover what it is that we should be seeking, so I like the prayer that the Corrymeela Community in Northern Ireland sometimes uses:

Show us good Lord the peace we should seek,
the peace we must give,
the peace we can keep,
the peace we must forgo,
and the peace you have given in Jesus Christ our Lord.

The traditional European, particularly the British, answer to the question of what kind of peace is possible in our world and how is it to be attained, is through a balance of power; that is through matching the military might of any potentially expansionist power with the military might of one or more other powers. This policy has not always worked; deterrence has failed; wars have broken out. Is there anything to think that the present balance of terror will succeed? There is one feature present in the current balance of power between the super-powers that has never been there before. Neither side could go to war with the other without bringing about totally unacceptable damage to itself. In the past, major powers have gone to war with the conviction that they could achieve their goal at a cost which, however horrendous, was acceptable. This is no longer true. The assured second-strike capacity of the super-powers ensures that *whatever* action one side might take the other side will retain the potential totally to devastate the mainland of its adversary. For the first time in human history war between the super-powers could under no circumstances be a rational option. Both sides know this and have admitted it publicly.

Have we then entered a nuclear Utopia, or at least a nuclear stalemate,[1] where total war between the major powers has been banished for ever? If so, then surely this is a desirable state of affairs and we must all be glad about it. Some would argue that it is not at all a desirable state of affairs because it is based upon the conditional intention to do something immoral, namely to use nuclear weapons. This was the most important argument in the report of the Church's working party *The Church and the Bomb*. Its authors argue on the basis of the just war criteria, that a policy of deterrence based upon the possession of nuclear weapons is totally immoral. I have tried to show, I hope convincingly, that the moral argument of the report simply does not stand up to analysis.[2] It remains true that a pacifist will reject a policy of nuclear deterrence but for non-pacifists it is not intrinsically immoral.

For the non-pacifist then, the final question is a practical one. Will a policy of nuclear deterrence continue to avert war between the super-powers? There is no doubt that many people who are opposed to nuclear weapons are opposed because they believe these nightmare weapons will actually be used. They think that deterrence is unstable and pre-carious; that war is bound to break out, if not next year, then sometime in the next decade. But this judgement is not shared by those who have worked at the heart of the system. Michael Quinlan has written, 'A lot of people talk as though the whole system of deterrence was desperately precarious and perhaps becoming more so. With all respect to those who deserve it, I believe this is mistaken....I do not claim certainty here; certainty is not to be had. But I do believe claims of perilous instability, of a world teetering on the brink, are neither well-founded nor helpful to peace.'[3] I have also heard Sydney Bailey, a Quaker, and one of the working party which produced the report, agree with the judgement that nuclear deterrence, at the moment, is fundamentally stable.

Shortly after the first explosion of an atomic device in the Arizona desert, Teilhard de Chardin wrote these words:

> We are told that, drunk with its own power, mankind is rushing to self-destruction, that it will be consumed in the fire it has so rashly lit. To me it seems that thanks to the atom bomb it is war, not mankind, that is destined to be eliminated, and for two reasons. The first, which we all know and long for, is that the very excess of destructive power placed in our hands must render all armed conflict impossible.[4]

The second reason he gave, that mankind would find a new unity of purpose in scientific research, has not transpired and it would be foolish to accept uncritically his first judgement. Nevertheless there is, without being complacent, a hope expressed in it that has been much neglected in the current debate over nuclear weapons.

The present nuclear stalemate is not without its cost and this must be fully reckoned with. First, because all of us, pacifist, nuclear pacifist and non-pacifist alike, accept that the worst possible evil that could afflict the world would be a major nuclear war, we are prepared to sacrifice other cherished values for this end. The West has not intervened in Hungary, Czechoslovakia, Poland or Afghanistan because to do so would probably precipitate a nuclear war. Under the nuclear umbrella injustices have taken place, injustices that we cannot afford to right. Secondly, the unceasing struggle between the two super-powers goes on in every form and place where it can take hold without actually precipitating a nuclear war. The most obvious example, as already mentioned, is in arms sales to the developing world. The nuclear stalemate does not mean the end of struggle and conflict; far from it. It ensures that ideological warfare finds new forms of power and influence.

Despite what has been said about the stability of deterrence, no morally sensitive person can remain content with the present world order for ever. The thought that our uneasy peace depends upon the conditional intention to annihilate millions of people, if the worst came to the worst, is rightly disturbing. We are clearly called to work for a world order in which international stability is achieved by more civilised means. So it is that the Pope, in pronouncing the present balance 'morally acceptable' hedges this support with qualifications: 'In current conditions...not as an end in itself but as a step on the way.' Only, in working for a world order which does not depend on the mutual threat of mutual annihilation, let us not delude ourselves that conventional war is somehow alright. Fifty million people were killed in the Second World War and far more people were killed in the conventional bombing of Japan than were killed at Hiroshima or Nagasaki. Since the Second World War there have been 140 wars in which over 10 million people have been killed. In trying to get out of the nuclear stalemate let us not move into a world of conventional killing. From the theological point of view the existence of nuclear weapons and the threat they pose is a kind of judgement. They are a continual reminder of the horrendous consequences of going to war. And when we consider the trivial reasons for which people have so often killed one another in the past — tiny patches of territory, considerations of honour and pride, and so on — it is good to be kept permanently aware that in war people, mostly innocent people, are killed. Nuclear weapons keep before us the unacceptability of war. Whatever world we manage to struggle into, let it not be a world in which conventional killing is somehow regarded as acceptable.

NOTES

1 See Neville Brown, *An Unbreakable Nuclear Stalemate*, Council for Arms Control discussion paper (available from 85 Marylebone High Street, London W1).
2 In *Christian*, vol. 7, no. 2, New Year 1983; and in *The Cambridge Review*, May 1983.

3   *The Tablet*, 18 July 1981.
4   Teilhard de Chardin, *The Future of Man* (Collins, 1964), p. 146–7.

People and the Bomb

JOHN AUSTIN BAKER

The publication of *The Church and the Bomb*, the report of the working party set up by the Church of England's Board for Social Responsibility, was one of the factors which during 1982 stimulated the present intense public debate. Had the report not included, in addition to nineteen non-controversial recommendations, three that provoked angry criticism in some quarters it would have done little to help forward that valuable result. But what has emerged from the debate so far?

First, I think that in the area of ethics the report raised at least five basic questions which will not go away. We all need to face them honestly.

1   Are there some weapons so dreadful that it could never be right to use them?

In fact some nations say 'yes' to this question, because they have signed, for example, a document outlawing germ warfare. Nuclear weapons are not just more devastating versions of ordinary weapons, like TNT and napalm, which are horrible enough in all conscience and getting worse. Nuclear weapons have three extra features: they inevitably harm the innocent, even in distant lands not involved in the war, by long-term fallout; they poison the environment by irradiating earth and water; and they strike at those yet unborn by genetic damage. Can we honestly say that we ought ever to use such things, whatever the danger of provocation?

2   Can it ever be right to threaten to do something it would be wrong actually to do?

In ordinary life we say 'no' to this one. It is all right to say to a child, 'If you do that again, Mummy will smack you.' It is not all right to say, 'If you do that, Mummy will never speak to you again.' In adult life, we accept laws which threaten the wrongdoer with fine or imprisonment, but we have abolished flogging and would not contemplate mutilation — not because these are heavier penalties, but because they are wrong in themselves, and therefore we cannot use even the threat of them to deter the criminal. We have to find other ways to defend ourselves. Why should we abandon this principle when it comes to national defence?

3   Do we have different standards for judging our enemy and ourselves?

Human experience gives an almost invariable 'yes' to this one. It is the hardest thing in the world to be fair to the motives and intentions of someone who dislikes us, or whom we dislike, a competitor at work, a sarcastic or bullying colleague. Fear or hate makes us read in one way something done by them, in another the same thing done by ourselves. The Soviets' huge military expenditure 'proves' that they are intent on world conquest, given the chance; but the West's equally huge expenditure 'proves' only our determination to safeguard peace. How can we overcome this built-in bias and learn to assess the world objectively?

4   Why is it right for us to have nuclear weapons, but wrong for Brazil, Israel, Pakistan and others?

Many countries signed the non-proliferation treaty saying they would not acquire nuclear weapons, provided those nations that had them reduced their stocks and finally got rid of them altogether. We among others also signed and promised to do this. Since then the nuclear stockpile has grown enormously. Any argument that justifies these weapons for us can also logically justify them for any other nation that feels threatened. If we want to prevent their spread, ought we not to do something at least to cut our own?

5 Can the values we believe in ever be defended by nuclear weapons?

Freedom and human dignity under just laws justly executed are a priceless blessing. Hardly any of us would willingly change our way of life, with all its faults, for the harsh and corrupt tyranny of the Soviet Union. But can our way of life be defended by visiting tens of millions of people with a cruel and lingering death? If we say 'yes', are we not admitting that, in the last analysis, people don't matter to us. If we can even contemplate inflicting nuclear horror, have we not already abandoned the values we claim to cherish?

The report also drew attention to some major areas of Christian theology which are essential to the forming of a Christian mind on this subject. They are: humankind's God-given responsibility for the world we live in, and for all its creatures; the need for realism in moral decision-making; the true nature of peace, which is far more than the mere absence of war; and the moral theology of war limitation, which is a description I myself prefer to the more usual phrase 'the doctrine of the just war'. Since the report appeared, it has been pointed out that there are other areas which need equal investigation: God's control of history; the biblical teaching about the end of the world; the depth and character of human sinfulness; and the teaching of Jesus Christ about non-violence (only partly covered in the report's analysis of pacifism). It will be a great step forward if Christians can pool their thinking — much of which has already been done, for example, by the Churches in the USA — on these subjects, and apply the result to the weapons problem.

One other very contentious area is that usually labelled 'the theology of power'. Here I have the feeling that we approach the most sensitive issue of all, the degree to which

Christian living can legitimately be conformed to the wisdom of the world. In this field much more work still needs to be done.

Finally, a word should be said about the logical basis of a document such as the report. As I see it, we came to a conclusion about nuclear weapons, their possession and use or threatened use, in the light of Christian faith and morals, namely, that they were unacceptable. This conclusion, if it commended itself, might as it stands be of help to an individual Christian in deciding about personal involvement with or protest against nuclear arms. But such a conclusion could never be more than the first stage in framing a policy to be suggested to a secular state.

The way forward which the report took was to say that if nuclear weapons are not morally acceptable, then it is of the first urgency to get rid of them. What would be the safest way of doing that, and the one most likely to succeed? Contrary to the popular impression given by the media and never eradicated, we did not advocate unilateral disarmament. The report recommended a modest unilateral reduction by the West, which would not in any way endanger security. We accepted that the nuclear deterrent had played a part in keeping the peace since 1945. What we urged strongly was that new developments were steadily eroding the stability of the present equilibrium, and that it could not last for ever. Balanced force reduction had not so far delivered the goods. Had not the time come for independent initiatives which were carefully calculated not to tempt anyone to the gamble of war?

I still firmly believe that this idea has not been defeated by argument. It has only been distorted by misrepresentation. That this has happened is partly our own fault. The Archbishop of Canterbury in the General Synod debate put his finger on the weakest point in the report, which was a failure to get to grips with the internal dynamics of NATO, and with the need to modify the nuclear weapons policy of the alliance as a whole, not just that of one member state.

Nothing has been said to change my personal conviction that an initiative by the West could usefully take the form of removing one nation from the world nuclear weapons line-up. But that result must be achieved by a different route from the one we suggested; and if that particular form of initiative cannot be agreed, yet substantial independent cuts by NATO as an alliance would still be of inestimable value.

In the end, disarmament has to be general. No one disputes that. But the question which more than any other those in power in East and West always evade is this: why do you cling to the theory that nuclear deterrence demands parity in weapons, when this is demonstrably and patently false? Nations do not need to match system for system, megaton for megaton, in order to deter. All that is needed is three things: sufficient power to inflict unacceptable damage; a reliable delivery system; and one that is invulnerable to a pre-emptive strike. Given these three requirements, everything else is superfluous. Where then is the risk in independent disarmament initiative? There is none. What they do offer is the chance of transforming the international atmosphere by a serious move away from the brink. I am certain that before long an alternative consensus will emerge along these lines to challenge the present establishment thinking in both East and West, and that such a consensus offers the best hope for the people of the world today.

But what about Russia?

LORD MACLEOD

An everlasting discussion now goes on in countless British homes as to whether unilateralism should not be the choice of Christians as we face the escalating arms race. It seems it should be, if only by the knowledge that in the Third World someone dies of starvation every fifteen seconds. But every fifteen seconds also, the nations of the world are spending £75,000 preparing for the next war — a war the experts assure us, neither side can possibly win. As no less a person than a recent Defense Secretary of the USA publicly declared: 'We shall fight with conventional weapons till we are losing; then we will fight with nuclear weapons till we are losing; then we will blow up the world.'

Thus and thus goes the conversation in so many homes. But more often than not, it ends by someone muttering 'But what about Russia?' and the conversation then moves to another subject altogether.

Well then, what about Russia?

I dare to attempt a short answer, because recently I have been to Russia twice, as I hold honorary office in the Christian Peace Council with its headquarters in Prague. It was inaugurated by the Eastern Orthodox Church as permitted by the hierarchy that is now the central government of Russia in Moscow. Twice this government (and not the Russian Church) paid my fare from Edinburgh to Moscow, via Prague, and back, and paid for my hotel accomodation everywhere, to hold conference with the government (and not the Church) officials.

'Ah, yes,' I can hear some readers say, 'that is the cunning way they do these things.' Then they add, 'That same Russian government also gives contributions to CND in Britain. It is the Russians' way of keeping Britain quiet.'

But, apart from the fact that the Russian government has never given a penny to CND, dare I ask you what the end result is going to be if we insist that Russia is deceiving us every time she uses smooth words? If we are for ever thus to scorn them, what can the end result be for both sides, other than nuclear war, or world bankruptcy? Is the Christian Church never to trust her enemy? Is Christ's commandment that we *must* trust them something for us to disregard? If so, we should stop saying the Lord's Prayer if we do not believe that 'His is the power.' If we are obedient, He will work things out for us.

I trust Russia. And we must be telegraphic in our answers:

Communist Russia is not faring well, agriculturally or industrially. After over sixty years of agricultural dictatorship, she cannot, despite her vast territories, grow enough maize to feed her people — she has to buy it from the USA. Nor can she produce enough butter — she has to buy that from her Western capitalist neighbours. Industrially, she cannot manufacture enough steel to build a pipe-line running from her capitalist neighbours as far as Moscow!

Again, Russia is not gaining followers in the rest of the world. Britain, for instance, has very few members to make up its Communist Party — some 30,000 out of millions of electors with alternative solutions. In a Scottish by-election early 1983, in a district where the Labour Party won the seat, the Communist Party lost its deposit.

In China, running hundreds of miles along Russia's eastern border, the Chinese have tried communism in vain, and are now seeking another style of government to appeal to its 1,000 million population.

Internally, the dictatorship of the proletariat has never come about. A dictatorial hierarchy is still in power, but can no longer afford to be truly dictatorial. They still do not allow independent groups to grow up such as CND. Such would be ruled out of order, but unorganised groups — such as millions of women — are secretly attracted to what they know the CND stands for.

Again, in the Stalinist period, dreadful were the persecutions of the Church, and many of the Eastern Orthodox clergy disappeared. But religion is now tacitly admitted: while the bishops of the Eastern Orthodox Church and the clergy of the Baptist Church are allowed to worship openly; and indeed are used by the hierarchy to further their hopes for peace, as I shall show in the final paragraphs of this article.

The Russians are far more afraid of the Chinese than they are of the USA or NATO. They are well aware that if they rushed their nuclear forces to combat the Western world, their eastern borders might well be invaded by China.

There is sufficient evidence of the constancy with which they have tried to convince America and the West of their efforts to prove the sincerity of their desire for peace. However, it is reasonable to ask, have our daily papers given prominence to most of their efforts? In the light of their reporting how justified is Russia to be exasperated when President Reagan introduces the MX missile system?

Finally, in the Spring of 1982, did you see any reference at all in the British press to the remarkable four-day conference held in Moscow? Representatives of ninety nations, covering many different faiths, met under the title 'World Conference: Religious Workers for Saving the Sacred Gift of Life from Nuclear Tragedy' from 10—14 May 1982, at the invitation of the Russian Orthodox Church. Five hundred and ninety eminent representatives of Buddhism, Christianity, Hinduism, Islam, Judaism, Sikhism, Shintoism and Zoroastrianism met to discuss 'in a spirit of brotherly co-operation the ways and means for strenghtening the contribution of the religious people of the world towards erecting an insurmountable barrier on the road to nuclear war and thus saving the sacred gift of life.'

The conference was held at the initiative of His Holiness Pimen, Patriarch of Moscow and all Russia. Messages of greeting were received from His Holiness Pope John Paul II, His Holiness the Dalai Lama, His Grace Archbishop Runcie of Canterbury. Several heads of government also sent messages. The International Fellowship of Reconciliation was represented by its President Ronald Beasley (a member of the Iona Community). The USA declined to be represented, but Dr Billy Graham, nevertheless, was present and was a prominent speaker. The conference was officially received by the hierarchy of all Russia.

Is it conceivable that all this could take place in Moscow if the hierarchy was secretly opposed to peace and disarmament? No! the Russian people are as human as we are. After all, in the Second World War when they were our allies against the Nazis, the Russians lost no less than 20 million soldiers. There is now hardly a home in the land which did not lose a relative or a near neighbour. Russia is as keen for disarmament now as any other government in the world.

The Simplicity of Death and the Complexities of Life

DAVID JENKINS

It has always been very well known that not a single one of us has an earthly chance of a future. This knowledge is kept pretty well at bay by most of us most of the time. But it is quite clear that we shall all, severally, die. What difference, then, does it make when it becomes publicly clear that there is a possibility of our all dying together, in a limited time span, in the immediate or near future? On the face of it, it makes a hell of a difference. First, it sets the fact of our fragile mortality firmly and frequently before us. Secondly, it threatens to deprive us of even a vicarious and quasi-immortality. There may well be no future for us to contribute to and no one to remember us, or to remember those who remember us. Thirdly, we face the monstrous possibility not just of universal death (*sic*) but of a period of totally inhumane and utterly hopeless dying, with all life-supports broken down. Finally, we are confronted with the obscene absurdity that by a human act all the rich and joyful possibilities which have been discovered and which might be discovered for those who live as long as they live, are likely to be blotted out once and for all. None the less, we may still reflect that in the not very long run life is like that. One day, and in any case, on this planet earth there will be none of us and none like us. Perhaps the bomb simply throws into stark relief what it is really like to be alive and to know that you die.

But clearly the bomb does more than this. It confronts us not only with the fact that we die, but also with the fact that we bring about death. Like the fact of our dying this is something which has long been obvious but which is usually ignored. Setting aside man's death-dealing activities throughout recorded history we may concentrate on our current 'achievements'. The modern use and abuse of motor cars, modern life-styles with their mental stress and obesity, modern pollution all bring premature death to millions. Routine wars and preventible famines kill millions more. The investment of limited resources in armaments and the over-production of consumer goods in certain parts of the world prevent possible developments in health care and agricultural growth, and leave innumerable fellow human beings to unrelieved misery and early death. Thus as human beings in history we both live under the threat of death and are ourselves the promoters of death. Now that the United States and Russia each possess, and have ready for use, means of destruction which are many times more than sufficient to kill us all in Britain and the rest of Western Europe and to let loose radiation clouds which have a fair chance of killing most, if not all, human life throughout the earth, it is publicly, universally and, so to speak, statistically clear as a mere and sheer matter of fact that we human beings are not only mortal but also mortally sinful. Our use of our fragile, insecure and temporary living is, as often as not, to promote death. We can kill, we do kill, and there is now a serious possibility that we shall kill, to the limits of life.

But generalisations about a 'we' which embraces the whole human race seem of singularly little use to any particular 'us', who are looking for concrete, urgent and possibly hopeful responses to this present and pressing threat. Surely menaces produced by men and women can be countered by men and women? It does not seem so. The problem is that while there is only one human race, nobody is organised to live like that, particular groups of 'we's' when organised for power and practice have never behaved like that, and there are few signs of any immediately available set of ideas and programmes to which enough people (and especially powerful people) are likely to turn in time. Neither past history nor present omens offer much to suggest that we have a reasonable chance of beginning to practise what the unity of the human race in life, mortality and sin now so clearly requires. All of us together (the human race) and each of us in our particularities (family, tribe, nation, group, class, ideological or religious tradition) would seem to have little chance of survival.

Might our chance as human beings, however, lie in the fact that it is now publicly and generally obvious that we do not have much of a chance? The simple and urgent threat of death could help us and compel us into new ways of getting to grips with the complexities of life. The threat of a last chance might really give us a good chance, if we can see it and grasp it. Certainly those of us who believe in God and hold that the records and stories of the Bible are authentic sources of validly revealing insights into the possibilities of men and women, the world and the Transcendence within us, around us and beyond us, could well interpret our present predicament in this way. For the message of God has always been 'Except ye repent, ye shall all likewise perish', and the purpose of God is held to be focused by and in that Jesus who, in the Gospel according to John, is portrayed as saying 'The thief comes only to steal, to kill, to destroy; I have come that men may have life, and may have it in all its fullness' (John 10:10). In the purpose of God therefore a threat of destruction is meant to be received as a compelling demand to turn from death-dealing to life-seeking. A last chance in the face of deadly things is always present in such a way that it can be turned into a good chance of better things by repentance.

From the time of the first great prophets of Israel onwards, however, it has been plain that religious and moral demands on their own have never been sufficient to turn a society or group of any size from developing destructive ways to pursuing constructive ones. Repentance is an insight and an offering of the few. The redirection and replanning of the many in a society, or of the whole of a society, comes about, if at all, through a bewildering and inextricable mixture of some creative moral and religious insights with the pressures of prudential self-interest, fear and force. This is why so much discussion about 'the morality of the bomb' seems so oddly forced or irrelevant. The problems are not whether the possession of thermonuclear weapons is 'immoral' or in what ways it is immoral, but how we are to prevent their going-off, and what chance we have of this. Moral clarity and agreement may assist in this prevention. There seems no sufficient reason to assume that it would achieve it. In a somewhat similar way the basic 'theological' problem posed by the present state of thermonuclear weaponry is not what bits and pieces Christians (and other theists) can contribute to the common task of the prevention of nuclear war but what it might authentically mean to believe in God in a world which has produced our present predicament. On the face of it the threat we are under makes nonsense of morality and absurdity of belief in God.

But this may not be so. Perhaps what 'the bomb' makes clear, in a way hitherto unequalled in human history, is that the responsibility of morality and the issue of faith in God are, quite simply and literally, matters of life and death. There is a universal purpose and hope to be discerned, precisely in our present predicament. The purpose of our being confronted, in a purely secular and statistical way, with the realities of sin and of death is that we may respond collectively to overwhelming pressures to work out those forms of political and practical rethinking (secular, prudential and social 'repentance') which can contribute to survival and creative life. And herein is hope, for many things more than morality and religion conspire to force us to newness. In this we may be right to discern the power and presence of God who is far more than any one system, apprehension or expression of morality or religion can contain.

The very clear threat of total moral nonsense and absolute human absurdity makes clear the terrible but still hopeful reality of what it is like to be in the image of God but not God. We are mortal but we have powers of life and death. Our freedom and our responsibility are god-like but we are not able to handle them on our own. We are 'as gods' but we are not God. Our last chance, therefore, can become a good chance of better things if, by a mixture of sacrifice, insight, calculating prudence and fear we can be somewhat enticed and greatly forced into learning and exercising a dependent godliness.

Dependent godliness is marked by four things. First it enables unquenchable hope. The last word on our human enterprise does not lie with ourselves but with the God who is more than ourselves, however much He has risked His very being, by being committed to our enterprises of freedom, responsibility and consequent sin. Secondly, it emphasises the possibilities and demands of our responsibility and freedom deeply compromised and questionable though they are. The absolute monstrosity of thermonuclear weapons must neither terrify us into apathy nor anaesthetise us into acceptance and a cowardly hoping against hope. Thirdly, it requires us to work out our responsibilities through a realism which fully and painfully appreciates the limits on the possibilities of political negotiation, agreement and control. We are all potentially destructive and dangerous sinners, especially when organised into groups, classes and nations who live largely by their own fantasies and partial truths. We have no grounds therefore for expecting (still less relying on) miracles of conversion and transformation. We may hope and work for miracles of patience, survival and the creation of yet one more chance. Fourthly, it relativises all ideologies, aims and commitments because godly dependence recognises that the only valid absolutes are God and human beings when they have the grace to be truly like God. Everything else is a temporary, partial and corruptible means to more or less questionable ends, themselves subordinate to the possibilities of continuing our human living and subject to modification and rejection.

Our greatest and most practical hope probably lies in the way in which the single and simple threat of death relativises the ways in which we face the multiple and complex issues of life. We may thus be set free to treat seriously but not absolutely the dangerous polarisations which threaten us by insisting that at all costs, 'we' are right and 'they' are wrong — that the West (or the East) contains all that is bad (or good). This is plainly blasphemous nonsense which is a form of making an absolute idol out of a fantasy like 'capitalism' or 'communism'. Now it is clear that we must all live together or else we shall all die together (some with merciful abruptness and some in a dreadful lingering). Thus it becomes clear that all political programmes have, as a priority, to enable survival and then an equally pressing requirement to work out ways by which it is less and less necessary to concentrate on survival alone and more and more possible to work for more expansive ends.

But first we must be clear that there is no 'right way' either of being a human community or state or of working towards the easing of the death threat we live under. That is to say there is no ideal way which guarantees the achievement of properly desirable ends nor a way which can be justified as 'righteous' (whether by canons of communism, capitalism, Christianity, Islam, scientific humanism, pacifism, or what you will). Everything must be potentially negotiable and flexible. At the same time, however, we must maintain a proper respect for and a proper loyalty to our commitments, visions and hopes. The necessity to negotiate and compromise in no way undermines the imperative to maintain long-term commitments to the increase of opportunities for freedom, justice and welfare. What dependent godliness does is to warn us not to be too sure that 'our' way of seeing things and doing things is necessarily in all aspects better then 'theirs' or that 'they' have no case. This does not involve any simple-minded trust. There is no realistic way forward which permits us to ignore the realities and inevitabilities of conflict, at both the pragmatic and the moral levels. Empires have always contended for power and influence, whatever ideological excuses or interpretations have been offered. There are also real and deep conflicts over what is involved in 'the good life' and there are serious grounds for abhorrence of what is done in the name of communism. Whatever criticisms are necessarily to be made against ourselves, the situation is not indifferent. It is quite clear that communism breeds totalitarianism and that totalitarianism is an evil to be resisted. So romantic acts of trust are no substitute for resoluteness in practicable self-defence. Trust is not a useful political virtue. But distrust must not be allowed to dominate political judgement.

It is literally 'vital' (a matter of life and death) to be able to appreciate the point of view of those whom we have real reasons both to distrust and to resist. Our opponents have a serious point of view. It is really held. It has much to be said for at least some of it. And they are clearly seriously threatened. Like us they are human beings trapped in a deeply threatening world. It is one world and we have all contributed to its threatening nature by various versions of idealism, sin and indifference. Dependent godliness should tend to set us free from turning possibly dangerous and to some extent wicked human beings into malignant and all-powerful demons, just as it should prevent us seeing ourselves as righteous angels of light. The task is to survive together so that we live together, and out of this living together to look for ways forward. We have to face up to the simple threat of death and in the light of this to negotiate our way through the complexities of life.

Some of the practical considerations which arise from the arguments and programme outlined above include the following. First, there is no sufficient case for Britain's retaining an 'independent deterrent'. It obscures our actual and total dependence on the wider US and NATO alliances. The case for having our own deterrent looks like a false and dangerous fantasy produced by that sort of independent and aggressive nationalism which is precisely one of the main contributors to the threat of death which faces us all. Arguments about and efforts for maintaining our deterrent distract attention from our main and vital concern for policies of survival and then reconciliation. And the waste of resources in the face of our local as well as global poverty is monstrous. Secondly, we have nevertheless to retain our membership of NATO and the process of giving up our own deterrent must be part of negotiations within that alliance. There can be no substitute for continuing, uncertain and compromising negotiations. There is no magic or miraculous stroke which will, overnight, multiply the chances of peace. Peace is a possibility derived from costly, hopeful and faithful persistence deriving from a realisitic awareness both of the threats and the possibilities.

Thirdly, everyone must be constantly reminded that the two overriding pressures upon us are the threat of death and the necessity of having to live together. The overriding aim of arms negotiations therefore is the prevention of war not the prevention of victory by the other side or the achievement of victory by our own. The immediate prize to be aimed at is survival and the opportunity to live together in the hope of better things. This means, for example, that negotiations about arms limitations must be based on *quid pro quos* about arms restrictions and inspections. Extraneous demands concerning such matters as human rights or withdrawal of influence from this country or that are not part of negotiating improvements in our chances of survival. They are separate matters to pursue as we survive.

Fourthly, on a broader front, more and more attention should be concentrated on the issues of economy and poverty. The relativising of our ideologies under the threat of death ought to help us to see that we do not have a crisis of capitalism with a saving communism waiting in the wings. We have a total human industrial and economic crisis with the communist countries sharing in the crisis of production and all of us without either the means or the will to organise ourselves to share resources effectively in a way which will also multiply resources and at the same time protect the earth. A principal prudential reason therefore for negotiating arms reductions and mutual systems of control is the crippling burden of cost. Neither the US nor Russia can much longer afford the consumption of such huge resources and nor can the rest of us. The waste of such resources is also a moral obscenity in the face of so much poverty that, probably, we might well deserve to destroy ourselves. But dependent godliness sees this as one more way in which pressures of self-interest and fear could come together with such moral insights and hope as we can muster to move us in a creative and morally desirable direction. For the same reason we must encourage continuing work with enthusiasm on all possible fronts and not become single-issue dominated. The fear of death must not become panic and hysteria in the face of the threat or tensions will be further heightened and possibilities of negotiation and manoeuvre further limited. Every negotiation, pressure group or campaign for wider welfare, justice or freedom is a worthwhile contribution to the human struggle for sufficient peace to enable survival, growth and search. As the bomb makes it clear that we must live together it may also free us to find better and more just ways of living together. Thus our last chance may still be our best chance.

The Heart of the Gospel

LORD SOPER

Nothing is more important than the issue of armed violence in general, and the nuclear arms race in particular. Moreover the capability possessed by modern weapons gives unprecedented urgency to the problem of avoiding a holocaust, for the world and everybody in it may well be in a terminal condition. Apocalypse was hitherto solely in God's hands. Now we possess a do it yourself kit. Therefore the widest dissemination of factual evidence about this crisis must be welcomed, and prosecuted with all speed; for we may not have much time left. This volume will, no doubt, provide a stock of such information to shock the indifferent into concern, and to correct the manifest nonsense that is being spread alike by the arms manufacturers and those politicians and propagandists who are either their tools or their sponsors. Others contributing to this document may demonstrate, as I believe they can, how foolish are the arguments that support the arms race and the need for the bomb. It may well be shown that in fact, those who 'take the sword perish by the sword'. Reason and logic are progressively occluded when once the so-called 'balance of terror' is involved, and so increasingly the future becomes a mindless hazard.

I could presume to add two considerations to this vital question and they both spring from the Christian faith

I endeavour to cherish and advocate. The first is this: mass violence is always inevitably wrong. There is no such thing as a just war, and the emergence of nuclear weapons only reinforces the argument that the Way of the Cross can never be pursued with a gun. The risk of taking the Christian road of pacifism is understandably great, but the risk of rejecting that road in the interests of so-called realism is much worse — in fact such a rejection contains the seeds of a total abandonment of the teaching and spirit of Jesus Christ.

The second follows as a necessary piece of theology. The responsibility of the would-be Christian, bidden to walk in the steps of the Prince of Peace, is first and above all to be obedient, rather than to endeavour to modify the Gospel in the interests of what he imagines to be practical politics. Obedience is the opening of the door to God's power. That is what the Sermon on the Mount says. God can use our obedience today to transform the situation tomorrow.

This is a tremendous affirmation. If it is true, as I believe it is, then all our prognostications about what will happen (if, for instance, we totally disarm won't the Russians be over next week, etc.?) can be transformed in an environment of obedience, while the failure to obey projects into the future the kind of fear and mistrust that poisons the present. This is, as I see it, the heart of the Gospel and therefore the programme of peacemaking.

The Epilogue?

PETER MULLEN

And it came to pass that he went into the region round Westminster and even unto the house which is called Church House. And there came unto him certain which were of the Synod and entreated him saying, 'What think ye Master, is it lawful to ban the bomb or no?'

And he answered and spake unto them and said, 'Ye know the commandment which saith thou shalt not kill. How readest thou? What thinkest thou?' And they say, 'Master, that is an hard saying and we cannot tell what it signifieth: for the prophet which is called Baker saith that verily the bomb is an hindrance, but our Patriarch Leonard hath spoken darkly unto the people saying that behold it happeneth there is greater evil in casting away the bomb than that which cometh from keeping it withal. Pray, teach us the right way that we may walk in it.'

And he began to speak unto them, teaching them, saying 'Ye know the bomb and its power, that there is nothing like unto it in all the earth and that great shall be the destruction it bringeth upon the earth even unto the end of the whole earth? Why tempt ye me therefore with these questions? What meanest thou?'

Then they that were of the Multilateral Party, which was of the company of Margaret and Leonard, opened their mouths and denied not but confessed, 'We perceive that

SALT hath lost its savour and behold an enemy raiseth up mighty megatons against us to destroy us, even to make altogether an end of us. Except, beholding our bomb and its power, he durst not do this evil for he is affrighted lest we might haply do unto him as he would do unto us.'

And behold he was angered and spake unto them saying, 'Wouldst thou cast out the bomb by the power of the bomb? And how sayest thou unto thine enemy, Come let us cast the megatons out of thine arsenals! Cast out first the megatons which are in thine own arsenals and then thou shalt see clearly to cast out the megatons that are thine enemy's.'

And it grieved their spirit and one of them which was of Leonard's party saith unto him, 'Master, we grieve not for ourselves but for our kinsfolk and our children and the stranger that is within our gate, that except we do gird up our megatons and the strength of our might, an enemy should loose destruction upon these which are without guile and which have committed no offence.'

And he waxed the more wrathful and upbraided them saying, 'Thou hypocrite! Behold thine enemy, that he also hath kinsfolk and children. And are there not strangers within his gate which also are without guile and innocent of great offence? Wouldst thou destroy them in the name of the commandment? And I say not unto thee for thy children's sakes only and for the sake of thine enemy's children, but for thy and thine enemy's children's children even unto the third and fourth generation which should suffer unto death if these things be loosed upon the earth.'

And they were pricked in their hearts and they cried out against him saying, 'This man is an enemy and blasphemeth!'

And they would have made away with him. But he withstood them and said, 'Get thee hence, for I perceive that in all things thou seemest holy and would fein make long prayers in palaces made by men's hands, but in thine heart thou rejectest the counsels of God and in thy deeds thou makest them to be of none effect.'

And they say again, 'He blasphemeth the temple that is

called Westminster! Now are we assured that he is an enemy!'

And he saith unto them, 'Love thine enemies.' When they heard this saying, they began to take counsel among themselves how they might put him to death.

Index

Adolfs, Robert 192
Afghanistan, Russian occupation
  of 11, 16, 26, 30, 72
Alliance, Liberal–SDP 161
  clergy support for 98–9
Andrews, Donald Hatch 145
antinomianism, secular 116–19,
  120, 122–4, 127–8
  and principle of love 131,
  135–6
arms race, nuclear 30, 38–40, 43,
  62–4, 67–8, 70, 150–2, 154,
  160, 236
arms reduction, negotiated ix, 16,
  21–2, 26–7, 42–3, 64–6,
  68–9, 81–2, 150, 161–3,
  203, 234–5
arms trade 40, 148–9, 154, 210,
  215
Aspect, Alain 145
Augustine of Hippo, St 93–4, 197

Baelz, Peter (Dean of Durham) 11
Bailey, Sydney 23, 214
Baker, J. Austin xi, 15–17, 19,
  21–6, 28, 101–2, 104–5,
  159, 238
balance:
  of power 189–90, 194, 213
  and Russian threat to Western
    Europe 2–3, 75–7
  of weapons x–xi, 9, 12, 24,
    36, 40, 182, 221–2, 236

Batovrin, Sergei 46
Bell, G. K. A. (Bishop of
  Chichester) 95
Blake, William 36, 146
Blanch, Stuart 121
Bohm, David 142, 144–6
Bowie, David 116–17
Brezhnev, Leonid 40
Britain:
  American nuclear bases in 6–7,
    18, 42–3, 68, 106, 125–6,
    135, 154, 161
  independent nuclear weapons 29,
    33, 62, 172, 234
  military build-up 39, 67–8
Brown, Peter 93–4
Bultmann, Rudolf 166–7, 169
Bush, George 135

Cameron, James 153
Campaign for Nuclear Disarmament (CND) 17–18, 21–2
  40, 42, 46, 126, 235,
  224–5
  on deterrence 24
  unilateralism and multi-
    lateralism 14, 70, 156–7
  see also peace movement
Capra, Fritjof 145
Carter, Jimmy 161–2
Carver, Lord 43, 80
Chardin, Teilhard de 215

Christianity:
  alternative tradition 85, 91—3, 95
  on arms and force 7—8, 85, 101—2, 236—7
  and clerical opinions 95—100
  established Churches 85, 93—8, 101
  and political order 85—91, 92, 93, 103—6
  political theology 100—1, 102
  secularised 110—11, 113, 127, 132
  symbolic models of 127—37
  and unilateralism 19, 23, 110
  see also theology
Church and the Bomb, The (report) viii, x, xi, 10—11, 15—17, 19, 21—4, 28, 33, 172—9, 181—2, 183—5, 187, 214, 218—22
  attitude to USSR 16—17, 24—6, 192
Church of England 10—11, 98, 172
  Synod 1983 viii, 10, 29, 31, 121, 153, 181—2
Churchill, Sir Winston 17
civil defence, inadequacies of, 47, 59, 149
coexistence, peaceful 57—8
Collins, John 105
Conservative Party 101, 159—61
  clergy support for 99
cost:
  of conventional forces 32
  of nuclear weapons 10, 32, 54—5, 160, 223, 235
Council for Arms Control ix, 27
Cruise missiles 16, 36, 48, 68, 16, 36, 48, 68, 125—6, 134—6, 152, 157, 162

crusade, doctrine of 198
Cupitt, Don 96

Dahrendorf, Ralf 207
death, threat of 227—9, 232—5
  and last chance 229—31, 235
defence strategies, alternative 66, 68—9, 203
  conventional 30, 32—3, 81, 107, 159
Dekker, Gerard 99—100
democracy:
  defence of 101
  and possession of nuclear weapons viii, 10
deterrence, nuclear weapons as form of 36, 43, 201, 212—15
  abandonment of 18, 234
  British 33, 54—5, 98, 101, 176—7
  denied 4, 6
  effectiveness of 24, 31—2, 55—6, 59—60, 78—91, 151—3, 158—9, 185, 221, 239
  erosion of 63—5
  morality of 24, 101, 105, 173—7, 181—2, 183—96, 214
Dickens, Charles 108, 112—14, 115—16, 119, 132
Duke, Michael Hare 103—4

education, role of 69—71, 236
Einstein, A. 141—5
Eisenhower, Dwight 25, 202
Eppler, Erhard 40
European Nuclear Disarmament, committee for (END) 45, 158, 162—3

Falkland Islands 4–5, 9, 66, 91,
94–5, 97–9, 106, 124–7,
131, 198, 208
fatalism 120, 199
fear 121–2
exploitation of 9–10, 15–16,
44
first use 55, 80–1
repudiated ix, 10, 27–34, 65,
69, 78, 181–2, 204
first-strike weapons 63, 152
Flessati, Valerie 109, 135
flexible response, doctrine of ix,
59, 77–8, 82–3
France, independent nuclear
weapons of 4, 9, 33, 65,
106, 160, 212

Geneva negotiations 66, 82, 156
Gillen, Ian 113, 115
Golding, William 207–8
Gordimer, Nadine 209
Gorshkov, Admiral 73, 74–5
Graham, Billy 165, 167, 169, 226
Greenham Common, women's
peace camp 109, 134–6,
152, 157, 161
Healey, Denis 82
Helsinki agreement 26, 73–4, 158
heroism 111–14, 122–7, 130
Heseltine, Michael 136, 160–1
Hinsley, F. H. ix, 31
Hoban, Russell 170
Hockaday, Sir Arthur 184
holograph:
human brain as 146
universe experienced as 144–5
hope, Christian 26–7, 231–2,
235
Howard, Michael 191–3
Hungarian Peace Council 46–7,
103
Huzzard, Ron 152

Illyes, Gulya 35–6
images:
apocalyptic 121–2, 165–70
Biblical x, 130–3
feminine 109, 127, 134–5
masculine 122–7, 133
popular 110–37
prophetic 168–71
of quantum physics 144–6
scientific 141–4
individualism, Western 89, 101,
111–16, 119–23, 125–7,
130, 136

Jam, the 113–14, 117–18, 126
John Paul II 10, 24, 27, 216, 226
Jung, C. G. 166–71
just war, theory of 94–5, 100,
131, 173, 184, 197–9,
201, 204, 214, 219, 236

Kant, Immanuel 61
Kennan, George 202
Kent, Mgr Bruce 135
Kitwood, Tom 119

Labour Party 42
clergy support for 99
and morality of nuclear
weapons 10
and Western Alliance 18, 158
land-based weapons 9, 68
Lennon, John 113, 114, 116,
135–6
Leonard, Graham x, 13, 238–9
Levin, Bernard 133
Levinson, Charles 147
Liberal Party, and morality of
nuclear weapons 10
Ligeti, Gyorgy 170
limited war, concept of 24, 54,
95
nuclear 29, 42, 59–60, 78, 82

Longley, Clifford 33—4
loyalty, group 91, 111, 116, 123, 136
Luckmann, Thomas 111

MacFarlane, Alan 114
McLaren, Malcolm 112
Mahler, Gustav 169—70
Marley, Bob 116
Martin, Bernice ix—x, 171
Martin, Laurence 80
Matheson, Donald 153
Messiah, symbol of 122, 129—30
Mitterand, François 106, 212
Mlynar, Zdenek 40
Montefiori, Hugh (Bishop of Birmingham) 29
morality ix, x, 6—7, 8, 98, 102, 107, 172—9, 181, 218—21, 230
    of dependence on US weapons 18, 104—5
    of deterrence 24, 101, 105, 157, 173—7, 181, 183—96, 214
    and government action 190—4
    morally acceptable and morally good 186—8, 193, 216
    and 'no first use' 28—30, 33—4, 182
    of peace campaign 10, 15, 42, 103—4
    of war 197, 199—201, 204—5
multilateralism 11, 27, 203, 238—9
    and unilateralism ix, 14, 62, 64—71, 156—63
multinational companies x, 147
    and arms race 148—9
    economic influence of 147—8, 150
    and risk of nuclear war 150—5
    and Soviet bloc 150—2
MX missiles 10, 36, 64, 225

NATO 50—1, 73, 150, 162, 181—2, 221—2
    and defence of Western Europe 75—82
    first use of nuclear weapons 28, 77—8, 80
    membership of, and British unilateralism viii, 18, 21—2, 158—9, 172, 234
    and 'no first use' policy 29—33
    nuclear capability 24, 38—9
neutralism 17—18
neutron bomb 162
Niebuhr, Reinhold 101, 211—12
non-proliferation treaty 26, 64, 219
Novak, Michael 101
'nuclear-free zones' 47—8, 64—6, 68, 163
nuclear weapons:
    actual use of 1—2, 22—3, 172, 183, 193
    possession of 22, 105, 157, 178, 193
    potential use of 4—6, 172—3, 175, 177—9
    see also first use
Nuttall, Jeff 118

O'Brien, Conor Cruise 195
Osgood, 67
Owen, David 10

pacifism x, 85, 91, 94—5, 98, 123, 133, 184, 214, 219
    absolute 23, 40—1, 92, 111, 157—9, 161
    Christian pacifism 198—205, 237
    nuclear 19, 23—4, 36, 41—2
    rejected 18—20
    state 157
parity of weapons, *see* balance

Parliament and nuclear debate 10

Partial Test-Ban Treaty 64

patriotism 111—13, 116, 122—6
    and Christianity 131

peace, nature of 194—5, 212—13, 219, 234
    and justice 206—7, 211—12
    and liberty 207, 211

peace movement:
    arguments against 14—15, 17, 152
    Christian 98, 100
    and Christian symbolism 131—6
    direct action by 41, 136
    Eastern Europe ix, 37, 41—2, 44—50, 103, 163
    importance of viii—ix, 11—12, 154
    international dimension 10, 48, 93
    Western Europe ix, 36—7, 40—51, 70
    women's peace movement 109, 134—6, 152, 157, 161
    see also Campaign for Nuclear Disarmament; morality; pacifism

Pershing missiles 50, 162

Polaris missiles 11, 39, 68, 107, 159

Powell, Enoch viii, 15—16, 91—2, 130

power:
    in international diplomacy 13, 188—90, 193—4, 208—9, 212
    theology of 219—20

Pribam, Karl 145—6

proliferation of nuclear weapons 11, 24, 63—4, 66, 69, 152—3, 159

Quinlan, Michael 214

Reagan, Ronald 26, 34, 152, 158, 161—2, 225

relativity, theory of 141—5

repentance, necessity for 196, 229—31

risk of nuclear war 30, 63, 203
    aggravation of 31, 106, 151, 153, 181, 211
    reduction of 34, 82—3

rock music, anti-nuclear 112—13, 114—16, 122, 126, 132

Rodgers, General 159

Roman Catholic Church, and denunciation of nuclear weapons 10, 11, 98, 105

Runcie, Robert (Archbishop of Canterbury) 94—5, 153, 221, 226

Russell, Bertrand 141—2

Ryle, Sir Martin 43

SALT negotiations 64—6, 160—1, 239; *see also* arms reduction

Schell, Jonathan 22

Schlesinger, Dr 79

Schoenbaum, S. 110, 132—3

second strike force 32—3, 63, 213

secrecy about nuclear weapons viii, 9, 37

security, national, and pacifism 203; *see also* defence strategies

Social Democratic Party 108
    'no first use' policy 28

Soviet Peace Committee 41

sovereignty, national 160—1

SS20 weapons 29, 31, 36, 48

Status Quo 109—10, 113—14, 121, 126, 128, 136

Steiner, George 128—30

Stockhausen, Karlheinz 170

Storr, Anthony 143
strategic weapons 9, 26, 63–5,
68, 152, 161
subjectivity:
as mode of knowledge 146
in quantum physics 144–5
rejected in mechanistic physics
142–3
submarine-based weapons 9, 39,
58, 160
Sutherland, John 121–2

tactical weapons 9, 59, 63, 68, 77
technology, nuclear, advantage of
contact with 6
test-ban treaty, necessity for 65,
69
Thatcher, Margaret 39, 91, 101,
124, 160–1, 238
theology:
and the nuclear debate 22,
135–6, 219–21, 230, 237
and politics 101–2
and war 197–8, 201
Third World, arms sales to 40, 66,
148–9, 154–5
Thompson, E. P. ix, 34
Treaty of Tlatelolco 64
Trident 16, 39, 64, 68, 107, 161
opposition to 11, 36, 159–60
Tsipis, Kosta 152

unilateralism, British 13–14, 24,
27, 42–4, 49, 64, 82, 122,
134, 177–8, 212, 221
and Christianity 157, 173–4,
176, 223
and Church of England 10,
21–2, 102–3
dangers of 14–16, 106, 159
exemplary effect 154
first-step unilateralism 157
and NATO viii, 18, 158

popular support for 110–11,
114, 117, 125–6, 136
see also Christianity; multi-
lateralism
United Nations 90
and arms reduction 66, 67, 69
and restrictions on war 52, 56
United States of America:
and defence of Britain 7,
104–5, 234
military build-up 38–9
nuclear capability 2, 9, 43, 63,
65
response to Russian threat
2–4, 32, 75, 79, 81, 107
weapons on British territory 7,
18, 42–3, 68, 106, 161
USSR:
desire for peace xi, 18, 25–6,
41, 46, 82, 225–6
military build-up 38, 40, 75–6
and 'no first use' policy 31–2
nuclear capability 2, 9, 24, 26,
38, 43, 63, 65–6, 74–5
threat to Britain 4, 39, 158,
223–4
threat to Western Europe 2–4,
11, 15–18, 29–30, 72–82,
203

Vance, Cyrus 161
violence, images of, and peace
movement 122–3, 136

war:
and Christian discipleship
197–9, 202
conventional xi, 29, 54–6, 63,
153, 202, 204, 216
in Marxism-Leninism 57–8
measures to avoid 52–4,
58–61

right of states to go to war
56–7, 60
see also just war; limited war,
concept of
Warsaw Pact 32, 150, 181
nuclear capability of 38–40,
46
and peace movements 67

and threat to Western Europe
72, 75–7, 81
weapons revolution 53–4
Weber, Max 146
Weinberger, Caspar 38
Western Alliance, *see* NATO
Whitney, Ray ix, 19
World Peace Council 45